MILK THE PIGEON

MILK THE
PIGEON

A Field Guide for
Anyone Lost in Their 20s

ALEXANDER HEYNE

Milk The Pigeon is a work of nonfiction. Nonetheless, some names and personal characteristics of individuals or events have been changed in order to disguise identities. Any resulting resemblance to persons living or dead is entirely coincidental and unintentional.

Acknowledgments

To my parents, for dealing with one cranky twenty-something as he tried to figure his life out. To all the twenty-somethings who feel confused and stressed about what to do with their lives, who *really* want to do something important and make their time on earth matter. Finally, to Paulo Coelho, for helping me get back on the path to my Personal Legend.

Preface:
The Field Guide I Wish I Had

What you're holding in your hands is the bible that I wish I had when I was twenty-two, or even eighteen. Life clearly has no guidebook, and the twenties are even harder—we go from the structured life of school, and are thrown into the daily mindless routine of working and paying bills, and doing "grown up stuff." When I entered my twenties, I wasn't well prepared, and it was my own fault. I didn't know how successful people thought, acted, and lived their lives. I didn't know how the best jobs were found, or how to start a business around something I loved.

I didn't know how to make genuine, life changing connections or, hell—*just friends*. I didn't know how to make those impossible decisions on moving, quitting, starting, or staying in a certain situation. I didn't know how to be successful at whatever it is I did, regardless of the economic conditions or the lack of success I saw everyone else having.

Most of all, there was no guidebook for getting through that dark night of the soul, which so often accompanies us on our journey to "figure it all out" and usually lasts the entire twenties, and sometimes, our entire lives.

This book is comprised of all the lessons that I would've killed to know when I entered the real world. It's filled with the lessons on figuring out the path to take when it all seems dark and foreboding and you're worried about making the wrong decision. It's filled with a roadmap to help you understand the "hidden game" behind those who find (or create) work they love, and do work they feel called to do. And at the end of the day, they are the lessons I wish I would've known about creating an awesome, meaningful life, beyond the shiny objects and ego attractions that often side track us.

It's about the most important thing of all: a life well lived. So find a nice café, grab a coffee, and enjoy the story.

– Alex
July, 2016. Andalusia, Spain.

CONTENTS

What This Book Actually Is
(and How It'll Help You)

Milk the Pigeon is part story and part how-to, but I can promise you'll leave with a few things—inspiration, direction, and a hell of a lot of motivation to get your ass moving. I'll share my story and what key success habits and principles helped me figure out the answers to the three biggest life questions I had on a daily basis in my early twenties. The point is simple here: to help you realize that if you consciously pick a direction, and work every day towards it, you are a serious black sheep in a world where people despise the black sheep and will do anything to kill them and make the world a little bit more vanilla.

This book is broken into three major chapters, with the first part being about direction and answering that burning question I had, "what the hell should I do with my life?" The second part is all about work, and about that age-old question of, "how do I find work I love?" The third part is all about fulfillment, and at the end of the day, what most of us really want on a day-to-day basis—to feel like our life was not only awesome, but that it mattered. This third part is for those of you in great jobs who don't have to stress about money and life is good, but still wonder, "why am I not happy? I have it all." Each section features a key lesson or theme, which are key success principles that I wish I had known. At the end of each chapter, I give you an action step and something to take home.

Behind all of this, I didn't want this book to be preachy or prescriptive (even though that inevitably comes through). Each chapter provides a story behind the success principle that eventually worked for me, and then a key habit for you to work on. Like I said, I can't imagine how much more painless my twenties would've been if I had this, so I hope this guidebook serves you well in a world (and human experience) where there is no map.

QUESTION #1:

"WHAT THE HELL SHOULD I DO WITH MY LIFE?"

CHAPTER 1

The Lost Years

*"Death is not the greatest loss in life. The greatest
loss is what dies inside us while we live."*

– NORMAN COUSINS

"Screw this, I'm moving to China."

That was my first "logical thought" in a long line of logical thoughts before boarding a one-way flight to China in search of sages, Kung Fu masters, and monks. The game plan was to move to China for five years, become a legendary ass-kicking machine, do six hours of meditation a day with some monks, and travel around in search of sages and wise men.

I could always come back to the comfy life in the United States, I figured. All day long I would talk to friends, coworkers, friends of my parents, and really anyone older than me, and I was always struck by one thing: the almost universal agreement that life sucked. It was boring. It was monotonous. It was filled with doing "grown up things" and certainly didn't involve all those cool things you dream up when you were a kid.

I had an irrational fear of ending up like everyone I saw around me—bitching and moaning about their jobs, laughing in the face of anyone doing anything remotely different or out of the norm (aka: dreaming). To me, it was an easy decision then—if this is the real world, and if this real world is always going to be here for me, then I'm getting the hell out of here and doing something I *want*. See you never.

***

The reason I left in the first place is an experience all too familiar to most human beings, especially twenty-somethings. There's that feeling you get when you sit down at the desk of your very first job, something that grows on you a bit day by day, month by month, and finally crystalizes anywhere from six months in, to three years in. *Is this it?* This is the grand purpose of my life? This is what I'm going to wake up and do for the next forty years? It puzzled me. Actually, it just felt weird and scared the crap out of me.

Why is it that as children we all naturally dream big and tell mommy, "I wanna be an astronaut!" Because as kids, no one has the heart to say "you can't" to a child. It's just not socially acceptable. You'd be an asshole if you said that to a kid. But as you grow up, something happens. Your mom, or older brother, or friend, tells you to "get realistic" and "get a job" and to "get a degree." And then we encounter society—a vast mass of people living largely miserable lives, doing work they hate, to support a lifestyle that is never good enough and then retiring half a lifetime later to start living.

The downers (society) eventually grow on us, and by the time we hit high school we join the "dreams are for kiddies" club. Might as well, right? Since you probably haven't met a single other person living the dream. I probably would have too.

But the fact that I knew not one friend, adult, parent or mentor pursuing their ideal lifestyle was my fuel. It was my impetus to work harder than those around me. And I swore to myself never to end up like so many of my friends or other adults who told me, "Enjoy college man, party it up, don't be in a serious relationship, and travel the world. 'Cuz it's all work from here on out."

There are a couple of reasons why you are here reading this right now. I firmly believe you have found this exactly at the right moment—because things happen at the strangest, most perfect times. I don't know why. I don't know how. They just do.

You feel like you were born to do much bigger things with your life. Being someone's coffee bitch, being told to work your way up the ladder, and the idea of waiting until you're so old that you *"can't even get it up,"* to start living makes you want to bring an Uzi into work. You feel like you were born for something great and there is some larger purpose out there for you.

Well, here's the good news – there is.

"Why Not?"

That was the question I asked myself, when I seriously considered buying a one-way ticket across the world. What's the worst that can happen? My life can go back to the way it is? I'll go back to a suck-ass life where I hit snooze six times in the morning, zombie my way through work, and dull the senses at home afterwards.

The weekend rolls around and I party myself retarded, because getting shitfaced five days a week was easier than looking at myself in the mirror and admitting I was unhappy. Once Sunday night hits I'm ready to slit my wrists in anticipation of work on Monday. And on Monday afternoon, racing home from work with the music blasting for seventeen minutes was the best goddamn highlight of my day. Yeah, *a life*. Really, you have no alternative when you think about it. Your choices are: live a life doing what you want, working towards what you want, *or*... not.

How is there really a choice?

***

"Hmm, what's that smell?" I thought, as I hopped off the plane by myself in Beijing. It was almost the smell of nail polish remover burning my nostrils. I walked around a bit worried, thinking there was a fire inside the airport and started to get a bit anxious. As I was looking around assessing my surroundings, I walked through the airport automatic doors, and walked into the musty Beijing summer air. Within a few seconds, I realized the obvious: that was just the smell of the air. I was pleasantly surprised to find that the U.S. State Department had a daily air quality update linked to twitter, and most days it was in the "immediately hazardous to your health" range. Awesome.

Even though most days you didn't smell that obvious nail polish remover smell (I never found out what it was), pollution was sometimes so bad you could see it in the long hallway of the dorm where I stayed. Still, I was pretty enamored—China—the land of ancient history, Kung Fu, tea, mail order brides, nerdy white guys, and Taoism.

The place where everyone meditates and trains in some sort of Kung Fu daily, where people discuss philosophy in the streets, and businessmen all read Sun Tzu's Art of War... if only that were true. In fact, just about the only stereotypically story-book things that exist in modern China are the following:

- Tai Chi (mostly old people, mostly 22-year-old "masters," lots of scam artists)
- Tea. Everywhere......
- and lots of squirrely white guys (don't know what that means? Picture a squirrel. Yeah, it's awkward).

Then there are the things you don't hear about, like the incredible food, some of the most beautiful scenery on earth, the pollution (bad, but not as bad as you think), and women that wear high heels in all four seasons, including climbing mountains.

A lot of the rest of the stuff is very romantic, old fashioned, fairy-tale junk that you don't see anymore. There's a lot to love, and a lot you may hate about it. But one thing is for sure: it's one hell of an adventure to live or travel there. Here's a run-down on some of the things I found hilarious. First, western-level manners don't exist. This may be a touchy subject, and my western bias is definitely at work here, but most mainland Chinese (by western standards), have God-awful manners. Really. Manners so bad my mom would have beaten the shit out of me in public.

Spitting inside restaurants, letting children urinate inside the brand new Beijing subway, grown men getting into fights as soon as they start drinking—it all exists. Yielding *doesn't* exist. Old women will shove you out of the way in the grocery store. There is absolutely no respect for other people if they are not part of your family, extended family, or contacts. If you aren't family, you ain't shit in China, and people act like it. Next, lines don't exist. Now this one's hilarious. The first time I went on a big solo adventure in China, I was heading from Xi'an, home of the Terracotta Warriors, to Beijing, the capital of China. I showed up plenty early to the railroad station alone and figured I'd have time to read a book while waiting at the station.

Boy was I wrong. As it turns out, there were three thousand other Chinese trying to get into the train station. And none of them lined up. They pushed each other like a mob of brain-dead kids getting on a bus. They shoved so hard, I saw two women crying and cursing at the crowd, they were injured so badly. And as it turns out, this isn't unusual at all. This is pretty much the norm. I'm proud to say that by the time I left, I learned the ropes—and shoulder checked an elderly Chinese lady who tried to cut me in line and steal my Chinese medicine I just paid for. Suck it, grandma. Those herbs are mine. She looked at me shocked at first, like, "what the hell are you thinking, elbowing a grandma?" and then laughed, and I read her mind: respect. White boy learned.

Third, connections get you anything (anything), but beware. Here's a very interesting facet of the Chinese: the concept of *guan xi* (loosely, connections) is what runs the country. Since corruption, cheating, and stealing are all still extremely commonplace, knowing people is the best way to get things done.

I was once in Shanghai with a young guy who was born into the "millionaire" club, aka second generation rich. He was young—mid to late twenties—spoke Japanese fluently, and had decent English. "If we go into a club together, you pick any girl. She's yours. I'll have a wall of bodyguards surround you so you can dance and they'll close the club for us," he told us at dinner one night. Awesome. And terrifying.

The scary part of connections is that it works "eye-for-eye" style— you better be able to pay back every single tiny favor. And the Chinese remember every single one. So it might go like this, after ten years have elapsed. "Remember that time, ten years ago, when I picked up you and your girlfriend in the freezing cold? Well, I've got to go to a conference for a week, would you mind watching my kids?" That sucks. The rumor is that they keep track of *every* single little favor.

There's also a widely circulated word of mouth story in Beijing about a police sergeant's son who was driving drunk and hit a family or a couple of kids on the highway and killed them. He got off scott-free because of his daddy's rank. Chinese *guan xi gets* you anything, and out of almost anything.

Beijing has one of the worst reputations for being a polluted city, but here's the truth: it's bad by western standards, but not nearly as bad as the papers in the west portray it. Yes, some days there is a burning nail polish remover smell. And yes, some days you can see pollution inside the buildings if the hallway is long enough. And yes, the Chinese organize their exercise days around the pollution (and are told to not go outdoors and definitely not exercise outdoors on the worst days). But usually it's just an L.A. haze or New York City kind of smell.

Next, there's the presence of poisoned, exotic, and chemically molested (but delicious) foods. Sometime around early 2011, when I was in Beijing, there was an exploding watermelon epidemic. The Chinese news reports were claiming that watermelons were exploding and I quote "like land mines" because they were so pumped full of growth hormones. And you know about the milk scare.

Well, if you ask the Chinese what things not to eat, they'll tell you: milk and watermelons. They're familiar with it. Here's another fun one. A new scary thing popped up recently in China, which was a chemical (a carcinogen, naturally) that can change any meat to have the appearance and texture of beef. Creepy.

The health scares exist - just try not to get too worked up about it, know that the foods you eat on a daily basis probably will not make you sick, and regarding restaurants, use local presence as an indicator of whether or not they're safe.

Oddity and local interest number six: the year-round mini skirt and high-heeled girl. First, as a confession and disclaimer, I'm not one of those "into Asian girls" guys. I like the Indian, Latina, Asian sort of look—but I'm not an anime watching Asian-fetish kind of guy. Having said that, China easily has some of the most beautiful women I've seen in my life. And in way higher numbers than I've ever seen in a club or bar in the United States. Lots of my male friends that lived in Beijing also agree. The interesting part of this vanity culture (if you want to call it that), is that a lot of them dress like they are going to a club on a day-to-day basis.

Even in winter, women wear heels. I've even seen women climbing some of the most sacred (and most dangerous), mountains in China while wearing high heels. It's madness. Vanity is absolutely huge in Asia. It's both good and bad, and the phrase in China for the extremely high-maintenance gold-digging kind of girl is a "Shanghai Girl."

Another aspect that goes along with being a woman here—if you're white—you might be an overnight celebrity (for no reason). Because of the cultural revolution, China has had a relatively short history of having foreigners within her borders. Ten or twenty years ago people were talking about how when you go to Asia you gain celebrity status instantly, with people (especially young girls), wanting to take pictures of you. When my mom came to Shanghai to do business, we were in a touristy area where there were temples and gardens in the center of the city, and my mom gestured to stand in a spot to take a picture. As I was taking a picture, I saw something out of the left corner of my eye—it was two girls trying to "sneak" up next to me while their friend took pictures. My mom apparently found this hilarious because she keeps telling the story, but this is pretty common in China.

In my experience, this is still the reality today. I'm not sure how or why it's like that, but I'd imagine it's due to the western media influence, novelty and the perception of beauty. My other Asian friends (going all the way down to Southeast Asia), even say where they live

(Malaysia, Indonesia, Philippines), it's the same. A tall white American guy is a huge status symbol for a girl.

So my advice if you're a white dude in Asia is simple - enjoy it. Be careful. And don't be a douchebag. If you're a white guy, you will probably have lots of girls and people coming up to take pictures with you. You will probably have girls ask for your phone number. You may have people come up to you asking if you want to model (pretty common in Beijing on university campuses). Enjoy the attention, don't let it get to your head, realize that there may be a lot of gold digging girls, and just use it as an opportunity to make friends.

This next one is a bit funny – people will stare at you. A lot. It's another thing that intrigues some people but bothers others. Even in the big cities like Shanghai and Beijing, if you're not at a foreign university, you'll have a lot of people staring at you. In Beijing, the gym where I would work out only has a couple of foreigners, and every single time I get into the elevator (six floors), there is some elderly Chinese man looking right at my face totally captivated. He looks at my face for a while, and then looks me up and down noting things about me. My shoes. My belt. My shirt. All examined from only six inches away from my body. It's as if I were a friggin' zebra with purple legs and the head of a human, and it was the first time he'd seen this endangered species.

The attention you get may or may not bother you. But the feeling I had from all these experiences is that the Chinese simply are new to the outside world, and any chance they get to see it first-hand, they'll take. Want the ultimate experience? If you speak Chinese and live in China, you're a half unicorn half minotaur-like creature. People will smile at you and ask where you're from in English, then when you speak Chinese, they'll go berserk and won't stop talking to you.

After I had explored the culture for a couple of weeks and learned a couple of these oddities, I went in search of what I came for: an internal Kung Fu master.

Everybody Picks on the White Boy: My Ass Kicking and Return to Reality

Li De, zenmeyang? Teacher Zhou said, after he did a fireman throw, throwing me completely over his head, onto hard gravel. *"Li De, you okay?"* He would always feign being worried, and once he saw I was conscious and wasn't dead, he would start laughing, the sick bastard. Zhou was, in one sense, what I came for. He was the disowned disciple of a famous Tai Chi master, and a current bodyguard for the communist party. And he loved to beat the shit out of the white boy and prove how good he was.

One time, Zhou was demonstrating a wrist lock, something that was old news to me, having trained in Kung Fu for about five years back home. My teacher back home was rough too—he didn't mess around, and he trained NYPD in New York, so I was used to rough punishment. One time he had us stretch until everyone in the room cried. Yes, you read that right. Imagine little fifteen-year-old Alex with tears streaming down my face as someone stared at me crying, while they were the ones pushing my legs open wider with theirs.

In any case, I was used to joint locks that hurt like hell. But this was a whole new level. After a sickening, crunching sound, the first time he did an arm lock on me, I was almost positive he broke my wrist, and if I wasn't afraid of going into a Chinese public hospital, I would've checked myself in pronto. I didn't, and thankfully it got better. When I was nursing my wrists another time, he laughed and said, "I'm going easy on you, my teacher was way worse, and I used to have to drink out of my water bottle like this" he gestured using his arms as nubbies, as if they were amputated.

My close friend Jeff, and eventually another friend Tim, would come and train with Zhou three days a week for three hours a night. It didn't matter if it was negative ten degrees in February, we always trained outdoors in a public park. It was the real China training experience, and it was awesome. Since I only had four months of Chinese night classes when I arrived in China, the first thing I did was to make arrangements at a local university for foreigners, because I figured that would spare me two huge headaches: where I was living, and learning the language.

There was also the added bonus of meeting people and making friends, which would be huge, considering I just moved across the world by myself. One day, after training with Zhou for about six months, and still being just as afraid on the way there every night as I was the first day I trained with him, he mentioned that his prices were going up. "It's getting expensive here in Beijing," he said. "So it's going to cost more." I was almost a hundred percent sure he was full of shit and looking to make some money on foreigners, which disappointed me, but he threw in something else, "*Li De*, since you brought your two friends here, you can keep the same price."

It was a nice gesture, but it was way more fun to train with my friends. One of the best feelings was waiting for the public bus in the middle of the night (after class), when we'd all put our legs up on the railing, stretch and talk about Kung Fu and life. It was one of those few times in my life I felt a real brotherhood with some close friends. In any case, my two friends didn't want to pay the increase, and I didn't want to either—I wasn't working, just living off of the money I had saved (around ten grand). Unfortunately, even though I stayed in China for another eight months, that was the end of my Kung Fu journey, where I realized that it wasn't the thing I was most passionate about.

The next semester of my intensive Chinese language classes (four hours a day) I just focused on learning Chinese. I would do class four hours a day, study in a café three hours a day, and then hang out with friends or try to make friends with locals. But at the end of the summer, it became clear that my quest for the monks, sages, and holy men, just wasn't going to happen, at least not at this time in my life. All my friends were leaving China, except Jeff (who decided to enroll at the Chinese Medicine school there), and I didn't have any clear next steps.

Create a caravan and go in search by myself? Just get an apartment and look to apprentice with someone? My gut wasn't giving me any good signs about what to do next, so I pushed the retreat button: a one-way ticket back to New York, and I moved back in with my parents trying to find the next step. Ugh.

The Dark Night of the Soul

When I got back from China, at first it was all excitement: holy crap, so that's what fresh air smells like! Sweet baby Jesus, life is good. Then I felt a pretty heavy weight on my chest. When I graduated college, I was ecstatic. I actually didn't want to go to college because there were all kinds of other things I wanted to do instead, and once I graduated it meant I could do whatever the hell I wanted. In other words, if I wanted to travel for ten years straight, I could. If I wanted to become a monk, I could. Finally, I had no one telling me what to do. That turned out to also be a curse. There I was sitting on my parents' couch, wondering, "what now?"

I had no clue. I wish I could tell you that some intuitive slap in the face came from God, but it didn't. I moved back home and had no friends. I had no job, and despite being from a top U.S. college with a Biology and Environmental Science degree, it took six months to get a job. A shitty job. And each string of jobs was worse than the next one, until eventually I fell into a deep depression. The next few years were one big haze, job after job, starting my income back at almost zero (entry level), wondering when I could plan my next escape.

When I finally escaped from the haze, around age twenty-six, it took me another three years to figure out why I was both so miserable and so unsuccessful. Unfortunately, my descent into my own personal hell, and dark night of the soul, was marred by making a lot of mistakes I now see other twenty- somethings making. The good news—almost anything is fixable. The bad news—some of us make these mistakes our entire lives.

CHAPTER 2

How to Mess up Your 20s (and Other Awesomeness)

Let's face it, many people tell you that your twenties are for making mistakes, right? People have told me that, "your twenties are your wealth building years." Yet another person has told me that, "your twenties are your last chance to be sexually promiscuous, participate in orgies, and do a bunch of crazy shit, so make sure you go full out." *Thanks...* However, very few people have told me there are life-changing mistakes you can make in your twenties when you don't have shit figured out.

These mistakes are the most common ones I've seen in my own life, the lives of my friends, and later, the experiences of some of my twenty-something coaching clients. Where do I see them? These "mistakes" are ubiquitous. Some you can fix. Some you can't—and they may alter the course of your life, forever. Also, let's be clear, I'm not a psychologist who has seen a thousand twenty-somethings and this is the "definitive list"—I have, however, answered well over five thousand of the exact same emails and have coached hundreds of clients, and you spot the same things over and over almost instantly. And of course, I made all these mistakes too.

Let's start with a not-so-obvious mistake that I made very early on, and I think many people make throughout their lives, but especially twenty-somethings.

Mistake #1: Avoiding Asking Yourself the Hard Questions.

Except for being the perpetually lost demographic, we twenty-somethings are also famous for avoiding our problems and running away from them. Some of us, a small percentage, actually continue to put off life... indefinitely. And you know why that is? It's not because we're slackers. It's not because we're lazy. It's not because we don't know what we want (even though that's true too). It's because resistance has beaten us, and we are too goddamn scared to ask ourselves the hard, scary questions in life. We're afraid of the answers that might bubble up. You'll be sitting on a beach in Thailand talking to one of these people and they'll go on some long diatribe about how, "it's bullshit how the world is run" or how, "money is everything back in my country" or how, "I'm trying to live a spiritual life."

But in reality most of them are cowards. It's easier to get shitfaced drunk, four nights a week, than stay sober and face the reality of your life. Guess what? Lots of other people hate their jobs. You're not special. But only a small percentage of people do something about it. They take the courses, they read the books, they learn the skills, they make the network and then they make a change. So what are the hard questions you need to ask yourself? If you're lost, just admit it. You aren't alone.

Don't want to go back home to live in the 9 to 5 grind? There are other ways around it. But we need to have the emotional maturity and the cojones to admit that and know that the road may be long and difficult. But that road is always more fulfilling than living on some beach in Southeast Asia, retreating, and just cultivating our little plot of land.

Somehow we all know what our path is, but many of us choose to ignore it for one reason or another. It's time to stop being afraid, and ask yourself the hard questions. What do you really want to do? Are you in the current life you're in because you're too afraid to go after the life you truly want? Or are you genuinely confused about the path forward?

Maybe it's your relationship that's imploding and you're uncertain about the direction it's going, and you need to be honest with yourself and break it off because you are completely incompatible. Maybe you're drinking excessively because you're miserable, but you just tell yourself that it's just a social thing (five nights a week). Or maybe something else is going on. Just be honest with yourself and face those hard questions.

Mistake #2: Living Someone Else's Life.

By far, and I mean by far, a major reason you see many adults freak out and join the half-life crisis club, is because they spent their youth doing things they *should* have done, instead of things they *wanted* to do. They spent that time becoming a New York City finance guy instead of backpacking in Thailand. They spent that time stuck as a corporate rat despite the fact that their inner entrepreneur was trying to claw its way out. They became a lawyer even though they always wanted to be a schoolteacher—because dad said you could never make enough money as a schoolteacher.

And guess what happens when you "wisen up" and "get logical" and "act realistic?" You harden up. You stop giving a shit about childish things like dreams, you think long-term travel is for hippies that live in Thailand and do drugs. You think that "pursuing your passion" and "living your dream" is for douchebag, college, twenty-somethings— not for mature, grown up, adults. But the worst part—and I mean, by far the worst part—is that somewhere down the road, maybe two years, or five, or twenty-five, this creeping dissatisfaction with life enters your world. "What the hell am I doing all this for?"

Whether that's at twenty-five or fifty, those little stirrings of discontent show up. First in your job, then in your life. Your relationships start going haywire. You start going haywire. Your life goes through a new incarnation. And it was all because you ignored your gut. You probably already know what you want, you just have to go for it. It will be one of the hardest things you ever do in your life. But it will be the single, most worthwhile thing you ever do. There will be a hundred and one reasons to be swayed by someone else and go into a life you don't want. There will be your parents who want you to grow up and be a successful, contributing member of society.

There will be your friends who want you to go off and do what you want. There will be acquaintances that tell you to hustle now and stack that cheese, and you can retire early—maybe as early as forty. But only *you* know what you really want to do, and at the end of the day you're only looking yourself in the mirror.

At the end of the day, it really doesn't matter to anyone but yourself, because you have to brush your teeth, look in the mirror and realize you're beyond miserable. Your parents won't be there, your school teacher from fifth grade that called you stupid won't be there, and all of society won't be there—just you. Are you happy? Are you living the life you want?

Mistake #3: Thinking You'll "Figure it All Out" and Then Go Do Something.

Guess what? Most people live their entire lives without figuring it all out, and they don't end up doing shit. You've heard this a million times before, but there is almost never a perfect time. Yeah, I'll admit some of us get lucky. We get that sweet business introduction. We get a scholarship to live abroad. We get a hook up from mommy and daddy. For the rest of us? The more time you spend thinking, the more time you spend screwing yourself over. I recently talked with a friend about how thinking is one of the major causes of unhappiness.

The same is true about "figuring your life out." Trying to think it through is the absolute worst idea. I can suggest this because I've done it myself and it didn't get me any closer to figuring out diddly-squat—and that's when I learned that it's fundamentally flawed. You truly don't know something until you've done it. So go do it. "Which one will I like more? Being a doctor, lawyer, or teaching English in Korea?" Here's what you do to figure that out in a month: Shadow a doctor. Shadow a lawyer. Talk to a family friend who is a doctor. Talk to a friend who is a lawyer. Go teach in Korea. Booya. In a year and a half you've answered the questions you would've guessed about for the next forty years.

Mistake #4: Making Expensive Financial Decisions When You Don't Have a Clue What You're Doing.

This is the "caveat" part of #2. Doing something is more important than trying to think it through. However, doing something—when you don't know what you're doing—that costs $100,000, like grad school, or an MBA, is one of the biggest mistakes you can make. Just my two-cents of course. "I'll see how I like psychology" is not the same as enrolling in a PhD program in clinical psych. If you want to know if you'd like a PhD program or would like being a psychologist, how about shadowing one first? Go into an office and actually talk to one. Creep around their place of work. See what they actually do all day. Sometimes it's a lot less glamorous than you'd think. Also, talk to PhD candidates and shadow them, because you'll be one of them.

The grad school life-postponement move that so many of us do when we're lost is beyond dumb. Yes, it's great to figure out your life. No, it's not great when it costs a ton of money just for an experiment.

You can often get the exact same insight into whether or not you'd enjoy the daily life of a profession by calling, shadowing, and talking to people working in the field. If they like their job, most people are happy to share.

That's one of the reasons I opted-out of being a conventional doctor. It looks great on the outside—I love medicine, biology and helping people. But when I did some research, guess what I found? You spend five minutes with a patient. You don't even let them talk and say, "So what's bothering you?" You are confronted by sales reps of pharmaceuticals, all the time. JAMA/NEJM and the other major research journals are filled with full-page pharmaceutical ads. Even the good physicians complain about the system. Not what I signed up for, or would be happy doing every day.

Go with the minimum viable product methodology—find a way to see what it's like before committing. And no, attending med school is not "seeing what it's like." That's called "an easy way to burn 200k" and "being dumb."

Mistake #5: Being Dissatisfied in a Job, but Doing Nothing About it.

Why do I consider this such a sin? Such a life mistake? I consider it a big mistake to stay in a situation you're unhappy with (when you're young), because it's one of the only times in your life when you can be uber-selfish and just go do whatever the hell you want on a whim. That means you can quit ten jobs and still have a safety net. You don't have to worry about a spouse or kids. The risk when you're young and have no dependents is zero. Literally. You can try business ideas, move across the world, and write as many failed novels as you want without any lasting emotional damage that'll screw you in the future. The only things holding you back then are typically:

- Fear of the unknown
- Laziness—looks tough; I'll pass.
- Lack of information (You tell yourself, but it's a lie, it's actually laziness. There's no such thing as a lack of information in the Internet age. It's lack of action.)
- Not knowing what you want (and feeling like you need all the info before you act)

• Money, to a certain extent (with no *real* worst-case scenario for most of us under thirty)

Well, guess what? I say this a lot but I'll say it again: your work occupies a ton of your waking hours. And when your work sucks, your life sucks hardcore. When I was going through a string of bad jobs in my twenties, I was shocked that people could spend twenty years doing that to themselves. I was beyond shocked. I was stone speechless and looked at my coworkers like they were child-abusing pedophiles with green heads from Mars. What in the hell is this world?

Spending seven am to six pm thinking about your work in some way, shape or form? It's awesome when your work is good, and terrible when it's bad. It's so far beyond terrible when it's bad, and it's almost all of your waking hours. Don't you think it makes sense then to make finding (or creating), work you love a priority?

This may be the last time in your life you can start or quit ten different jobs (been there), or businesses without losing much (done that). What's holding you back? When you get married or have kids you have 1/2 the time, 1/3 the money, and five times the responsibility. There will never be an easier or better time to quit a million jobs until you find one you like, or go into business for yourself.

Mistake #6: Getting Too Comfortable.

Guess what? When you die, your coffin will be really comfortable—lots of nice padding in there. Many of us looooove comfort. We love sitting down with half a box of Krispy Kreme Doughnuts® in front of a nice movie on the couch. Many of us would rather write about (or read about) interesting lives, than go do it ourselves. It's like this epidemic of twenty-something male wannabe MMA fighters. They watch MMA all day, and then start weight lifting. Three months later they think they are the ultimate fighter. Come on. Wake up.

This is a big gripe I have with many bloggers and writers talking about living "big lives" and breaking the mold. Many of them live ordinary lives and they just write about the life they wish they were living. The problem with comfort is that it's boring. You don't acquire life experience through comfort and familiarity. Flow happens when you get slightly uncomfortable. It's like when you're learning a new language and you show up to class sweating through your clothes.

You have no idea how to say the words in the new language, so it's nerve wracking. But six months later you have some basic skills.

It's just like going on a date. You "paper towel" your armpits (don't lie, you know what I'm talking about), like thirty-six times in the bathroom while you're talking to this guy or girl you're really into, you're always paranoid about food being in your teeth, and you triple check your breath every six seconds. At first, things are stressful, because it's just out of your comfort zone—then you enter flow and things are amazing.

That's how *life* is. When we start doing things that make us uncomfortable we grow. If you want to know the secret to getting good at just about anything, it's this—as soon as you get comfortable, find a way to make yourself uncomfortable again. Choose growth. We are happy when we're growing. That sweet spot between anxiety (just out of reach) and boredom (too much within reach) is often where we thrive.

Mistake #7: Settling and Giving Up.

Settling, rather than being a "mistake" is pretty much the path that the vast majority of people take. We decide to make a bargain with life. "Alright, I'll get the job that I may or may not like, you pay me, I live a quiet life, get drunk on Friday and Saturday, and then suck it up. I'll meet a nice girl and marry her, and then we'll have some kids. I'll play with those kids for 20 years, spend 20 years in retirement, then die a quiet death." The people that stop fighting have unfortunately believed the lie that it's time to "get realistic." It doesn't matter whether it's the job or the girlfriend—people always tell you to get realistic, as if there's something wrong with you for wanting even 1% more than what the average person has.

So what do they do? They hunker down, get a job, and get a life. Unfortunately, I've received 100's of emails from just these kinds of folks who woke up one day and said, "Ugh, this is not the life I wanted." They tell me that life sounded a lot like the following.

College and debt, work (to pay off debt and "be realistic"), get married, have a family, buy a new car, stay in debt and continue to work. And then, around forty or fifty, that creeping feeling that they haven't done anything with their life other than purchase things, comes crawling in. I recently knew someone that died from cancer in his late thirties—and one of the things he just could not shake was the one thing he kept telling me over and over: "I spent my entire life buying stuff. Buying a nice apartment, filling my nice apartment with nice stuff. Buying nice clothes. Not even going on vacation. And now I find it ironic that I'm giving it all away to friends because none of it matters. So what else do I have to show for my life? Nothing. I spent thirty years accumulating nothing."

It was scary to me. And unfortunately that's where I find most of my friends who have "given up." They just settle in and buy all the trappings of a comfortable but boring life. Don't let that be you, if you want your life to matter.

Mistake #8: Believing in the Retirement Lifestyle.

This might sound funny—but how is believing in retirement a mistake? Here's why: believing in retirement (and acting accordingly), is a totally different way of living. If you ask me, the entire idea of stacking cheese today so you can save it for tomorrow is flawed. Yeah, of course you need to save money. Yeah, of course you need to plan for tomorrow. But deferring your happiness for forty years and then you start living?

I have friends that got jobs right out of college, and being "settlers" they settled down into comfortable but boring lives. Four or five years later, they're still doing that. Some of them are still dreaming about starting businesses or traveling. They fantasize about waking up without an alarm. They wish they could work on stuff they love. But unfortunately, the idea of "deferred" gratification is so built into our society, I know that very few of them will ever escape. They'll get so stuck into their work that twenty-eight, twenty-nine, thirty roll around, and they'll get married—and then they get really stuck (often in a good way, but still more stuck than they want to be).

One of my friends finally decided that he was tired of it and wanted to make a change, so he asked me when the perfect time was. So I told him this:

For many of us the stars never align, the clouds never part, and the sun never shines. You just have to pick a day when you're in a good mood for a damn good adventure, and go for it.

You can't store up happiness. You can't store up life stories and experiences. A lost day is a lost day. One day putting off your dream is just another day you're getting further away and losing time. You and I both know that "one day" never, ever, happens. One day becomes forty years. Ask your parents. Ask them what dreams they've put off.

One day becomes forty years very, very quickly.

Chapter Recap: The Biggest Life Mistakes People Make in Their Twenties

☐ **Ask yourself the hard questions.** The biggest mistake I see others making now is avoiding the difficult questions—what's my dream career, what do I want from life, what kind of person do I want to marry, what do I really hope to achieve—because they're difficult. The flaw in thinking is that these questions magically resolve themselves, but here's the thing—they don't. They just get harder to solve the older you get.

☐ **Be deliberate, on paper.** If you write down every aspect of your life, from your finances, to your health, to all the things you want to achieve, what does that look like? Personally, I carry around goals in every aspect of my life on paper, which I keep folded up in my phone case so I can review it daily. If you don't have a vision for the direction you want to go (an "X" on the treasure map), what are you going to work towards?

☐ **Denial only works if there's an exit plan.** It's pretty common for us to just ignore something when it's not working—going into debt? Go out for a drink and forget about it. Underperforming at work and you think you'll get fired? Go crazy partying and do drugs to bliss out for a while. See yourself gaining weight? Stop stepping on the scale. Denial only helps you avoid short-term pain, but the long-term pain is way, way worse.

CHAPTER 3

The Bad News and the Good News

The Bad News: You Have a Terminal Illness.
The Good News: You're Not Alone.

"Raymond, you are going to die tonight." he said.

"Is that your mom and dad?" he says, gesturing to the wallet he has in his hand.

"No, no, no!" Raymond says, as he gets down on his knees with a silver revolver placed up against the back of his head.

"Your mom and dad are going to have to call up doctor so and so. You wanna know why? Because there's going to be nothing left of your face."

"An expired community college student I.D. What'd you study Raymond?"

"S-s-s-stuff."

"Stuff? Were the mid-terms hard?"

"Biology, m-m-mostly."

"Why?"

"I don't know..."

"What did you want to be Raymond K Hessel?" RAYMOND. *The question was what did you want to be?"*

"A v-v-veterinarian."

"That means you're going to have to do a lot of schooling."

"Too much school..." Raymond says, whimpering and crying.

"Would you rather be dead?" Would you rather die here, on your knees in the back of a convenience store?

25

"No... please.... Stop..."
The gun cocks.
"I'm keeping your license. I'm going to check in on you. I know where you live. If you're not on your way to becoming a veterinarian in six weeks, you will be dead. Now run on home."
The accomplice chimes in: "I feel ill. Come on man, this isn't funny. That wasn't funny... what the fuck was the point of that?"
"Tomorrow will be the most beautiful day of Raymond K Hessel's life. His breakfast will taste better than any meal you or I have ever tasted."

***

"On a long enough timeline, the survival
rate for everyone drops to zero."

– FIGHT CLUB

As sick as it sounds, for some people, putting a revolver to the back of their head and telling them they're going to die would be the best way to motivate them to take action. It's such a strange facet of human nature that we never act until things get to the absolute worst level— for example, the worst clients are the ones that are already the most comfortable, in a good life, a good job, with a great paycheck. Money isn't called "the golden handcuffs" for no reason. They're golden, because it's great having money, which allows you peace of mind and freedom, but at the end of the day, they're still handcuffs that you have a hard time giving up.

People that are comfortable are often, by default, way too comfortable to want to change anything. If everything implodes and goes wrong, then who cares? You can go back to a life that's "alright" and not wake up wanting to kill yourself or drive your car off the bridge on the way to work.

Twenty-somethings are equally curious: even though this is the most important time to be ambitious in your life—because of the lack of responsibilities, bills, and time commitments—this is the time when people most often just chill out and do nothing. Here's the thing, if you feel lost and confused, like you're wasting your life and your time, and you beat yourself up internally for it...

YOU ARE NOT ALONE!

There, I said it, so that you can chill out and stop beating yourself up. You aren't alone—this is normal. In fact, I would say that most grown adults with kids, families, and more who "appear to have it all together" are screaming and dying inside. This is that "life of quiet desperation" that Thoreau talked about. So, in fact, it's not just a condition of twenty-somethings, but really all humans. We aren't born into this world with a roadmap, we don't have instinct to guide us, and our lives aren't just guided by sex, food, and staying alive. The human mind is both a gift and a curse.

I was struck by a business insider article I read the other day, called *"This is what millions of young people in China and India REALLY think."* A photographer, Adrian Fisk, traveled all over China and India interviewing youth, asking what they thought about life. His project, iSpeak, started in China in 2008 and eventually moved into India as it gained momentum. He simply asked each person he randomly chose, to write what they thought about life, about their future, and about their purpose.[1]

The responses are more than interesting, and are an incredible reminder that you probably aren't alone in your thinking, no matter your age. Here were some of the responses from the Chinese, many spoke some English, and a few were illiterate, so I leave the responses as-is.

- "I'm worrying something. Girls in China is becoming materialistic. Without house, my girlfriend would not marry me."
- "I can not plan my destiny. Therefore, I do not plan my future!"
- Another from a country peasant, "When I watch TV I have a lot of ideas, and thoughts, but I have no way of realizing them."

These were some of the responses from India:

- "No point being a part of the rat race. Even if you win, you are still a rat."
- An illiterate Indian—"Like you, we need the same things in life."
- "We are evolved, give us a chance!"

There's obviously a trend here, yeah? Interview a bunch of young Americans and you're very, very likely, to get similar responses. So what are the trends? There's a lot of pressure to follow expected life routes, and for tangible, material achievement (often by parents or the overall culture).

Many of us feel powerless and in the grip of the hands of fate, rather than empowered. And there are feelings of hopelessness—the general perception regarding dreams is that "they are impossible to achieve."

To me, that raises an interesting point. These are some of the exact same emotions I've heard described from many of my own clients and students, and have felt myself, like:

- Powerlessness. "I can't control my future so I'm not going to plan my it."Dispirited. "I have a lot of thoughts, dreams, and ideas, but know I can never achieve them."
- Boldness. "Live your life, you may die tomorrow."
- Pressure, expectations, and criticism. "I'm supposed to follow a certain life path, and if I don't, I'm opening myself up to massive criticism."

What I'm saying is this: every culture in the world deals with generational problems, like feeling lost in your twenties. But on top of that, you also find cultural expectations, which further strengthen those feelings. You find traditional cultures, like those in Asia, where there's a much stronger familiar pressure to succeed and "stop thinking about yourself so much," and in the western world, individualism is prized.

At the end of the day, though, most "youth" are still just as frustrated, lost and confused as you might be, and are trying to figure out what path to take.

However, there's a catch here: yes, you are not alone, and it's okay (and natural), to feel lost—but you don't have a lot of time. In *Tuesday's with Morrie,* Morrie says that we're all born with a terminal illness—it's called *birth*. That means—no, you don't have a lot of time. No, thirty is not the new twenty as *Meg Jay* points out. No, you don't have all the time in the world to experiment, to not be serious, to chill, or to sit on your ass and do nothing. In fact, time is even more precious now. If you're reading this, you feel lost, you're probably in your twenties or thirties, but even more, that's a big window to 10x the amount of hustle you want to put in to finding work you love, figuring out a direction, and taking a step towards that meaningful life.

Chances are, if you're in your twenties, one day you want to get married or at least have a serious relationship. You might want to have kids, and you might want to settle down. All of those things are going to occupy a lot of your time later, so even though you might have a 9 to 5 now, don't piss away your 5 to 9.

Here's the thing: everyone goes through this. Literally every human being goes through phases of feeling lost, confused, and not having a damn clue in which direction to go. That includes ambitious people, lazy people, smart people, dumb people, good students, bad students, and everyone in between. And here's what else is interesting: your elders, including your parents, often haven't figured it out. The reason why they haven't figured it out is because they haven't thought deliberately about it. For many of us, it doesn't just magically go away if we wait long enough—it's something we need to consciously direct ourselves towards. Personally, I've found that not that many humans have actually thought about this to the point where it becomes a burning obsession to figure out.

So far in my life, the only people that haven't appeared to be lost at some point are: people who are truly so busy working multiple jobs just to pay their bills, and liars. We all know the goody-two-shoes A-student kid, who always got good grades, always appeared to have their shit together, etc. Many of those are just as lost but just don't admit it (or won't, due to ego issues), but they feel it just as much. The third thing here is that a lot of people just self-medicate by getting hammered on the weekend or picking their own vice, or giving up and cultivating their little garden.

The twenties are the highest risk period for depression for most people in their entire lives, up through the retirement and elderly years.[2] So it's not surprising to find a lot of us just getting hammered four or five nights a week to fill the void, or smoking weed throughout the day to turn off the brain. But like all distractions, those only work for so long, and in the worst case, we just end up repeating, year after year, because we're too gone to even be present and figure out what needs changing. The ultimate reason that self-medication is so deadly is because you turn off the single thing that's the most important tool in finding your path: your intuition.

Most people get lost, many people self-medicate, and no, there's nothing wrong with you, cool? So stop beating yourself up about not having this life shit figured out. Most people *never* figure it out, but then again, that's not surprising since most people don't think. Obviously, if you're reading this, you think about life and want to live more deliberately.

***

"The boy didn't know what a person's 'destiny' was. It's what you have always wanted to accomplish. Everyone, when they are young, knows what their destiny is. At that point in their lives, everything is clear and everything is possible. They are not afraid to dream, and to yearn for everything they would like to see happen to them in their lives. But, as time passes, a mysterious force begins to convince them that it will be impossible for them to realize their destiny."

— THE ALCHEMIST

Why is it so easy to get lost? I mean, what's up with all of these hallmark headlines, like, "Gen Y, the lost generation." What's up with all of this? Was it always this way? I think so, but I think the difference is that we Gen Y just want more from life, and want a different one than we saw our parents have. But the biggest reason is that this whole "lost" thing is a human phenomenon.

I promise you, between eating bananas, picking lice out of his mom's hair, and getting freaky with his monkey girlfriend, Mr. Bonobo doesn't think about his life purpose on a daily basis. Animals are lucky in one sense, in that they're guided by instinct, which is more or less eating, sleeping, and having sex. Not a bad life if you ask me, but then again, Paris, New York, and lambs with two heads wouldn't exist without humans.

The first reason why this is so hard for humans is that while animals are governed by instinct, there is no map for humans. Not only is there no map for what to do with your life, there's definitely no map if you want to do anything other than the normal stuff you see people in your culture doing. In the U.S. we joke about the white picket fence accountant with 2.5 kids. His life usually consists of going to college, getting a degree, getting a good job, getting married, having kids, and so on. If you want anything outside that cultural norm, there's no map. There are pieces, but there's nothing that can get you from A to Z without any thinking. You have to create the map.

The second thing is that we spend twelve years in school, where every day is structured for at least nine hours, and then suddenly we're let loose in the real world, where we work for nine hours, not because we have to anymore (we don't legally need a job), but because we need to pay rent. And then those after-work hours end up being a big question mark. So many readers have reached out to me saying that they got a good job, and are making good money, but they aren't happy. Why not? They don't feel like they have a reason to wake up in the morning. Work, pay bills, commute, work, and so on. Life loses its luster and its excitement. Why bother with it all? When there's no structure in the real world (outside work), which means conscious, meaningful, directed work and specific goals, it's easy to feel like life is this big, sixty-year long tunnel of doing the exact same stuff every day. As Earl Nightingale says, a rut is just a grave with the ends kicked out.

The third reason we get lost is because we lose touch with what we want. Of course showing up to a job you hate, or is meaningless, doesn't give you much reason to wake up. It's a job just to pay the bills, which is, essentially working nine hours a day just to exist on a plot of land. It's not like you're using the money to fund a passion project. One of my obsessions since I was a kid was seeking out holy men, sages, and wise men to learn their wisdom and see what feats these modern day sages are truly capable of. If I had this goal tacked on my bedroom wall, and I was using my work money to pay for a trip each year, then suddenly there'd be a huge purpose for me working a meaningless job.

Since I didn't direct myself like this, work was pointless, and I figured I'd rather be poor temporarily than do work I hated. Knowing that I could get hit by a bus, crossing the street, it seemed like an ass-backwards way to live, working all day for literally no reason.

At some point during childhood, we get talked out of most of our dreams. It's no wonder we get lost.

So how do you create a great life when there is no map? You create one.

Chapter Recap: You Are Not Alone

☐ **You are not alone.** In case you were wondering, no, even that one kid that seems to have his shit all together still does not know what's going on. I once observed this guy I knew, who never seemed to get frustrated, lost or confused, who seemed to ace every class in school, and was really calm on the outside. It was almost supernatural. All was fine and dandy until, of course, he had a nervous breakdown, was hospitalized and was the talk of the town.

☐ **It doesn't naturally resolve itself.** You definitely aren't alone in feeling frustrated, lost and confused, but here's the catch—it doesn't magically resolve itself. I know just as many forty and fifty year olds who are the same people because they never asked themselves the hard questions. That's not always a fun truth to admit, but problems don't go away from avoiding them - they go away from confronting them, no matter how much that may suck right now. Take the time to plug along 1% every day.

☐ **Ask yourself the hard questions.** There's always good news, and the good news is this: that feeling can and will go away, with consciously directed effort. That means asking yourself the most frustrating (and scary) questions about your career, your relationship, the direction in which you're moving and more.

CHAPTER 4

There Is No Map

One thing I wish someone would've told me a decade ago, is that "there is no map" for most of the things you want to do, if you're not following the beaten path. There really isn't one. That means there is no guaranteed path to finding your dream job (but there are plenty of strategies that almost guarantee it). There's no guaranteed roadmap to writing a book that changes lives and sells well (although many people have done it). And there's no map for creating a unique life, aligned with your strengths and passions (although many people have done this too).

So here's the thing: half of the process is just throwing shit at the wall, seeing what sticks, and doing more of that. It's way less sexy and linear than most people think, which is why so many of the greats in history took time to get to where they wanted to be, aka work they felt was their calling.

Look at some of the "greats" we remember today, and the timeline it took them to become household names for how skilled they were. Colonel (Harlan) Sanders was a "failure who got fired from a dozen jobs before starting his restaurant, and then failed at that when he went out of business and found himself broke at the age of 65" before finally creating and selling his first store (Kentucky Fried Chicken[3]).

Remember Charles Darwin? That scientist dude with the big beard who spent time on a boat or something, studying barnacles or something? The man with that pesky little theory of evolution? Yeah, he published that when *he was fifty*. Ray Kroc, founder of McDonald's, also bought his first restaurant at fifty. Martha Stewart worked on wall street and owned a catering company but her real success came in her mid-forties with the launch of the *Martha Stewart Living* magazine.

Vera Wang was a skilled ice skater and editor of a fashion magazine before deciding *at age forty* that she wanted to design dresses. The couple who wrote the Zagat guide that almost every restaurant craves, were in the legal profession up until the age of forty-two, when they launched the famous *Zagat* guide (now a part of Google). We could go on and on here. JK Rowling was on food stamps, her mom had died, she had just gotten a divorce, and was a single mother that was the "biggest failure she knew" (her own words). She was the biggest failure, that is, until one of her first books was bought after the editor of a publishing house's eight-year-old daughter read the book and loved it. Some of the editor's last words? Get a day job, because it's impossible to make a living writing children's books.

The path is exceptionally winding for most people, far more winding and non-linear than we'd like. Otherwise, how do you explain hard-working, ambitious people, taking thirty years to have their "big break?" It takes time, experience, and failure to find the work you love, to have enough experience (and failures) to learn where you aren't showing up 100%. The good news? You only have to get it right once.

Putting the Puzzle Pieces Together

So how do you put the puzzle together? If what you're looking for is the dream job, the side business, a cool life, or just another adventure, how do you get there?

First, it comes back to this idea of stacking the bricks. Second, it entails getting experience as quickly as possible, with minimal navel gazing. Third, it means forcing yourself to take action even if you don't know where the "X" is on your map. Fourth, it's about rapid iteration, trusting your intuition, and quitting quickly when things don't feel right. Don't even waste a week in the wrong situation. Cool? Let's jump in.

Stacking the Bricks

In one of Will Smith's interviews on how he became so successful, he said his dad taught him a key lesson when he was young. Here's a snippet of the story featured on the *Charlie Rose* talk show.

> One summer his dad tore down a brick wall in front of his business and told twelve-year-old Will and his brother to rebuild it. It took them a year and a half and they did it. And he said, "don't you ever tell me that there's something you can't do." You don't try to build a wall—you don't say "I'm gonna build the biggest, baddest, greatest wall that's ever been built." You don't start there. You say "I'm going to lay this brick as perfectly as a brick can be laid." You do that every single day, and soon you will have a wall.

Not much later, I came upon an article written by Amy Hoy called "stacking the bricks," where she builds off Will Smith's concepts to talk about how people truly build their own empires.[5] From the outside, we often think that a big author, business owner, or Olympian just had talent, got lucky with that book deal, or never encountered any roadblocks while building their businesses.

When you look deeper, what you often find is that their career was a lot like stacking bricks that made no sense (and often felt like stacking bricks or taking steps in the dark), but over time, when you step back, you see the end result—an incredible wall that's a masterpiece. The ultimate paradox is that when you're in the thick of it, it all appears to be a complete mess, but when you look back five years later, it makes sense.

You just have to stack the first brick before you can see where you lay the second brick. This is huge, because we often wait to stack any brick before trying—but the paradox is that you have to stack bricks (try things out) before anything becomes the clear path to follow.

When I went through that agonizingly frustrating period of trying to find a job at the peak of the recession (I graduated college in 2009), I did what everyone else did originally: I would shotgun resumes out each day in the hope that some soul would take pity on me and offer me something. Unfortunately, it didn't work, because I was yet another resume in that damned resume machine. Also, with how few jobs there really were, I was just another vanilla candidate bitching about his life and asking anyone for any job. The irony is that people don't want "anyone" for "any job"—they want people that have a specific skillset for a specific job.

When things didn't work (for over six months), I had to keep stacking the bricks and trying something new. The first brick was this idea of shot gunning out resumes. It didn't work, so I moved on to brick #2: trying to be more personal. Around that time, I ended up trying to learn video for my own business. I had been blogging for a little while, and now I was trying to learn video to upgrade my skillset, and an idea occurred to me: everyone was submitting written resumes, so why not submit a video cover letter with my written resume? The first person I sent it to instantly responded, and I was applying for a job paying double what I had been applying for, with my shotgun strategy. Just being 1% less vanilla had a huge payoff, and even though I didn't get that particular job, it was an "aha" moment like no other.

When it comes to applying for jobs, sometimes you have to stack the first brick, before you finally strike gold on the second, third, or twentieth.

Building my health business was another frustrating mess altogether. I came into the game with no skills other than being a personal trainer, being fit and having a desire to spread a different kind of gospel about health, weight loss and wellness—the habits message. I showed up as someone who studied biology and environmental science, who thought that business was stupid and that I'd never end up doing it. Thus began my long journey of entrepreneurship—with blogging. Since I had been writing on my personal blog (Milk the Pigeon), I had seen other sites that had taken off quickly, so I modeled them.

Eventually, over the months and years, I got a feel for how to write content that connected with people, how to write epic articles that were so valuable people would link to them, and then eventually, how to shoot videos that were not only great video quality, but were on point with my message and with my audience. After writing for a while and building an online audience, I started learning about launching my own online courses, because it was time to create a business. Most of the big people in the wellness space promoted other courses for a commission, but that made me feel slimy since I had no idea about the quality of the courses and the message the author was sharing.

As a result, I created my own. That by itself was one hairy endeavor—I had to figure out what my audience wanted, what was a reasonable price for what I offered, and then how to create the course, sell it and more. Most people never get past this phase, because one or two course failures in, they just give up and resort to slapping ads on their site or quitting altogether. The course creation process was an up and down journey, but it led me to my next brick: Webinars.

Webinars were yet another skill that I didn't have yet. Because webinars were live, you needed to be a good presenter and public speaker, you needed to create engaging slides, and yet again, you had to sell if you planned on feeding yourself. So I slogged through the process here, with up and down results, and never really "figured it out." But, are you seeing the trend, webinars led me to my next thing—my book.

After the webinars became an up and down success for me, and my audience, I thought of another unique way to really spread my message that I hadn't used before, and I had another aha moment: a book. Wouldn't it be cool if I could share my core message just in one book, so I wouldn't have to send people to a list of blog articles, they could just buy it and then also share it with their friends? It would be like my one stop hub for people to see if they liked me, and if my message would help them, before they decided to read any articles, waste their time following me, or potentially, joining a course.

The result? The book was the brick that finally took off. The book received awesome feedback from most people, tons of reviews within the first year (over 106), and the royalties became a series source of income for me—and every single one of these results was a big surprise.

Can you imagine if I had never started my business though, and I just assumed I would always get mediocre results? If I never started, I never would've accumulated the failures and frustrations (initial bricks in the wall), which led me to the important bricks (like my book, certain courses, and I'm sure many more things in the future). At the outset, I never could've predicted that this would've worked, but I persisted long enough to see that brick being stacked successfully. Hell, at the start, I never even thought I'd write a book (in my life). Ironically, here am I finishing my second one.

There's one final story here on how I found "my calling." Maybe the most frustrating and discouraging process I went through in my twenties was the process of figuring out what the hell to do with my life. You know, finding my work. The work I want to wake up to every day for the rest of my life. At the start, I didn't know if this was true or not, but I was desperately hoping that I could at least find work I really enjoyed and looked forward to (or at least didn't complain about). I was really, really hoping, this was a reality, but most importantly, I had the pig headed discipline to keep going and not give up during the process.

To be honest, if I reached thirty-five, after seriously searching and thinking about it every day (for fourteen years), I probably would've just jumped off a bridge. So to me, in an oddly dark sense, the stakes were very high. To me, life wasn't worth living if I couldn't find work I loved. Even though I didn't know too many people who did work they loved, that didn't discourage me—it inspired me, because I realized it was even more important that I kept going and showed others it was possible.

During the messy twenty-three to twenty-seven period, I promised myself one thing: I would do whatever it took to keep working on side projects that I actually enjoyed, that could possibly lead to something good. There were no guarantees, but here's what that meant:

- I worked part time for about four years (and moved back in with my parents until twenty-six)
- I went through *nine or ten jobs in less than four years*—yes, that's a shit load of quitting and starting
- I earned less than $30,000 for my entire twenties, before I started my own business
- I had to also freelance on the side to pay my bills (and afford to continue to travel)
- From the age of twenty-four on, I always worked at least two jobs, and in the worst year, worked four of them, which included my business, for three hours a night. I would go to the first job by seven am, the second one by one pm, the third one by four pm, and then my business at seven pm.

I really was paying the price and doing whatever it took to really live the life I wanted—quitting, starting, and staying focused on that core vision. Here's how stacking the bricks eventually led me to finding out my work—Chinese medicine. I would take jobs that I knew would give me something (a skillset), or otherwise interested me, knowing full well that I had no interest in doing them for longer than a year.

In the next chapter of the book on finding work you love, I'll drag you through the messy weeds called "Alex's twenty-something work life," but for now, here's all that matters. As one of those final jobs in my ten-job quit-streak, I ended up becoming a personal trainer. I was getting older (twenty-six) and despite actively working my ass off since twenty-three to try and find my dream, I wasn't any closer. My girlfriend mentioned personal training, and I figured I had nothing to lose—so I went to a high-end gym (knowing they'd pay me more) and asked them what it would take to get started.

The woman at the front desk said, "We'd love to have you. No problem, just go take the certification exam." The exam was basically my last $600, and once I got that shiny piece of paper, I went back.

"Here you go," I said.

"Oh, that's a shame," she said. "You don't have any personal training experience. Go get a few clients for 6-12 months and then come back."

Shit.

Talk about a punch in the groin—she had "casually" failed to mention that to me, which in retrospect shows just how naïve I was—thinking that the piece of paper would be my ticket, instead of experience and a core skillset (which is the only thing that employers really care about).

I went back to square one. Got another piece of paper? Check. Punched in the balls? Check. Back to the drawing board? Check. Shit nuggets. So I spent a couple of weeks testing new things out— how could I put this to good use? I realized that I didn't actually like personal training, but maybe I could leverage it for something new. I had seven years of experience in the gym, training myself. I had also trained a few friends to get some results. Then I thought about my personal blog again—Milk the Pigeon—and realized I could do something similar online.

The rest became history—even though I didn't use any of those ten jobs in my twenties, and even though I didn't become a personal trainer in a big globo-gym, it led me to the idea of doing online training, which became my online wellness site, blog, business, and book. That business eventually earned me my freedom once and for all, and in another weird twist of fate, led me to discover my own calling: Chinese medicine. Through a few more stacked bricks (aka what was missing in my approach with clients, what I loved, and what I wanted to study for the rest of my life), it made perfect sense for the coming year.

From the outside, the process is painfully messy (and often very painful and discouraging internally). It feels hopeless most of the time. But the most important thing to remember is that you have to stack the bricks. Your map will create itself, but if you never try things out and stack brick one, you'll never find the life changing bricks somewhere in the mess. That could be brick six or brick twenty.

This is true whether you're trying to find your dream job, what to do with your life, or even romantic partners. It's often true that one brick will lead you to the brick you're actually trying to find.

Experience > Buddha

Coming back to this brick idea there is something I've noticed to be particularly true of twenty-somethings: we spend a lot of time navel-gazing and not taking action. As someone who spends a lot of time thinking about life, I can tell you definitively: it's about as useful as a poo-flavored lollipop. Not one of the books on finding your passion gave me the entire box of pieces to the puzzle, although each one gave me a very small piece.

For example, going after all those job pieces and stacking the bricks of your career—you can't just be doing the What Color Is Your Parachute Exercises. That stuff is great and will provide insight into understanding yourself, but it's kind of like dating—some things and people sound great on paper, but when you meet them, there's no spark. In fact, there are tons of similarities between dating and finding a job or business you love, but at the high level you have to trust your gut more than anything you see or write down on a sheet of paper. At the highest level, the most successful people are intuitives.

Finding a job for example, you have to be regularly taking those coffee meetings with people to see if a career is something you potentially like, but shockingly, most of us get stuck in the research and thinking phase. The only thing that matters is the time in the trenches. When I've coached people in their twenties or thirties, 95% spend an inordinate amount of time thinking rather than getting their hands dirty, and seeing first-hand if they'd like a career. No doubt that's because action is harder than thinking.

With finding your passion, the same thing is true. It's really easy to get paralyzed into not taking action, because you feel like you might go down the wrong road and waste a ton of your time, potentially ending up worse than you were before.

At the end of the day though, it's just about the action that matters, even if you don't know which direction to go. If you read this right now, and think to yourself, "okay, only five percent track their action daily, so I'm just going to do that" I'm confident you'll make leaps and bounds, unlike most of the world.

What If I Don't Know Where
the "X" is On My Map?

Naturally, there's another question that comes up. Okay, I get it. Basically set a goal and go after it. That's fine and dandy, but what happens if I don't have a clue about what I want? Why would I bother taking action when I have no idea about the path I want to go down? What if I waste time going down the wrong path and screw myself even more?

I was stuck in the longest rut for more than a year in my early twenties, and the primary reason was because I had this exact mental philosophy: it's better to take no steps, than it is to step in the dark, right? Wrong. For example, I told you about my very short-lived personal training horror story. I spent six hundred bucks to get the piece of paper, and the hiring manager implied that I'd get the job if I did, and when I went back they treated me like they didn't even know me and told me to get more experience.

Going into that, I knew personal training wasn't my passion. But I also knew that it would provide something for me, and some ideas about how I could move forward and get ahead. What I didn't realize was that this step into the dark would provide a lot more insight about how I could step forward. That training example introduced me to the idea of just training my clients online so I could travel. That led me to building an online health business. And that lead to a whole bunch of other cool stuff like writing my first book, Master the Day, which helped a lot of people.

It was also the momentum from that step, over six years ago, that led me to finally find the work I love: Chinese Medicine. If I never took that first step into the darkness, I never would've set into motion the series of events that led me to where I am today. Sometimes you have to step before you see the "X" on the map, and it will reveal itself with time.

***

One other thing: much of this process that I'm talking about, is more of an intuitive path. In other words, you can't iron-discipline your way to finding it, because it's more about sensitivity and listening to your gut than grinding out painful days in an office. This is something that can't be taught to another person easily, and I had to re-teach myself, since I found myself ignoring my gut for a bulk of that lost period of my life (no coincidence, what a surprise).

Along these lines, what should you be doing if you feel like you're on the wrong path, and after sticking out the first few months in a job or situation you really are unhappy with, you still want to run away? Follow the example of startups and the idea of rapid iteration. When a company releases a new feature, they often look for feedback immediately to see what people think. If it's great feedback, they keep it, if it's not, they drop the feature and pull in a new one soon to iterate and test out. This is how the best companies in the world ensure constant innovation—they are always testing, tweaking, and trying little things out (little bets) that give them data.

When things aren't working out right, they iterate, pivot, and do something else. Just like a lean startup, you need to quit quickly and iterate as soon as you feel something is wrong, or you don't want your boss's job in five or ten years. If it's obvious that you hate the work, and it's not where you'd like to be in the future, start planning your escape.

The same happens in relationships quite a lot too. We stay because at least it's a guaranteed partner, just like we stay in a job because at least it's guaranteed income. And on and on we go in the relationship that's making us sick, because we're so used to the person and we have so much history together, we stay rather than doing what we know is right. Just like in relationships, the amount of people I know that told me that, "the day they got fired was the happiest they'd been in a decade" is almost scary. When things don't feel right, move quickly.

A year turns into ten faster than you think.

Chapter Recap: There Is No Map

☐ **There is no map.** Here's the thing about being a human being (versus a broccoli plant growing in someone's garden), and being a younger human being. It sounds scary as hell, and it sometimes is, but there's really no map. There are likely tons of people who have done what you want to do (or maybe there aren't a lot), but overall you are unique, and your life is going to be unique. As a result, you're going to have to piece together the puzzle a lot by yourself as you go.

☐ **Stack the bricks.** The vast majority of people that have "figured it out" did it through action—each day they stacked a brick, worked hard, and pushed forward despite not knowing where they were going. Each time you stack a brick, try a new opportunity, and test something out, a new door opens that wasn't there before. But you have to keep stacking and testing things out to get any real clarity on where the "X" is on your treasure map.

☐ **Model the masters.** Let's be honest here, we're all special snowflakes, but we really aren't that unique. Unless you're the first person to do something in human history, others have been through what you want to go through, so there's enormous value in modeling. For example, if you're a painter and you have no clue how to get paid for it, can you find ten other contemporary painters who are making a living? Can you interview them or just email them, and find out how? That could save you a decade (or more) of struggle.

☐ **Fail—and quit—quickly.** Flat out, bottom line—if something doesn't feel right, get out fast. I don't care how good the job is, or how good the relationship is in your head, if something is screaming in your gut, it's time to split. Easy in theory, hard in practice. Take the data this experience gave you, update your treasure map and jigsaw puzzle, and move on.

CHAPTER 5

Where's Your Ladder? Do You: Rebel, Conform or Evolve

When I was first trying to figure out all the possible career paths that I possibly could've taken, I broke down the advice most people gave me, and it fell into two distinct categories. The first category was that most people do what they see most other people doing: they become accountants, bankers, marketing folks, or just do what their parents did. In other words, they conform. It makes the decision really easy.

Then you have the second group. These are the preacher's daughters that end up getting smashed and contracting STDs because they party so hard to rebel against their rigid upbringing. These are the teenage goth kids, the lesbians-who-aren't-really-lesbians, the surfer stoners who move to Costa Rica or Thailand, and the permanent travelers who swear off the white picket fence lifestyle. In other words, they're rebels. But they rebel not because they want to, but just to emotionally push back on something (or someone). This kind of rebellion never produces happiness, because it can't.

And if you look at things closer, 99% of people fall into this dichotomy: they conform, or they rebel. But guess what? I found that neither of these things made me happy, and likely won't make you happy. And that's because there's a third group almost no one thinks about: you. The problem with the two of these is that they're unconsciously reacting to the world around them, and thus are slaves to the world around them. If we were more conscious, we'd consciously sit down and actually try to think about the life we wanted, and then plot it out.

Group three seeks an awesome life through deliberate living, which is being conscious about what you really want, putting it on paper, then going for it. And guess what? You don't have to be either of these, or do any of the shit they say you do. You just have to do what you want.

This was a pretty huge revelation for me when I realized it, because I discovered that neither of the extremes produce fulfillment, because they're still unconscious. It appears that we either do what daddy says or become a rebel dropout to tell daddy to fuck off and get off your back. But both groups aren't conscious. Behind all the partying and "freedom" you see in them, rebellion doesn't make anyone happy, and they often aren't behind the scenes. It's only once you think strategically about the life you want—even if it's conventional and vanilla—that you really find fulfillment.

The Rebel, Conform, Evolve Exercise

The exercise I want you to do here is all about clarity. To be honest, it's designed to help you figure out down which path you've been going, if it wasn't immediately apparent reading the previous analogy. Have you been "going with the flow?" or have you been really sticking it to the man (but not getting any closer to your own dream?). This exercise will help you get some clarity.

First, take out a piece of paper and draw three columns. On the left column, write "conform" at the top. If you're realizing that you did "all the stuff society tells you to do" just write down your current life here. Write down the version of "you" that does all the stuff daddy and mommy wanted. Okay, I'd just get some boring ass banking job like most white people in Connecticut. Now, what about the rebel version of myself. The rebel version of myself would go be a ski bum or live in some monastery. Then create the third "evolved" column. The evolved version of myself? He'd start an online business, create a cool community, write books, travel when he wanted, give back, and pursue things that were personally fulfilling and not simply a matter of just making more money for the sake of making money.

I find that sometimes if you just get yourself to write out the rebel, conform, and evolve aspects of yourself, you can easily spot the middle ground (your "truth"). Let's go a bit deeper into this now and paint the whole picture.

The Rebel

The next phase of this exercise is an extension of your "one-liner." Really paint the full picture over the next three to five years.

For me, the rebel would partly be an extension of the Alex that went to China. I would say screw off to money, bills, and to the expectations of society. I would say screw off to the white picket fence lifestyle, to six figure incomes, to being judged solely on how much money I earn, and more. I would wear whatever the hell I wanted to wear, just be a monk or practice Kung Fu all day, and avoid working full-time as much as possible. Basically, I would do whatever the hell I wanted, would have no interest in slowing down or settling down, and would pick a pretty easy life to avoid the dreaded 9-5 grind.

The Conformist

The conformist version of myself would probably mean getting a job based on my major—most likely that would mean working in a biomedical lab, hating my life (while making mommy and daddy happy). It might mean staying in the tri-state area of New York, New Jersey or Connecticut. It would definitely mean settling down and finding a good wife with a good job and raising a few kids. It would mean slowly dying inside and just sticking with that same job, not taking any risks, and not really doing anything "cool" with my career. It would basically mean doing all the "right stuff" that's vanilla enough so that everyone gets you and you aren't considered too much of a black sheep.

The Conscious Alex

Now, the million-dollar question. Well, if the rebellious Alex who says "screw you to the man" would stay in China and not do much, and the conformist Alex would just make mommy, daddy and society happy, what would the conscious Alex do? If I could do anything, be anything, have anything—*what would that be?*

Obviously, that's the million-dollar question. And that's why you're here. It's also not an easy question to answer, and it's something that's constantly evolving as we get older. But for now, the most important thing is that you do the rebel, conform or evolve exercise—see which side of the spectrum you fall on, and as you go through this book, work on figuring out what the 100% conscious version of yourself would want. What *you* want. Ultimately, the only path to greatness, happiness, and fulfillment is found in just one thing: deliberate living.

For me, deliberate living was simple. I realized that I wanted to build an online audience around something I was passionate about. I wanted to learn and practice Chinese medicine. I wanted to keep traveling, and most of all, I wanted the freedom to be able to fill every single day with work I enjoyed. The bottom line was that I wanted to consciously *choose* my day, and live my life based on things I had *chosen*, not a bunch of crap I was forced to toil away on to exist on a plot of land.

The Mid Life Crisis

It's not uncommon to find people who are thirty, forty, or fifty who are still rebelling against mommy and daddy, and it's very clear that they haven't created the life that they wanted. They were too busy rebelling. See, in their head, they thought that they were, "living their own life" by being little rebels, but that forty-year-old is still the sixteen-year-old goth kid painting his nails black so he can be different and feel special. He didn't listen to his gut which said, hey, maybe I actually do like being an academic after all? But no, that's way too conventional, God forbid he did something that would make daddy proud. Always gotta' be the little rebel.

It's also a lot more common to find people who just did what mommy and daddy wanted, and even though they are providing for themselves financially, they're spiritually bankrupt. The entire inner experience of life (enjoyment, fulfillment) is missing. Here's an example of the type of textbook emails I get from people over thirty.

Hey Alex, I realize I'm not your typical audience of twenty-somethings, but I feel the exact same things you write about. I was the good kid, the ambitious first born who did everything right. I went to medical school, and I'm about to become a doctor, and now I realize: holy shit, I hate medicine. And I don't want to be a doctor! My parents are thrilled that I'm the "pride of the family," but inside I'm dying. What am I supposed to do?"

The emails I get from people under thirty-five are almost always about trying to figure out "the path" in life. The emails from people over thirty-five are from people who took the conventional path and are materially rich, but internally broke.

The question for you is simple: if you were a hundred percent honest with yourself about what *you* really want, what would you go after?

Chapter Recap: Do You—Rebel, Conform or Evolve

❏ **The rarest thing in the world is a person who thinks consciously about what they want.** We can easily put the majority of people into two buckets: they do what they see other people doing, or they rebel and fight against "the system" and "the man." The paradox is that the rebellious types often feel like they're not being sheep— but they are, because they're just pushing away from conformity, not because it gets them closer to the life they want, but just for the sake of rebelling. It's still being unconscious and thus doesn't (can't) lead to progress.

❏ **The 100% honest look.** Up until this point, which bucket would you say you fall into? Obviously, your situation is unique and different but the majority of readers I've talked to either were plugging along living the "normal" life, or pushed hard in the other direction and went unconventional. If you were completely honest with yourself, which path would you say you've been going down up until this point?

❏ **The third way.** Much like Buddha, who tried the two extremes in his quest for enlightenment, I want you to become your own little Buddha. If you had to be 100% legit with yourself, what does a cool path seem like to you—whether it's really conventional (like becoming a doctor), or really off the beaten track, like leading adventure expeditions in the third world? The most important thing is to make the decision based on what *your* gut says. Sounds easy, but it is way messier in practice.

❏ **Don't bullshit yourself.** The bottom line here is simple: the more you bullshit yourself, the more you get off track. We don't have to be brutally honest with other people or the world, but we *do* have to brutally honest with ourselves. Any lack of consciousness in decision making just causes that "ugh, how'd I get here?" feeling later.

CHAPTER 6

Deliberate Living: The Path Out of the Average Life

"Many men go fishing all of their lives without knowing it is not fish they are after."

— HENRY DAVID THOREAU

The Flaws of the Bucket List Life

A few years back, I thought the dream life just involved traveling long-term, going to kickass places all over the world, making my friends envious of my travels and… doing that forever. So I did what any of us would naturally do: I created a sweet bucket list.

Swim with whale sharks, jump out of airplanes, do some of the highest bungee jumps in the world, learn to speak another language, write a book, live abroad for a year. I did it all. And some people were envious. But an interesting thing happened: once the experience was done, I was no happier than before. In fact, I wasn't any happier than if I were just sitting at home having a beer with friends and talking about life. Exactly. The. Same. It freaked me the hell out.

How was that possible? I traveled half way across the world, I did all this conversation-worthy stuff, I crossed things off my bucket list, and everyone knew if they wanted to hear the coolest stories, they just had to ask me. That's when I realized that the epic life that I always wanted actually had nothing to do with a bucket list, because a bucket list was filled with *events*. One-time events. Happiness, and the great life, conversely are *processes*. They're built up of the things we do every single day, day after day, so one-time events (whether good or bad), usually don't affect our happiness levels long-term.

I made the biggest mistake imaginable, which was confusing short-term pleasure with long-term happiness and fulfillment. What I wanted was a great, meaningful life. What I *got* was a life filled with random (cool) experiences, but no underlying narrative or story that tied them together. I was essentially just a drug addict bouncing from high to high, never quite feeling fulfilled because I was just thrill chasing.

Very few of us consciously think about what we want from life—from our relationships to our health, finances, and more. And the paradox is, we often have to go far to the right side—we have to go do all the mid-life crisis stuff before we realize what actually makes us happy. Naturally, to the person stuck in the cubicle job who just wishes they could go sit on a beach and do nothing, you'd never want to tell them it's boring as hell after about two hours. The same is true of this bucket list stuff. I once told a friend that quitting his job and traveling the world wasn't going to make him happy, and he verbally kicked the shit out of me.

Remember that rebel, conform, or evolve thing we talked about earlier? Most people just push to the exact opposite side of the spectrum, not because it consciously pushes them *closer* to where they want to be, but often because it's the only way for them to get as far away as possible from where they currently are. This only works for so long.

It's extraordinarily rare to find somebody who consciously, deliberately thinks about what they want their health, financial life, relationships, happiness, and physical surroundings to look like.

My Quest for the Beyond-the-Bucket-List Life

It was around this time that I realized that this fundamental life philosophy wasn't making me happy. I realized that, okay, clearly sitting in a cubicle didn't make me happy, but I also realized that doing adventurous stuff every few weeks also didn't make me happy in the long run. It was cool. And it looked good from the outside, and it was fun. But it didn't produce the long-term purpose and meaning I was looking for. I felt a bit lost, because in the west isn't that how movies often portray the life well lived? James bond, right?

I decided to sit down and jot out all the aspects of my life, and how I wanted them to look. Health? Okay, I need to fix that nagging G.I. problem that has been going on for a few years. Fitness? Let's go for thirty pounds heavier, with a six-pack. Happiness? I want to wake up, do work I love, pay my bills, have an awesome woman in my life, travel internationally once a year, and have close friends. Spirituality? I want to meditate forty minutes a day, and read one spiritual text for a few minutes each morning. Contribution? I want to earn enough that I can comfortably give away 10% of my income (tithe). Relationships? I want to have an awesome woman in my life that invests as much effort into the relationship being awesome as I do, and who also wants to travel. Financial? I want to earn six figures doing what I love, literally, 90% of my days, I want to wake up feeling happy and excited.

I just kept writing—on and on and on. I painted the entire picture. If there was something I didn't know (like where I wanted to live, or the house I wanted to live in, or what my "dream job" was), I just tried to paint as much of the picture as possible.

Then, I put them all on one piece of paper, a Google doc that I shared with my mastermind every Sunday. I put another sheet in my wallet, and every morning, using an app on my phone, I texted myself about why I wanted those things. This turned out to be pretty interesting. For the first six months or so, the why behind it was pretty crappy—I want freedom from the man! Blah, blah, blah. It had no passion or fire behind it. It was emotionless. Gradually, over the next few months, I realized why I did what I did: because I wanted the freedom to have certain experiences, any time I wanted them, like one particular experience I had with my girlfriend.

It was a lazy morning in Cartagena, Colombia, in the summer of 2015, and we didn't have anything on the agenda. So we decided to go for a walk to find a nice breakfast or brunch spot, but since everything was closed on the main street, we ended up exploring, and going through side streets to try and find something new. After a while, we came across a beautiful side street that was reminiscent of Cuba, with every door painted a different color, and then a small little European café. We walked into the café, and there was only one other group of people there—a French mother and her son.

We ordered a bit of food, sat down to an amazing omelet, and just looked out the window and took a big inhale of the coffee we were served—*this is the good life*. It was the simplest, cheapest experience, but it made me realize that sitting down in little European cafés and just breaking bread with my girlfriend, or a friend, or my family, was one of the highlights of the ordinary days in my life. For some reason, that memory was so strong that I ended up writing "The Cartagena Vision" in the app. Each morning, I would re-live that moment, and think, "that's what I want more of."

See what I mean? I wasn't writing down "go bungee jumping again or skydive in the Maldives." I realized that the great life was a lot simpler during the day-to-day, and it mostly involved just two things: work I loved, and other people.

"How Did I Get Here?"

I was once sitting outside my parent's house on the back deck during a family gathering, and a friend of my dad's was talking with me.

"I'm telling you dude. You have to make sure you do all the stuff you love now, because it's a lot harder when you get older. You sometimes just wake up and wonder—how the hell did I get here? This isn't what I had planned when I was young."

You know what else is weird? The two biggest audiences that read my personal blog, Milk the Pigeon, are the following: lost twenty-somethings, since it's a blog for lost twenty-somethings, and then another group—lost forty- and fifty-somethings. At first I thought it was weird, because when I started it, I was just some twenty-two-year-old kid throwing out advice on how I thought people should live their lives—a philosophy I was testing out as I lived my own. So I figured, who am I to give people two or three times my age advice? But they said that it helped them, and it helped a lot.

The most universal email I get from that older age group is a clone of the conversation that I had with my dad's friend: how did I get here? Is this all there is? I feel so stuck. I thought life would be better by now. In other words, they don't feel like they're on the path they wanted for themselves when they were younger.

Well, what are you supposed to do then? Look for the patterns in people who got what they wanted.

***

Einstein was a huge douche. Yup, in-case you missed that one, let me repeat it again: Einstein was a douche. That was my primary "success lesson" from reading his biography, when reading the biographies of the "greats" became an obsession in my twenties, when I wanted to "become a great" myself in something (what, I had no idea). Okay, so he won the Nobel prize, became a world famous physicist, and is widely regarded as one of the most brilliant humans ever. I think a lot of that is exaggerated, now that I "know him" better, but having about a dozen (maybe more affairs), wrecking his personal life (and that of his children's), and literally doing nothing besides physics in his life, made me realize something: if you don't consciously think about what you want in every aspect of life, you only get what you think about.

Earl Nightingale, in many of his books, says that he realized the secret to success in his late twenties, and it was the following: We become what we think about. That explained Einstein a bit better to me. He didn't think about his health. He didn't think about his relationships or being a good partner. He didn't think much about his kids even. He just thought about physics. As a result, weeds grew in the other aspects of his life. When you think of it like that, it's kind of crazy. So it's not only important to write (on paper) your goals for your career, or dream job, or bucket list, but truly every aspect of your life.

Rockefeller was meticulous about keeping the books, Elon Musk is crazy about this space-age vision of the future, Earl Nightingale wanted to bring the gospel of personal development to the masses, Walt Disney had a huge vision for a land of imagination, and more. I realized one thing after going through the biographies of others: the people that get what they want, think about what they want constantly, and work towards it 1% every day. It's slap-in-the-face simple. That's the path out of the zombie, "holy shit I'm having a meltdown, how did I get here?" life.

Over time, when I started applying this idea—just writing down what I wanted, looking at it daily, and working 1% towards it—small things started happening. They all took longer than I wanted, but they happened. I got closer to the body I wanted, I started a business and eventually quit my job (3+ years later), I wrote a book that helped a lot of people, and took many more trips like that Cartagena trip with my girlfriend and with my parents and siblings. This new kind of daily journey towards a mission (that picture I painted) became my new North Star.

It sounds crazy, and I don't expect you to know even close to 100% of what you want (otherwise you wouldn't be reading this, right?), but just start thinking of this. Better yet, take out a piece of paper, and just write down: My vision of what I want, as far as I know right now. As

Earl Nightingale says, most people would rather resort to crime than even think just a little bit.

Having a Reason to Wake Up

In 2015, I started a habit to religiously ingrain this in my mind: I wrote down what I thought I wanted my life to look and feel like on a daily basis, in each aspect of my life, and then put it onto a piece of paper. I folded the piece of paper into a 2" x 2" square, which I then put into my phone case. For the year previous, I had been working on just reviewing it each morning, but long morning routines quickly became a chore to me, especially on the weekend where I just wanted to get out of the house.

So my shortcut was to lower the friction of the habit: just carry it on me at all times. Now, anytime I was waiting on public transit, had a spare moment, or hell, was walking down the street, I could quickly review and think about my goals. The first thing I noticed was almost instant: on a typical Saturday morning I would have no reason to really get up, and would laze around until going to my favorite coffee shop for four or five hours to hangout and "work."

When I woke up, and quickly looked at that sheet, it was as though I had woken up with a treasure map with an "X" marking the spot: this was the road to start walking down. So rather than sleeping in, I suddenly had a focal point for my time and energy. I would open that up, and look at some of the "ideal" goals I had listed (really, directions to travel). For example, one of my goals for the relationship column was to have an almost jockish social life, because that's one area I've always struggled with since I was a kid. I consistently have no one to do anything with on the weekend other than my girlfriend, and it's completely my fault. I don't work on creating new friendships or maintaining the old ones.

I was also working on writing a book at the time. Now, when I woke up around 9:30 I had a treasure map: here were two of my goals I could work towards. Not too long after, the coffee shop morning routine became my favorite time to work on books and do any kind of writing work. Get me a big window with lots of natural sunlight and a good coffee, and I'm ready to roll.

You might be thinking, "Okay, if I *knew* what I wanted, then I would be working towards it daily. But I'm not sure what I want." In that case, as it was for me, the most important thing to focus on is the direction that you're traveling, and the best way I've found to do that is to write out these "progressive visualizations." I'll give you a few examples of mine to help you write out your own.

Progressive Visualization

"Success is the progressive realization of a worthy ideal."

–Earl Nightingale

One of the weirdest, most paradoxical assumptions many of us have is that once we're successful, we'll be happier. I quickly realized this wasn't true once I got the fittest I had ever been in 2015, wrote a #1 Amazon bestseller (in three health categories, and I'm a nobody), and just got back from spending two weeks in Colombia with my girlfriend. All of those things were awesome, but the day after they ended, it was back to my normal happiness level. As Earl Nightingale says, Children are happiest Christmas morning, with the anticipation of opening the presents, but by the afternoon they are their regular old cranky, tired selves. We're often happier during the days leading up to vacation than we are when we get back, and it's the *process* of achieving goals that makes people happy, not reaching them.

So success is *the process* of being successful, the daily routine that you enjoy that will inevitably "get you there." A bit paradoxical, right? Because of that, this next exercise I want to introduce you to, has the explicit purpose of painting the daily vision of the life you really want. A direction in which to travel.

First, I want you to write out the major categories of life, including the following:

1. Relationships
2. Health
3. Finances | Career
4. Spirituality | Purpose | Meaning
5. Contribution
6. Fun and Leisure

Next, as best you can, *write out* a description of what the ideal aspect of that life looks like. Here are some of mine.

Relationships. When the weekend rolls around, I have multiple people texting or calling me to hangout. For the first time in my life, my close friend group is like the living room from the Big Bang Theory or Turk and JD from scrubs. I always feel like I have a core crew of people I belong with, and have my own tribe of people that get me. My girlfriend and I have a ton of fun on a weekly basis, with date nights, going on trips, and we always make sure to save $150 a month so we can take that yearly trip to a new country each year. If I'm not living within an hour drive of my parents, we talk on the phone once a week and I'm there for Christmas, for at least a few weeks per year.

Health. The first thing I notice when I wake up in the morning is that I feel flexible, strong, and energetic. I feel vital, like I have tons of energy. All the stuff in my day-to-day life excites me and energizes me, so I'm happy in the morning, I'm calm, and I have a hell of a lot of fun. Physically, I weigh 185 pounds with the same body fat level I have right now, and I have the flexibility of a yogi. The most important aspect of my health is internal, and everyday I wake up feeling like there's a reason to wake up, because my life is awesome.

Financial and Work. The most important experience of my daily work life is that I enjoy my work and it contributes to someone other than myself. I wake up and see myself writing the first hour of my next book, then heading into my busy clinic to see patients for six or seven hours. In the evening, before heading home, I shoot videos and write articles before hitting the gym and heading home. The most important aspect of my work, juggling Chinese Medicine and an online community and business is one thing: Mastery. Mastery is the be all, end all, reason for what I do and why I wake up. If all the money in the world disappeared, the only thing that would matter is my mastery in the service of my patients. My reach is incredible: I have over a million YouTube subscribers, a million fans on Facebook, and I make an income well into the six figures, positively impacting other people. But more than all of those, because I'm focused on mastery, well-known public figures from across the globe come to me to be cured of their illnesses. The level of meaning is off the charts.

Spirituality, Purpose and Meaning. Each morning, I see myself meditating for at least forty minutes, because by the time I get into the clinic, the level of my calm should be so palpable that all my patients feel it. I should have such a high level of internal calm that they leave *thinking, "Weird. He just feels different, special somehow." That's how good my own personal cultivation needs to be. I see myself getting into arguments with people or having financial stress, and still being calm and tranquil. I'm always on a "borderline laugh." An inner smile.*

Contribution. *I give away 10% of my income to charity, or 10% of my time treating patients for free that can't afford my services.*

Fun and Leisure. *Each quarter, I start a new project, whether it's family, fun with friends, or just work related—that I'm intrinsically motivated to do and has no ulterior purpose—just fun. On the weekends, I always have friends to go out with, to talk about life with, or to go on trips with, and my girlfriend and I prioritize our own annual trip. I regularly go to seminars that interest me (either as a speaker or an attendee), and as general rule try to take as many trips with friends and family as possible.*

Okay. So that's a ton of stuff, yeah? Do you see how there's a world of difference waking up with all this written on a piece of paper versus… having no piece of paper?

One is waking up with a treasure map for an awesome life, the other one is just waking up into this haze of confusion we humans call "life." Big difference. If you really don't have a damn clue what you want from a certain aspect of your life, just write down what you think sounds cool. So if you're in the "ugh I have a million ideas about careers" phase, just write down Anthony Bourdain, for example—he just travels, eats, and talks. That sounds cool. Remember that it's a direction to travel in. And waking up with any direction to travel in is better than waking up without one.

And again like Earl says, we humans are like ships. If a ship leaves a port without a destination, then it doesn't matter how fast it sails the seas and which direction the rudder helps it go—it won't reach its destination. But when a ship has a destination, it doesn't matter if it gets blown off course, because it can always course correct, since the destination is still listed on the map. But most of us not only don't have a map with a destination, we don't even have a rudder to steer.

Don't you think that, even if it takes a lot longer than you think, waking up with your own personal treasure map will *guarantee* you eventually get there?

Chapter Recap: Deliberate Living

☐ **Deliberate living is the rarest thing in the world.** Imagine how fulfilled we would all be if we literally wrote down *exactly* what we wanted in each aspect of our life—health, happiness, career, finances, relationships, marriage, travels, contribution—then worked towards it. Okay, so maybe you don't really know what you want in some aspects of your life, but don't you think the chances of living an awesome life would go way up?

☐ **My little phone trick.** When I first started thinking about how simple (at a high level) deliberate living is (see the previous paragraph), I took an afternoon and simply wrote out all my goals on paper for the six or seven major categories of my life. Then I wrote down what, as of that year, I thought I wanted in all those categories. Then I started looking at it twice daily, and visualizing it in my head. To make sure I always get a chance to review the goals daily, I fold it up into a little square, and stuff it inside the back of my phone case.

☐ **The power of written goals.** There are all kinds of urban legends about the power of writing down your goals, but I think the most powerful "proof" is logic—imagine waking up and just getting started with the day, versus waking up and looking at all the stuff you want to get done in your life, and then thinking about it throughout the day. Is it really rocket science to suggest that you'll make a lot more progress when you think about your goals more often?

CHAPTER 7

Not Deciding Is Deciding:
Impossible Decisions for Dummies

There was this horrible, long period in my twenties where I was just stuck. I was stuck in this ridiculous period where I was doing all the work to try and find a job, but I couldn't get a single one for almost a year. I had moved back in with my parents and I was doing plenty of naval gazing. I'd go to the same coffee shop every day, read all the books on life coaching and figuring out your dream career, and I took all the personality assessments.

But I was stuck. I wasn't making *any* forward progress—things were just messy and nothing lined up—no matter how hard I was working. At first, I figured I just needed to work harder if I wasn't getting the results. So I would personally go and visit companies that had posted jobs, I would network, and I would try to do fun things with my very few friends to ward off that depression and stuck funk.

When that didn't work, I assumed that maybe things weren't lining up because I wasn't actually interested in any of them. I mean, I honestly did not like most of the jobs I was applying for, so maybe I was self-sabotaging because I didn't really want them? Entirely plausible. So each day I would carefully and meticulously listen to my intuition. What kind of jobs called to me? What kind of cities should I move to? What kind of adventures should I go on instead? Should I go back to graduate school or just go somewhere abroad for a year?

Nothing. Nada. Zilch. Not one intuition about the direction I should be going. And since I believed that my intuition was my guide, I just kept waiting, and waiting, and waiting and… I waited a very long time. And since there were no intuitions, I didn't act for an uncomfortably long period of time. I kept the silly part-time jobs I had, kept reading the same books, took endless personality tests but wasn't one inch closer to really anything.

Then I got stuck.

It took me a much longer period of time to realize something extra important for twenty-somethings: *not* making a decision *is* making a decision.

***

It's often hard to spot how not making a decision really is making a decision, so let me explain it a bit better.

Have you ever been in a relationship (or know someone who has) where you're so uncertain about the future that you're afraid of making a decision? Do I stay, or do I go? You spend night after night with that damned knot in your stomach, confused about which direction you want to go in. You say that you love the person, but there are a few things that have really been annoying you lately, and you're trying to decide if they're deal breakers or not. You figure you're safer by not deciding—because at least you won't make a wrong decision and break up with them, then really regret it.

Then the bomb drops: your girlfriend or boyfriend decides to break up with you. While you were thinking, analyzing and deliberating, the worst-case scenario happened anyway. Sometimes when we're really afraid of messing up something important, we just don't act, because we think that not acting is a safe decision. In reality, it isn't.

What about figuring out what to do with your life? Going back to my own example, I didn't make a decision because I was waiting for that slap in the face from some deity up above and the crystal clear conviction of a direction to go in. That never came, and it rarely comes like that (at least early on), so the years went on and on and on, and eventually I was twenty-five and twenty-six and still hadn't made progress—which was the most terrifying thing of all to me. The world couldn't have cared less that I didn't decide—time kept quickly moving along, as did my anxiety about time passing and me not having achieved anything.

Any action, in any direction, is better than doing nothing. When I went deep into that funk, after doing "nothing" and naval gazing wasn't working for about six months, I did something different and made a promise to myself. I promised myself that if I was just going to be miserable forever like the way I was, then screw it, I was just going to work my ass off for the next five years and see what happened. If that didn't work, and I was working way harder, I could always change my plan. I figured, even if my gut wasn't giving any clear signs, I could steamroll my way to progress, since I was already miserable anyway.

Well, as the story goes, the rest is history, and it was a great lesson for me. Sometimes when you're really stuck and there seems no clear path to follow, you just force yourself to pick anything. At first, I took a job working at a local Chinese medicine clinical practice. That made me consider studying Chinese medicine, but I forgot about it after a year or two. That added a new piece to my potential life jigsaw puzzle. Then, I worked for a company that specialized in digital marketing, which wasn't a dream job but made me think a lot more about the Internet as a business.

At one point, I worked for an influential online marketing guru, which made me realize that I don't ever want to be in the business of coaching business. If I have my own business, I just want to be world-class at it, rather than teaching it. Another job I took was a God-awful door-to-door sales job, which taught me a few things and added a few new potential paths to my "what the hell should I do with my life?" playbook. It made me realize I hated selling, and even more, selling products I didn't believe in. It also taught me that I personally like a lot of alone time when I work.

Again, most of these were not dream jobs or ideal opportunities when I took them. Instead, I forced myself to act, to see what would happen. The very act of picking something and maintaining momentum led me to my next step, which led me to my next step, and so on and so forth. That last job made me realize that a part-time remote job would be best—so I took a remote job, working as a nomad out of the Philippines, Taiwan, and other locations, realizing I hated work and travel, so I stayed in one spot. Eventually, it was the fusion of all of these, the health and wellness, the online stuff, the Chinese medicine practice (two actually), that eventually led me to the opportunities that were goldmines, and the decisions I had a hard time making.

Sometimes when you're stuck, the solution is simple: act. Do anything in any direction, even if it isn't ideal now. It often leads you to your next stepping-stone. Besides, life is a lot like stumbling home drunk from the bar. As you take one drunken step after another, up your dark stairway, each step becomes more and more clear. The trick is to have faith that the staircase is there in the first place.

Chapter Recap: Not Deciding *Is* Deciding

☐ **Clarity comes from action.** You've heard it before, but I'll share it again—none of my big, pressing, troubling questions came from thinking about them, even though I spent an insane amount of time trying to ponder my way out of the box.

☐ **Almost nobody just "figures it out."** This idea of "figuring shit out" is almost an oxymoron, since I have never just "figured out" a major life problem by thinking about it. I have never just "figured out" what I wanted to do with my life, or where I should move, or what business to start, or what book to write. What you never hear in the stories of people who are "figuring shit out," is that they were constantly trying things, iterating, seeing what they liked and didn't like, and then they finally stepped in the direction they wanted.

☐ **Take a step in any direction.** The bottom line here is to take a career step in any direction. If you've been stuck for a long time, this will open up new doors. Sometimes it's the new people you meet, the experiences you have, or realizing that you *really, really* hate something, which leads you to the next step, but it always does. Just step.

CHAPTER 8

The Drunken Staircase Dream Job Process

Trying to figure out what to do with your life is like trying to stumble up a staircase blasted drunk on a Friday night while using your iPhone flashlight. You can't see the rest of the steps, but you know that if you just find the first one, you'll be able to find the second one. So you flip on that flashlight, stumbling around, and just make sure you don't eat it on the first step, and you know you're pretty much guaranteed to make it into your bed, safe and sound.

The horrible irony of course is that most of us tend to do the opposite in life. When we don't see the path ahead of us (because it all looks like we're heading into the darkness without any kind of GPS), we stop and stay still. I mean, it makes sense, right? Who in their right mind keeps going when they're stepping into the darkness? All the fairy tales of humankind have warned us about the dangers of the woods—the trolls, bears, witches and child molesters (or eaters). The problem occurs though, when you keep staring into that abyss of darkness and don't do anything. That's how you get stuck.

Unfortunately, that's exactly what happened to me. In my early twenties, I was doing what everyone else was doing—just trying to get a job, and ideally, a job I loved. The problem was that literally none of the jobs I found was speaking to me, and since I was looking for my passion and my dream job, I found myself not acting because none of them were the "big kahuna." Months and months went by because I wasn't taking good opportunities, because I was too busy waiting for the great ones. And unfortunately, many more months went by before I was forced to take a new job that I didn't care about, to pay my bills. I was stuck, but at least I was stuck and making money. What I would've killed to know back then is was the idea called "stacking the bricks." The same stacking the bricks idea from Will Smith has infinitely more applications in finding work you love.

Stacking The Bricks to Find Your Dream Job

One of my Chinese Medicine mentors loved sharing this idea with me that seemed to make a lot of sense: everyone tries to control life and expects their future to be linear. We expect that we can fully control everything, and that it's going to be such a neat, straight line, to finding work we love, or our passion. But take a look at your past for a moment: even the city you live in now, how'd you get here? Was it completely planned and linear? Or are you almost like, "eh, I don't have a clue how I got here," or "I never expected I'd be here." Think about the people you've dated and the jobs you've had, or even your current job. Did you plan that fully? Or is it a little bit different than what you planned?

Clearly, for most of us, our past has been winding, up, down, left, right, and overall very winding and twisted. In other words, it's been anything but a linear, straight path. So why do we assume our future is going to be so neat and predictable?

I'll tell you the exact insanity of all the jobs I had before I found work I loved in part two of the book, but this idea is really important to grasp. I found myself paralyzed like so many twenty-somethings— no job spoke to me, so I just didn't act. I was stuck in the mindset of trying to find my dream job on day one, on brick one. In reality, it was closer to brick twenty that I finally arrived and figured it out. My first job out of college was being a teaching assistant in Rye, New York. I loved teaching, but I hated teaching high school kids that were close to my age who couldn't care less about being in school. Was it my dream job? No. But I took the job anyway, stacked the brick, and learned that I loved teaching (in some form). The next brick I stacked was a part time job at a Chinese medicine practice. Did I like being a college-educated biology major working the front desk of a clinic? Hell no. But I stacked that brick anyway. It showed me that Chinese medicine *might* be the thing I wanted to study in the future. It also taught me important insights about working for other people, self-employment, and more.

After this, I started a business with my friend, which we ended up working on for six months straight, and even though we never made any money, it introduced me to this word: "entrepreneur." Next, I started my own personal blog—Milk the Pigeon. I had a ton of fun with that, but it was just a passion project I would write on the side. Did it "lead" to anything? Well, now it has with this book, but for many years, it didn't. I stacked that brick, and moved on. Five years later I decided to write a book. Talk about being completely backwards. What it taught me was that I loved sharing and creating content online, and that it might lead somewhere. After this one, I got a bunch of B.S. part-time jobs that I hated, so that I could learn more about entrepreneurship on the side. The last string in this series of side jobs was becoming a personal trainer.

Yet again, I knew going in that being a personal trainer wasn't my dream job. I told you about the front desk person who told me to come back with a certification—so I took the $600 exam with my last dollars, showed back up two months later, and she said, "Oh, cool. I forgot to tell you, just come back when you have more experience training clients." I was beyond pissed off, and besides training friends, never ended up training any clients until much later. The brick? It helped me fuse two interests and life experiences—creating content online, and training—which became my health site, a bestselling book, and a business too.

Finally, the last part-time job that I had was working for another Chinese medicine person that was treating me for some G.I. issues. I started off as a patient, but because he ended up helping me so much I asked if I could just pay him to hang out with me and teach me a bit about Chinese medicine. He asked if I just wanted to learn more first-hand instead, so I worked there a few hours each morning before going to my second job. The brick? It solidified that Chinese medicine was what I loved, he became a huge mentor, and it got me on the path to studying the work that I later referred to as my calling.

***

What's the point of all this stacking the bricks stuff? What am I rambling on about? My point is simple: if I never took that first step, stacked that first brick, even though my future was dark and I had no idea what I was doing (and knew those jobs weren't my passion), I never would've gotten to where I am now. If I never stacked the first brick, it never would've led me to the second, third, fourth, fifth, and the much later bricks: having a bestselling self-published book, building a business, traveling all over the world, finding the work I'm most passionate about, and so on.

If I never took the first step (despite all the uncertainty) I never would've been led to the second. It's often after taking each step and stacking each brick, that you clarify what your next step is. Sometimes, if there are no opportunities now, when you take a step and make an action, new ones show up. Movement creates new opportunities—ones that you can't yet fathom. That's why it's such a paradox—the tendency is not to act, when you're staring into the abyss, but you have to keep moving.

Chapter Recap: The Drunken Staircase Theory of Finding Your Dream Job

☐ **Your 20s and your career search are a drunken staircase.** The paradox is that we have a tendency not to act when we're staring into the darkness with no clue about which direction to move—but we have to step anyway. Just like when you're drunkenly stumbling back into your apartment late Friday night, you use your phone light and as soon as you get that first step, you're mostly golden. Then you can find the next one.

☐ **You have to step before you can see the whole staircase.** Maintain momentum: this should be a mantra for twenty-somethings. If you find yourself, like I found myself, not making progress for at least six months, force yourself to act and just take something.

☐ **It's messy when you're in it, but incredible once you look back.** Many successful people have talked about how you can only see how the pieces connect when you look back. Steve Jobs' quote is particularly well-known, but most successful people that found work they loved had a similar story: it's one hell of a winding road. When you're on it (trust me, I was there for years), it can suck. A lot. But when you look back, as long as you're taking action and making progress, it's incredible how all those pieces help you put together the puzzle later.

☐ **Skills you acquire now are worth 10x later.** Here's another thing that it made me really think about: skills that you acquire now are worth infinitely more later, because you have no idea where they are going to re-enter your life and be useful. This was one of my strongest motivations, to learn new, marketable skills. Sometimes it's the fusion of skills that you have acquired that become your ticket to freedom.

CHAPTER 9

Ignore Everyone

"Remember what Bilbo used to say: It's a dangerous business, Frodo, going out your door. You step onto the road, and if you don't keep your feet, there's no knowing where you might be swept off to."

– J.R.R. Tolkien

I'm lucky. When I was a kid, I was one of those few kids you could tell had already found his calling. I would spend hours each day by myself outside meditating, learning medicinal herbs, and reading books on mysticism. By the time I was eighteen, most of my closet was filled with several hundred books on meditation, shamanism, and medicinal herbs. So if anyone had an early predisposition towards some kind of career, mine was definitely in natural healing.

But then an interesting thing happened. Around my late teens, I started talking to zombies (aka adults) who said, "natural healing? Is there any money in that? Why don't you just become a real doctor and make tons of money? Then you can do natural healing on the side." Guess what happened? I didn't have enough self-confidence or life experience to trust myself, and I gave up on the dream somewhere mid-way through college. As a result, I got extremely lost. I was depressed for multiple years in my twenties. I moved back in with my parents until I was twenty-six. I worked a bunch of shit jobs that made almost no money and gave me almost no skills. I got stuck.

It wasn't until years later, almost ten to be exact, that I finally rediscovered Chinese medicine and no longer felt lost in life (around age twenty-seven). But what happened in the in-between says everything (more on that later).

Another time, when I first started my online community and health business, I would work on it on the side every day for two to three hours, after working a full-time job. My life was pretty rigid: Get off work around five, head to the gym, be done around six-thirty, then go to my favorite café until they closed at ten to make sure I did the work and didn't go home.

One day, I ran into an old high school buddy with his parents at a favorite weekend café of mine, where I liked to work. I mentioned what I was working on, how I was juggling a bunch of part-time jobs while building my business and blogging on the side.

"So… how's your *blog?*" he asked sarcastically.

"Great dude! I'm well on my way to earning my freedom."

"Well, yeah, just don't give up that day job too quickly, you know?" he said.

And then I replied, "Actually, *I'm creating jobs.*"

He left with one last quip, "Okay, Obama." And just laughed.

The reality is that most people flat out give shitty advice, mostly because they themselves aren't living the dream and thus aren't fulfilled, but sometimes it's because they genuinely don't know this "other world" actually exists.

When I wrote my first book, *Master the Day: Eat, Move and Live Better With the Power of Daily* Habits, I encountered a lot of the same resistance. People would say things like, "who are you, to be writing a book? You're twenty-six. Where'd you get the experience to write a book anyway, are you a Ph.D. or a doctor? Aren't you afraid that people aren't going to think you're an expert?" I encountered mindless loads of discouraging shit like this (and half of it was from my own brain—typical).

But guess what? I wrote the damn book. I ignored every damn person, and their crappy advice, and you know what else happened? It changed a ton of lives. I get emails (every week) about how my book has been one of the best books in the weight loss space (better than many "gurus" that are household names). I just focused on what I thought was true—I knew that my message was unique enough, that there needed to be a book on it, to help everyone going after their wellness and weight loss goals. I wrote it, and it's been a big success so far.

Travel is another situation where you encounter bad advice a lot, too. At this point, I've been to somewhere around fifty or sixty countries, and still, almost every time I travel, I hear the same schtick, "travel is scary, everyone is a rapist and murderer (in that country), and holy mother of God, don't go anywhere near the middle east." Ironically, the only time I've even been close to being robbed was in downtown Zurich, Switzerland—one of the safest countries on earth. Oh, and you know what country has the most gun-related crimes… by far? Yup, the good 'ol US of A. 'Merica. People often feed you the advice that they believe in their own mind, which is filled with the fear-laden stuff you see on TV, the ignorance of the individual, and more. Be very careful who you take advice from.

Here's one final story to illustrate this. Throughout my twenties I prided myself on never taking a job for money, but instead, taking jobs that interested me or gave me the opportunity to learn skills that were valuable (or would be later on). Guess what the advice was I heard though?

"Oh man, dude, you only earn twelve dollars an hour? My son earns like seventy grand and he's twenty-one, why don't you just go into engineering too? Wow… that's rough dude, why don't you become a CPA and get a really secure salary?"

I moved back in with my parents until I was twenty-six—I went through a half dozen jobs in less than five years, and all the while I was building my side businesses, failing, trying new things, writing, creating, shooting videos, just seeing what things would work, and throwing that spaghetti at the wall. I had to ignore everyone—including my own parents and closest friends—because I believed that my vision was correct.

Where am I now? While all of my friends are complaining about their jobs, I'm writing this book in southern Spain for a month, while still running my business, working on projects I choose (and love), and earning more than I did at my previous jobs. And this is just the third year. I can't imagine how good it'll be at year ten.

The Dirty Little Truth About Advice

In every single situation, it was exactly the same and became an almost eerie prophecy. Taking advice is one of the most dangerous things in the world, and you really have to be careful about who the advice is coming from. Are they living their own advice? Do you feel it's good advice?

It all comes down to knowing yourself, having that vision of what you think you want (it's always evolving), and then plugging away every day, 1% more towards that dream. Things change, and so do people, but shitty, unsolicited advice is always around ready to stab you in the back and sabotage you. It's always there, so you always need to be on high alert for the dream stealers.

Here's another thing to consider: advice is so dangerous because we often get advice from the average person, which means we're getting average advice. Think about the advice you'd get around the Thanksgiving dinner table if you wanted to become an Olympic sprinter. Your grandpa would say one thing, "Just run every day, son." Your grandma would say another thing, "Olympians take tons of supplements, son." Your aunt says another thing, "I heard Michael Phelps eats 12,000 calories a day." And then your mom says another thing, "You have to eat really clean, no candy, no soda, none of the unhealthy stuff." But here's the thing, none of these people have ever been an Olympian, none of them have researched Olympians, and none of them have probably even *met* an Olympian. So you really don't know if it's good advice or not.

Most of the advice we get from people is based on what people *think* is right—not things they've lived. It's the classic broke relative talking about how to get rich; it's the fat mother-in-law giving weight loss advice; and it's the wanna-be author telling you how to write and sell a book. The most important thing is the age old advice from people who have made it: have the vision of what you want your life to look like (as best you can), and then work towards it daily with bullish determination and discipline.

As another cliché saying goes, "do not seek to follow in the footsteps of the wise; seek what they sought." Your path is going to be a lot different, and more fulfilling, but only if you listen to yourself.

Chapter Recap: Ignore Everyone

☐ **Be very careful from who you take advice.** Listen, everyone wants to give you advice about something in life, and some of it's going to be good, while a lot of it will suck. But the most common category is people who are giving you advice based on a life they haven't lived. Like a person watching sports who thinks they know what it takes to become an Olympian, rather than talking to an Olympian or someone who trains them.

☐ **The most important voice to listen to is your own.** This is something that comes with more experience and confidence, but the most important voice to listen to is your own. Yeah, you can punch me for being such a corny bastard, but it's true. If everyone around you (all the people you respect and admire) is telling you to go down a certain career path, but your gut is screaming no, what do you think is going to happen if you listen to them? Exactly what you think. You'll make everyone else happy and yourself miserable, and a lot of us do it all the time (or our entire lives).

☐ **Seek the vision you want, not what a mentor wanted.** There's another subtle mistake people sometimes make, which is finding a mentor in their chosen field—business, writing, sports, etc.,— and trying to emulate every little step they've taken. In reality, it's very hard to take those same steps and end up in the same location—your own path to becoming successful at your chosen craft is likely to be much different. If you try to blindly follow in the footsteps of the people before you, you often miss good (or great) opportunities.

CHAPTER 10

Go Towards, Not Away: Impossible Decision Making for Dummies

The first time I went on an extended trip around the world for a few months, it was for adventure—every time after that, it was to get away from something. There's an inside joke among most people who travel for a long time—when you meet people who travel for extended periods, they're almost always running away from something. A relationship gone sour, a job they hated, a death in the family, or just society. And, if you're one of those people who travels long-term just because you love it, it makes you furious that I just said this. *See what I just did there?*

Unfortunately, for me, I was no exception to the rule. Every time, after that initial trip, when I would travel for more than two weeks, it was to get away. I wanted to get away from shitty jobs paying me minimum wage, from "the man," from this messy thing called society, from being an adult, from responsibilities, from the ups and downs of life, and from the *weight* of life. It usually took shape in the same way, "Why would I work all these hours, just to earn this money, just to exist on one piece of land? This makes zero goddamn sense."

I would ask myself the same question before jumping ship: Should I just stay and try to find that dream job, work hard towards advancing my career, or just say screw it and travel? I could never make a clear decision. It was always either/or, and every time my intuition was confused.

So I ran away. I would take remote jobs and go to the Philippines with my girlfriend, and when she went back to work, I went off to Taiwan for a month, or more. From my Facebook newsfeed, it looked like life was awesome, but internally, I felt like any old drug addict picking the next high to distract myself from my meaningless life. It unfortunately took me years to realize one key growth principle: always run towards, not away.

Running in the Right Direction

Here's a typical scenario of a twenty- (or fifty-) something: you're in an "eh" job, in an "eh" relationship (one you aren't sure about), and you have no particular attachment to where you live. Do you stay, or do you go? If you go, where do you go? New York, San Francisco, LA or maybe somewhere in Europe? Those are cool cities, right? Everyone says you should live in one of those cities before you die. Plus, we all know that the center of the USA doesn't really count. So you decide New York—yeahhh, baby. NYC, the city of dreams; it's the one Frank Sinatra sang about, the city of hustlers and hipsters, and the hardest working folk around. You settle in, get a job there (impressive, if it's not being a waitress or making sixteen dollars an hour), start partying, and a few months later wonder what the hell you thought you were doing moving to New York. Why did you go in the first place? What are you doing there? You're feeling listless - did you make the right decision? Is this the right place for you?

It's pretty typical for us to make reactive decisions and just go in the opposite direction of whatever we've chosen. We talked about the rebel, conform or evolve idea already, and here's an iteration on that. The way I've learned to decide which decision is the best (e.g., it results in growth and I won't regret wasting time), is the following: what involves running towards that deliberate life, and what involves growth?

Here's an example: you're in a relationship that you aren't 100% sure about. Maybe it just started off as a fling, and you aren't sure about it. Now it's been several years, and one partner is asking "where is this going?" Almost always, we stay in relationships we know aren't right for us because of comfort. It sure as hell isn't a growth decision most of the time. What's the growth decision? I guess in a lot of cases, it's marriage. It's consciously (e.g., something you chose deliberately) upgrading the complexity and value of the relationship.

You're moving towards something. It's the opposite of staying in a non-serious relationship because you're afraid of the truth, or just pushing away from marriage.

Remember the analogy? Towards or away.

Let's say you've gotten a job just to pay the bills. That's okay, and it's understandable. But now you're realizing that you've been there a while and you aren't sure where it's going, or if it's what you really want. You figure, eh, let me just get another job, because this one is kind of boring and it sucks. So you just get another job.

Okay... so this new job is cool. I'm a barista, it's new and exciting, I'm in a chill part of Brooklyn, and life is cool. But a few months later you find yourself in the exact same spot. Weird, I was doing this same thing November of last year.

How come? You were running away from the bad job you didn't want, instead of running towards one aligned with what you want. If you're not sure about what path to take for your career, keep the job for now, but start using that time to think deliberately—okay, I hate my job, but what can I take from it that results in growth and involves me going further down the path I want. Otherwise, you end up like a lot of people I talk with: people who weren't conscious and deliberate about what they wanted in their twenties, thirties, or entire life, and now they're sitting around without much to show for it. They took jobs just for shits and giggles, they didn't think about the overall trajectory of their life, they didn't think about what jobs resulted in growth and acquiring skills (rather than "just being cool"), and they were winging it.

Newsflash: the awesome life doesn't just drop into your life. It requires strategy, a lot like doing anything else in life that works out pretty awesome in the end. It rarely just happens.

So if you're in a job now that you hate, and you're thinking of quitting to travel the world—is that a growth decision (running towards your dream life, dream job, a skillset that will help you) or just a running away decision? Are you ready to tear the hell out of there just to get away from your douche boss and crazy work hours, or is it because there's very clearly a growth move there to make your life awesome a year from now?

One more example: should you move away or should you stay? I moved apartments and cities sometimes as often as once a year during my entire twenties. I thought I was doing it because I wanted an adventurous life, but it took me a few years of being unhappy to realize I was doing it because I was just unhappy, bored, stuck, and figured that moving would kick start the process. Nope, it didn't. Yet again, I was making a running away decision, not a growth decision, that forced me to move closer to something I wanted, rather than moving away from something I didn't want (being stuck).

Here's how I evaluate whether to move to a new place now: Is there an obvious job there for me, or better job market aligned with what I want? If I have a job (and can keep it), is this for a relationship that I am actually planning on seeing where it goes a few years down the line? Finally, if those obvious two growth decisions don't work (relationships and work), is it just a damn cool city you'd want to live in before you died, which also allows you an opportunity to explore different types of work, or a part of the world you want to see? I'm a little bit extreme, where I almost never move (ever) if there's no benefit to my career also, but now that my work is digital and online, I can do that anywhere. The paradox is that decision making just got a whole lot harder.

For example, right now I'm writing this from Barcelona, Spain and I'll spend three weeks in the southern Andalusia region. I could've spent a month anywhere in the world to write this—which makes the decision making process a hell of a lot harder. You know what's even funnier? I'm realizing that I could've been just as happy sitting near my apartment in one of my favorite cafés working. It's a double edged sword when you think moving or changing things can make you happier or somehow provide an opportunity you aren't currently getting. Sometimes it's true, but most of the time it isn't. Most of the time, for me, it never improved anything. It was just a new city with new faces, which is sometimes exactly what taking a new job means (if it's a "running" decision).

Most of the time, we just end up exactly where we were—no doubt with some awesome travel experience, for example—but feeling that same sense of anxiety about time passing and not living our lives well. I saw this all too well after leaving China. So many of my friends and Chinese school classmates from there, ended up vagabonding for several more years after school. I had Koreans going to Canada, Canadians going to Korea, Italians going to Spain, Americans going to Europe, and Europeans going to every other country, other than their own. But most of my friends just felt that same sense of listlessness. In other words, we were all just moving places for the sake of moving places—getting whatever job could sustain us, partying, learning the language, and then moving on after two years.

Years would pass, and even though we acquired language skills, *that stuck feeling never went away.* This was maybe my greatest lesson here—if you move "just for shits and giggles," without any kind of positive growth for your career (or career exploration, or relationship exploration), you grow exactly 0%. You can have fun, and you can learn a language, which is great, but in my experience when it comes to fulfillment and feeling like, "damn, I've made so much progress in my life," this doesn't do anything.

When I flew back into New York City from China, I spent hours writing out this long personal essay to myself about trying to "move" as an attempt to run away from my personal problems (like being lost in life). At the end, I concluded it with one last thought.

The grass is not greener. Put that in your pipe and smoke it.

Chapter Recap: Impossible Decision Making 101

☐ **Choose awesomeness and growth.** One reason why decision making is so difficult is because you never know if you're going to end up worse off than before. How do you know you're not screwing yourself over and you're not going to end up worse off? You don't. Choosing to avoid something because it might cause your life to implode is much different than choosing something because it upgrades your life.

☐ **Consult your inner schizophrenic.** The heart versus the brain. Your brain will tell you all kinds of stuff, stories, logical ideas, and you know, stuff that *just makes sense.* And then your heart will be telling you to do the opposite. What do you go with? The gut instinct, 100%. The brain will tell you about some awesome job paying tons of money, but inside you, your guts are already turning over because it's so boring and you know it. These days I'm pretty tapped into my intuition, but in the beginning, I literally wrote on paper "Gut/Brain" and wrote out what each wanted. When the two are in resonance, you're in a good place.

☐ **The grass is only greener on a "growth" decision.** It's extraordinarily tempting to think that the grass is greener—in relationships, in careers, in moving. I made the "move" mistake about a half dozen times, assuming that each new move would mean I'd make friends easier, find cooler jobs, or somehow magically realize what I wanted to do with my life. Newsflash: it never happened. I only ended up in a worse position, because I was more socially isolated than before. My number one metric I use to make decisions now is simple: *Does it help me grow in the direction I want to grow?* It can be easy, or it can be hard, but does it at least help you grow 1% in the right direction?

CHAPTER 11

Follow Your Flow

When I was almost twenty-two, I had a dream that forever changed the trajectory of my life. To this day, I don't know if that dream was "supposed to happen," because it changed my life in a big way, or if it was just a weird coincidence. In any case, I'm waiting in line to do my interview for a medical school. When I walk into the room, there's a man in glasses and a striped shirt, and a woman to his right—they're both my interviewers. They asked me what's rumored to be the most important question in a medical school interview, which is, "Why do you want this? Why do you want to become a doctor?" I don't remember my answer, but I remember it feeling *really* powerful, like I had this in the bag. But they both stared at me, confused. "That doesn't sound like a very good answer," she said to me out loud.

Then, I woke up.

The dream disturbed me for a while. If there was *ever* one of those people that knew what he wanted to do since he was a little kid, that was me. When I was thirteen, I started accumulating what would later become a very large library of books on spirituality, shamanism, medicine, herbs, meditation, and more. I started a (legit) garden in my parents' backyard to make my own teas, I took a home study course from the modern order of Druids in the U.K., which taught me about the history, meditation, herbs, and practices of the Bards, Ovates and Druids.

Finally, when it came to college, I didn't want to go—because I knew what I wanted to do, clearer than anything. I wanted to go into natural medicine, or become a doctor, then study natural medicine. I didn't actually know if there were options for that, so I figured I'd do something conventional and then get the additional training. Why would I want to waste four years doing something I didn't like if I already knew what I wanted?

So when that dream came to me, for some reason it punched me in the gut like a ton of bricks. I *knew* I wanted to do this—so why had the dream rattled me so much? Something in my gut felt weird, so I went back to doing some research. Okay, I figured, the main question I had was the following: Is there any money in natural healing, whatever that is? Then I came across an article from a disgruntled naturopath, complaining that she paid almost a medical school-priced education, but going into private practice for herself ended up making 30k a year, and with 200k+ of debt, couldn't hack it and decided to go into "another profession where she could really earn some money."

She left this scathing article on the Internet, criticizing natural medicine and how the entire system was set up, and went on and on. She bitched and moaned about her lack of success and how she was "conned" into a natural healing profession. In retrospect, I realized that she was essentially just a loser—someone who couldn't make it happen in her own life, and was complaining. The successful ones didn't complain, right? There were thousands, I just didn't see them writing about how awesome their life was. Something about it bothered me though, and I went deeper into Google before regretting ever having opened my laptop. Some forums said to get a conventional medical degree to "fall back on," and others said to just avoid natural medicine.

The biggest blow came from a martial arts forum that I used to hang out on. There was this guy, "Doc S" that I used to respect quite a lot, who was a martial artist and also a doctor of Chinese medicine. I personally emailed him hoping he'd give me the "thumbs up" green light to go full steam ahead and go right into school. However, his exact words were, "I used to earn a six figure income, but now with some of the changes with insurance and so on, I can barely feed my family. Regrettably, I can't recommend it as a good profession."

My stomach filled with rocks, and that sealed my fate—at least temporarily. Right then and there I decided that I wasn't going to do what I deep down wanted to do. Little did I know that right at that moment, literally that day, I turned off my gut and my intuition for another six years, and every year after that would be a non-stop struggle, slogging through mud, feeling tired, depressed, lost and discouraged, before I finally had the *courage* to live my own legend.

The One Thing That Changes Everything

*"The secret to happiness is freedom. And
the secret to freedom is courage."*

— *THUCYDIDES*

There's only one thing you need to live out "the dream"—whatever that might be for you. It's not hustle, it's not money, it's not time, it's not support, and it's none of the stuff you read in books about success.

It's courage.

Yeah, that's it. It takes fucking guts to stick with *your* gut, when your parents are telling you that you're being a dumbass for going down a certain path. It takes fucking guts when the world says you will never succeed, but you trust yourself enough and have enough faith that you know you will succeed. It takes fucking guts to Google all the negative aspects of your profession or your dream, read the thousands of stories of failed souls, and then still show up 110% every single day. It takes fucking guts to listen to a mentor of yours discourage you, belittle your dream, or tell you it isn't possible, and then to ignore them anyway.

It takes fucking guts. Because at some point, the whole world is going to be telling you that you *can't*—and *you* are going to have to *know* that you can. You know the reason why I shut off my intuition then and didn't plow along toward my dream? I didn't have enough life experience to have the self-confidence to know that I could be the exception. So when a mentor said, "Sorry, you shouldn't do this," that was it. End of story. Finito. Man, what a naïve little kid I was! If only I had known the truth.

The truth is that most of the people that give you life advice are average, and thus, give average advice. The truth is that most people aren't successful, and it's entirely their own fault, and they'll try to talk you out of being successful. The truth is that most people that haven't lived their dream are bitter and envious of others, so they'll try to talk you out of taking the risk of going after it. And the truth is that, ultimately, whether or not you get what you want in life (for me, it was finding my calling and being successful at it), is up to you.

I *wish* I could've teleported back in time almost a decade ago, after I had worked for an ultra-successful Chinese medicine guy, who was so good at what he did that you couldn't even Google his name and yet he had a packed practice for decades—well through the recession. I *wish* I could've had the life experience I have now, after building my business, realizing that the girl complaining about her naturopathic school was—for lack of a better word—a loser and a not a top performer. I *wish* I could've seen the success I was now having in my own business and with my book, when before I would've just told myself the statistic, "almost all businesses fail within five years" and "almost all authors sell less than a thousand books in their entire lifetime." (Last month, over 200 people bought my first book, *Master the Day*). I *wish* I could've seen all those people discouraging me from the one thing I wanted to do most, laughed in their face, and said, "fucking watch me do it, then."

There are many things I wish I would've known back then. But most of all, I wish I had the *courage* to have trusted myself, when the world was telling me to pack my bags and go home.

***

Because I didn't have the courage to trust myself, to have crystal clear faith that I could accomplish everything I wanted, I became a lost soul. I turned off my inner GPS, and the next year after graduating school, I got whatever job I could—working as a teaching assistant. The year after that, I moved to China, and the year after that I worked remotely as a digital nomad and just made enough to travel full-time. The year after that I settled down a bit, and in the next four or five years, I went through over a dozen (yes, that means twelve) jobs, always searching, searching, searching—yet I had no idea what I was searching for.

In retrospect, it makes so much sense now. It's like being handed a map directly to your treasure, and someone lies to you and tells you that the walking path listed is incorrect—so you erase it from the map, and then try to find a million other paths when you had the correct path the entire time. No wonder it felt so confusing and alienating to me.

Knowing what I know now, one of the biggest reasons why people get, and stay lost, is because they turn off their intuition. Bottom line. End of story. What we've talked about up until this point, are some of the tactics for finding direction in life—there is no map. You have to think consciously about what you want, you have to keep throwing things at the wall, and always making decisions that take you in *some* direction (even if you don't think it's forward right now). But none of these are the underlying philosophy that keeps you on the path that leads you to your destiny.

That underlying philosophy is following your flow. It's funny, as a kid, and really into my early twenties (not surprisingly) I realized that I was always following my gut in almost every decision. I ignored almost everyone's advice unless I personally found it to be true. And then in my twenties, when I started getting lost, and no direction seemed to be calling out to me, a book that helped re-introduce me to this philosophy was Martha Beck's *Finding Your Own North Star*. Let me paint you the picture of how it feels when you're living in flow, following your gut, and listening to those hunches, versus the opposite (listening to your head). The difference is night and day, and most importantly, living this way just makes life easier.

Making Life Effortless: Living in the Zone 101

In Your Head Living:

- **Effort and resistance.** Bottom line, shit is just hard. You're investing tons of energy to accomplish things, you aren't reaching the goals you want, and everything you do feels like pushing a boulder up hill. For example, taking a job you don't like for the money. Every day *takes* energy out of you.
- **Nothing lines up.** It seems like you're unlucky, things never work out and shit just isn't working.
- **Internally, you don't feel well.** Externally, your life might look awesome. The great guy or girl, the nice car, the house, the good job. Internally, you feel like garbage and you feel like you're imploding. Sometimes, no one else knows or suspects it. Example: being with a great partner or spouse that everyone loves, but you just don't feel right with.
- **You decide with your mind.** You make your decisions primarily with your mind, based on what *sounds* like the best scenario—but you later regret them a lot or they burn you out and make you unhappy. You may actually go through cycles of taking things that sound great or look great on paper, but make you sick (sometimes literally, so you can self-sabotage and get out of a job). Example: choosing a job with great pay and benefits, but internally you have zero interest in actually taking

the job. Every day you die a little bit more as your bank account increases.

- **No guideposts.** Nothing really calls to you or speaks to you, so you just figure you need to push along harder. There's also no feeling that you're being guided or pulled onto the right path—you're always pushing.

In Flow Living:

- **Internally, you have a lot of energy.** For me, this was the biggest difference that I noticed immediately. When I "realized" that Chinese medicine was my thing, I immediately felt this sense of energy that I hadn't before. That's that nuclear reactor feeling—and eerily enough—when I just re-read Martha Beck's book, she used the same word to describe the feeling: nuclear energy. Example: Compare *internally* how you feel going to your job, or working just as many hours on a passion project. If you don't know how you feel, video yourself (your face) as you talk about it, and listen to the tempo and cadence of your voice. It'll show you some interesting things.

- **Opportunities materialize.** This one is really interesting. Another surprising aspect of following your intuition is that lots of freaky coincidences start happening. I don't really know why or how this happens, all I know is that some interesting things started happening to me—cool book opportunities, business opportunities, life opportunities, and very obvious paths I should go down because they'd make me happy.

- **You're actually excited about each day.** Another very big difference here, is that regardless of how successful or unsuccessful you are right now—you really enjoy the hour by hour projects that you are working on. You're happy working on them even if they implode or go nowhere, you just feel like you're *supposed* to create this work.

- **You primarily make decisions based on your gut**. A day-and-night difference is that this flow living entails making decisions almost 100% based on the gut feeling. That includes what you should eat, what job to take, who to date, what to do today, and so on. Another indicator that you're really following your gut is that when you take jobs that internally resonate, they feel good later. There isn't any of that "buyer's remorse" where the job looks great from the outside, but internally you're dying.

- **You feel guided.** This sounds hippy-ish and woo woo, but at the end of the day, when you're living in the flow zone, going with your gut, you start to have faith that life is going to be ok. It doesn't matter how messy it is now, you know that what got you to where you currently are, was the fact that you listened to your gut—aka, the signs. And the signs are still going to be there for your next journey, and for every day that you're still alive. What do you really have to worry about?

Okay. So you know the differences now, but what happens if you aren't in flow living, and life is hard, takes effort, and there's tons of resistance every single day? That's what we're going to talk about now. If you're anything like me when I was at my worst, every day was definitely *not* living in flow. It was stuck, painful, frustrating, miserable, and ultimately depressing.

What to Do When the Only Thing You Feel in Your Gut is The Bloating After a Cheeseburger

Unsurprisingly, the worst part of my twenties was when nothing was really calling out to me and making any sense or connection. Sometimes, what intuitively draws you towards or away from things, stops working, or maybe we just turn it off. The short answer is listen, and then track your experiences, which proves that your intuition actually does work, and then keep listening. If you can't feel anything, it often means you've suppressed your emotions for so long that you've "turned off" the gut switch, at which point you have to be conscious about asking how you feel.

Dudes are experts at turning this off, because we're told that being emotional is for little girls (and are literally bullied into being emotionless). The same goes for smart, intellectual people. Intellectuals are an interesting bunch, because they're so dominated by their mind that they don't even realize it. It's like they've been brainwashed in this weird cycle: they honestly believe being intellectual is a better way to live, which just reinforces mind thinking. Ambitious people are sometimes the worst, because they strong-arm anything and plow through life, with 5 am workouts, twelve-hour days, and gut-busting hard work. Why listen to your gut when you can just head-butt your way through the brick walls? The irony is that it works—but it comes with a very large price, internal stress, frustration, and *effort*—lots of effort.

The way back to becoming more sensitive to your gut is exactly what you think: practice. It's a lot like a dude in a relationship who is God-awful at being sensitive and listening to his wife—he has to literally, consciously, practice turning towards her to listen, acknowledge, and then respond. He needs to practice being more conscious about that behavior. For me, I started making little bets. For example, today is a rainy Saturday, what do you want to do today? Go to a coffee shop and read a book? Chill at home and catch up on some reading? Go walk the dog and enjoy the rain? Work on a side project you've been meaning to work on? Something else? Just write five things down and decide which one *feels* like the most fun. Pick it—and go. Later that afternoon when you've hopefully enjoyed yourself, reflect on what just happened. Again, it sounds corny as all hell, but when you realize what just happened—you listened to your gut, you enjoyed your day, and things went well—you can start cross-applying that.

Tomorrow, it's lunch time. Well, what do you want to eat for lunch? Don't listen to your mind fully—I should eat this to be big, skinny, chill out, etc.—listen to your stomach. Does it want a light meal with lots of veggies? Does it want to avoid coffee today? Does it want meat? Maybe just soup? Then go eat it. When you realize damn that tasted good, you reinforce this ability. Gradually, when you start making more and more of these daily bets and prove to yourself that your intuition ensures that you make the right decision, you're sold. And when you're sold, you start living that way more.

The way to start waking up that intuitive way to live your life is initially with little bets. To those of you ambitious and intellectual-folk, this might sound completely alien. To some of you (I've found that women are genius-level at this), this is extremely obvious. What I can suggest is that this has become the most important underlying principle that has gotten me to where I am now—a life I consciously created and wanted, particularly my career.

What if You Really Don't Know Which Direction to Go In?

One of the things that scared me the most was the phase from twenty-four to twenty-six where every day I had a seriously losing mentality, "none of this has any purpose. Life is so pointless. Get a job? So I can just exist on this plot of land, hate my daily life, and hate forty hours a week, when there's all this other stuff I'd rather be doing?" What made it worse was that nothing was calling to me. I was listening to my gut. I was doing the flow living stuff. I was trying to find work I remotely cared about. And yet every job that came my way, I hated—either I quit after six months, or I just stuck with the part-time job I had (twelve dollars an hour, about $24,000 per year).

Nothing was a clear winner to me. It's like the intuition switch had been flipped off, and it felt like each path might be wasting time by going down it. How did I know I wouldn't waste three years by trying out a career that I wouldn't like? If I tried out two, and neither were the careers I liked, that would mean I'd be thirty and effectively still at zero. That was scary as hell. What did I do? Depressed, lost, broke, living with my parents, I finally made one promise to myself on an extremely pissed off day.

"Okay, so this intuition muscle is broken for some reason. Screw it. I'm just going to work agonizingly hard for the next five years, even if I don't like the work and even if my intuition is screaming no, at least I will have made progress. If I'm still unhappy with my progress in five years, then I can do something drastic."

Obviously, the rest is history—that little bump to "force myself" to do anything, take any job, pick any opportunity, just start gaining momentum, lead me to the next one, and the next one, and the next one. Five years later, life is very different, a lot more effortless, and the intuition muscle is working again. So if you truly have no idea after all of this, force yourself to make a decision. It will give you momentum and put you on a new path that will lead you to where you are trying to go. That new path will lead to more data, more options, and more variety. Ultimately, that new path is going to unlock doors you didn't see a year, a month, or even a day ago. And that's when things get awesome.

Chapter Recap: Finding Your Flow

☐ **Don't forget the highest principle to guide you along your path.** This is something that you don't often hear people explicitly say is the highest principle that guides them, but I find it often to be true. Everything we've talked about thus far are considered tactics, but the high level principle that should guide you is this idea of following your flow. If I could circle and star one principle to live by, this would be it.

☐ **Living out of flow.** We're all familiar with not living in flow. Everything takes effort, it takes energy, it's pushing the ball uphill, it's forcing things to work out, and it's often exhausting. There's little to no serendipity. This is the state of living that you want to avoid.

☐ **Living in flow.** Living in flow (pursuing the things that naturally call to you the most) makes life way more effortless. The first thing you feel is purely physiological—you are way more interested in the projects and the work that you're doing. You have more energy. You're more motivated to show up. You're more excited. From there, there's a lot of other stuff that "just lines up for you" and either way, the work is enthralling.

☐ **It's this intangible underlying thread that guides you.** It's very hard to explain this concept, but when you start living more intuitively, life just gets easier. Things work out. Opportunities materialize. It's an incredible experience the first time it happens, but eventually, it can be the guiding thread that helps you lead your life. If you want to just keep this conversation very material, hordes of successful people I've talked to mentioned this idea of almost blindly going with their gut regarding moving, dating people, job opportunities, and their entire life. Several of them mentioned blindly moving to other states or countries just on a hunch, and when I asked them why they just shrugged and said, "it just felt right."

Ending That "What the Hell Should I Do with My Life?" Feeling

As you can tell, trying to figure out what the hell to do with my life was a long and winding road. And I was very lost for a long period of time. This is really important, because even people that "figure" it out get lost for a very long period of time in their teens, twenties, or even thirties. The most important feature in my own journey was that I never lost that hunger—I promised my soul that I would do whatever it takes, as long as it takes, to find work I loved, and then do whatever I need to succeed.

We've talked about a few key principles so far: first, avoiding the big mistakes that twenty-somethings make, which mostly revolve around not asking yourself the hard questions, and being conscious and deliberate in thought and action. Next, we covered the brutal facts around being human: there is no map. There is no guide map for creating a life you love that works for everyone. You have to create the map and figure out where the "X" goes that marks the treasure. This often means going against your own culture, your parents, and your mentors. The way you figure out where the "X" goes on your map is through deliberate living—not rebelling against your parents or society, and not conforming, but thinking consciously about what you want.

We then talked about the danger in not taking action for fear of making a mistake, and the fact that most of us in our twenties feel like we're staring into the abyss and have no idea in which direction to go. But you have to keep stepping and taking action.

Finally, we talked about ignoring everyone who isn't already living their own dream, and the high level philosophy to follow: follow your flow. And at the end of the day, the most important decision of all: no matter what you end up doing, always make decisions that lead to growth

Whew. Hopefully you've made it this far. Now it's time for part two, on finding or creating work you love, and the painful, winding path I had to traverse on my own journey.

QUESTION #2:

"HOW DO I FIND WORK I LOVE?"

CHAPTER 12

The Quest for Work I Love: Startups, Suicide and the Winding Path of Finding Your Calling

The quest for work you love is more like a "straight line" drawn by a toddler with a crayon, than a "real" straight line. Let that one sink in. After spending hundreds of hours buying all the books on finding your passion and calling, hiring coaches, plumbing the depths of my own mind and trying to relive childhood memories, I've realized that the process was a lot less linear than I thought it would be. I want to show you the trajectory of finding what I think is my own calling, so that you can chill out and not think you're an idiot for not having figured it out in a year. From the day I seriously started searching for my "calling" to the day I found it was almost five *years*.

I want to show you how each job I liked or hated gave me an important brick for building my own dream job empire, to illustrate first hand that it's *just a matter of iteration* and showing up daily, changing fast when things don't feel right, and always valuing learning over the money in the short run.

Alex's Bizarre Job Trajectory—The Bullet Points

First job, age 22, worked as a teaching assistant, in a high school. Realized that I loved teaching, and also realized that I hated having students that were sometimes my age (from abroad). Also realized that I didn't like being around sixteen-year-old girls in miniskirts, especially when a jealous girl spread a rumor that I was sleeping with another girl. After getting called into a panel with the vice principal, principle, school psychiatrist, and more, concerning this imaginary incident, I couldn't wait to get the hell out of there. **Brick:** I love teaching, but to the right people. Hated being in an institution-like school with massive amounts of politics and red tape.

Second job, age 24, teaching English part-time in Beijing. I moved to China with about ten grand saved from the first job, so I basically just worked my ass off, studied Kung Fu, learned Chinese, and got a part-time job near the end, since they were paying $30 an hour cash for virtually no work. I was a full-time student studying Chinese while seeking out mystics, monks and masters in the after-hours. I never went there to teach English, it was just the last month I was there, but it still counts as job experience. **Brick:** Kung Fu, medicine, and meditation are awesome to me. I definitely want those to be more present in my life somehow in the future.

Side business #1, age 24, "Where the f--- in the world?" This was inspired by vulgar and hilarious websites that creatively show you where (and what) to eat. With a buddy overseas, we decided to create a series of quiz questions that college students can use to ask themselves where to travel to next. After spending about six months writing out seventy pages of questions, answers, responses, and more, my friend's laptop gets sat on at a party, and he loses his half of the data. When I follow up with him, I don't hear anything for months. **Brick:** There were lots of lessons here on entrepreneurship, the first being that the market rewards speed, the second being that we never actually validated the idea with customers (no revenue model), and the third being that partnerships are tricky—they're a lot like a marriage.

Side business #2, freelance blog consulting. When I got back from China, the first thing I did was start my personal blog, *Milk the Pigeon*, since I saw all my unhappy friends still in the same jobs and boring lives. I strongly consider stripping, and post the following ad in different health food stores with lots of hot, rich mommies:

Over Qualified Multi-Talented Man for Hire

Tough times call for **hustle.**

I am a (totally legitimate) jack-of-all-trades Top (#22) college graduate who,
can provide any and all of the following services:
- **Tutor Mandarin Chinese & Study Skills**
- **Babysit** / drive your kids anywhere
- **Organize** your office, home, or living space
- **Move heavy furniture or help re-arrange**
- **Clean your yard**, prune, cut, rake, shovel
- **Sell items on Ebay or craigslist** for you
- **Establish an online presence** for your brick and mortar business
- And **many other freelance jobs** (inquire for full list)

Contact Alexander for References, Rates and Availability

Man-Slave for Hire
Over-Qualified, Multi-Talented Man for Hire
Ad description: Tough times call for hustle. I am a totally legitimate, jack-of-all-trades, top (#22— Clemson University) college graduate, who can provide any and all of the following services:

- Tutor mandarin Chinese and study skills
- Babysit / drive your kids anywhere
- Organize your office, home or living space
- Move heavy furniture or help re-arrange
- Clean your yard, prune, cut, rake, shovel
- Sell items on Ebay or craigslist for you
- Establish an online presence for your brick and mortar presence
- –And many other freelance jobs (inquire for full list)

Contact Alexander for references, rates, and availability.

Brick: First, despite being funny, this ad is God-awful from a marketing perspective, but that's neither here nor there. I loved blogging, even when I had no followers, and realized it was a great way for me to start writing about stuff that I didn't see anyone else writing about, which often leads to a following, and/or a business. It taught me that blogging is the way of the future businessperson and personal brand, no matter what industry you're in.

Third job, age 24, employee at a Chinese medicine clinic. When I get back from China, I see this dream opportunity—working at a Chinese medicine clinic drinking tea, talking about cool stuff, and more. Turns out the boss is a slave driver, and I realize that after about thirty days, I've learned everything and find myself bored as all hell. **Brick:** This was the first time I realized that I need massive amounts of intellectual stimulation and challenge at work. Besides, most jobs I hated within 1-2 months. It wasn't because of the jobs themselves, but because of something in my character that required learning and growth to enjoy work. I also got fired for mentioning I was working on a side business, even though I was making zero dollars per month.

Fourth job, age 25, employee #4 at a startup. I figure, "Shit, this corporate stuff blows, maybe a startup is what I want? Freedom? Flexibility? People that say "fuck" in every other sentence like me? This has got to be a dream job." I end up sending 300 cold emails a day, and thank Jesus I only worked for them part-time. After a week of sending thousands of emails, I'm ready to slit my own wrists and write off startups. **Brick:** I realize this kind of startup is not what I want (and certainly not the stereotypical venture-backed startup). I remove that from my list, and realize that I want to emulate some other kind of entrepreneur.

Side business #3, age 25, a bunch of crappy niche websites. Around this time, I had started Milk the Pigeon, and realized that I liked blogging quite a lot. I also realized I hate creating a business that I don't like doing five hours a day, and that "wanting a business" is a dumb reason for being self-employed. I get inspired by "Internet click millionaires" and create a dozen stupid niche websites to try to make money in sketchy ways, like curing heartburn during pregnancy. I realized that, having never been pregnant and having never had heartburn, I would rather get punched in the balls ten times a day than write about those things.

Brick: Never—ever—start a business just to make money, do it to add value, or because it's building off something you like. Even bigger brick: if you don't like doing something five hours a day, you'll never become great, so start thinking about the process and whether or not you like it enough to actually show up five hours a day. If one week is living hell, then you're not really going to make it happen.

Fifth job, age 25, remote data entry. I decide around this point that I need a more remote job since I miss traveling and hate monotony. I moved back with my parents so I have no overhead, take a minimum wage (~12 an hour) data entry job, and just travel. They let me log my own hours, so I work two hours a day, get a check for $500 every two weeks deposited in my account and just do whatever the hell I want. I end up having way too much free time, get bored of long-term world travel, and realize something important. **Brick:** Sitting on a beach in Thailand with time, enough money, and freedom illustrated something huge. It wasn't the lack of work that I wanted—I actually wanted to work all day but on things I loved. It perfectly crystalized that nobody actually wants to retire and sit on a beach, what we want is the feeling of being retired (e.g., each day being enjoyable, and effortless). That becomes my new focus for work, and I don't try to find ways to avoid work.

Side business #4, age 26, another stupid niche website, about knee pain. After having dealt with pain for quite a long time, I figured, "let's talk about it, since I fixed my own pain!" I launch a site on knee pain, and once again forget my five-hour a day rule, and ditch it after thirty days. **Brick:** Don't be dumb, and stick with your five-hour a day rule. If you don't like working on something, you won't succeed.

Sixth job, age 26, random craigslist sales jobs (commission only). After driving around all day in a car with a bunch of sweaty, sketchy salesmen, trying to push products on local businesses, I realized that I hate this kind of business. I think I hate sales, but later realize I only hate selling things that I don't believe in. After getting screamed at, in my face, "I told you bastards to never come here again," I get offered the position out of thirty-two applicants, and decline.

Seventh job, age 26, my mom takes pity on me. My mom still sees me living at home, unable to get a traditional job, and "building my silly blog." Mom is one of three partners at a small biz, they take pity on me and hire me very part-time, since I wanted to avoid corporate like the plague. I get paid $12 an hour and am thankful that I now have enough money to "rent a gun and buy a bullet." **Brick:** This taught me a lot about going through your personal network for introductions. I never once reached out to people to see if they knew someone who needed work, a huge rookie mistake. One person can get you a job you are seriously unqualified for, which is as close to skipping the line as it gets. I was constantly pulling out my hair when I was 100x more qualified than someone, but because they "knew someone who knew someone" they got all the dream jobs and I was sitting there slamming my head against a wall.

Eighth job, age 26, I attempt personal training. Around this time, after being stuck for six months and still at home, I just decide to become a personal trainer at a local high-end gym (that charges $100 an hour). I figure rich people will love to pay anything to train them. I go to the gym, talk with some people, and they tell me "get this $600 certification then come back and we're good!" I get the certification, then go back, and they say, "Oh, you don't have experience. Go train people for six months then come back." **Brick:** People actually don't give two shits about your piece of paper, they just want to see a skillset and proof of results. This is something that would serve me for life, both in creating my own business, helping others find jobs, and later, hiring people. But, this also led me to starting my own business—the one I actually got right, this time around.

Side business #5, age 26, Modern Health Monk. I realized that I had been working out for almost six years at this point, and got lots of questions regarding fitness, losing weight, etc., that I could easily answer. I'm not an expert, but realized that I didn't see anyone talking about habits in regard to losing weight and living better. I start working on it three hours a day, after my 9-10 hours a day working. My routine for multiple years becomes the following: Work, 9 to 5, gym, 5:30 to 6:30, side business 7 to 10, when my favorite café closes.

Brick: This was the first time I learned about the "Dilbert skill acquisition" principle. It turns out to be a fusion of interests: teaching (that I learned from the school) with online content and courses, community and blogging (that I learned from Milk the Pigeon), and something I could deal with five hours a day.

Ninth job, age 27, the online guru. I'm on a guru's mailing list, and I win a free ticket to his live event. I offer value, and don't ask for advice. He gets sick, and I add more value. I end up working for him part-time—one of the bigger names in the online business world. I work for him for six weeks, with the promise of great experience, remote work, and making a valuable connection and friend. Within a week I realize that it's a living hell, being contacted all hours of the day, and adrenaline shooting through my spine every morning when I hear the

Skype blip go off at seven am to set my tasks for the day. **Brick:** This taught me the value of intuition over intellect. Things internally felt bad, horribly stressed, yet intellectually I kept telling myself that it was a once in a lifetime opportunity. Why did I feel so shitty then? The gut knows things that the mind does not. Trust it—blindly. Trust how you internally feel, over how you intellectually feel. It's a big mistake to trust your brain in a lot of situations. Smart people are the worst here, because they view intellect as superior (it isn't). Put that in your pipe and smoke it.

Revelation: I'm reading *Mastery* by Robert Green and my sister comments that I was smiling a lot while reading it, and asked why. I realized that I'm visualizing the exact kind of person I wanted to be, a Doctor of Chinese medicine. It becomes so crystal clear I get chills, and for the next six months I can't stop thinking about it. I fly to California and Oregon and get into my dream school, and have dreams about it every night. It makes sense. It's a similar feeling to falling in love, in the sense that "it just makes sense" and feels right. Intellectual people hate hearing this explanation, so I stop hanging out with intellectual people.

Opportunity: Around this time I realize I need a few more pre-requisite courses for graduate school. I spend twenty hours per week at job #1, twenty hours per week at class, twenty hours per week at job #2, and twenty hours per week on my business. I hate my life. I get sick and my digestive problem has gotten worse, from the stress. I use the only thousand dollars left to my name to get treated by a Chinese medicine doc. His entire approach blew my mind and I offer to pay him just to talk with me about the medicine after-hours.

Detour: Age 28. Closest friend commits suicide. There's a weird feeling you get when you meet someone that you *instantly* get along with, and feel like the friendship is almost cosmic. That's how it was with my friend Clint. We instantly hit it off, we were both ravenous for success and creating a better life (he had turned his own life around *way* more than I had). We constantly shared book recommendations, created masterminds, and shared our plans for world domination on an almost daily basis. One day I woke up and he was gone—with no warning to anyone, including his own soon-to-be fiancé. It almost felt like a glitch in the matrix, like there was a mess-up in the fabric of space and time. The lessons here were myriad: you never know what's going on behind the scenes; make sure to enjoy life, because it's short;

make sure you really, really like the process of achieving your goals; have the right goals, and do things for the right reasons (no ego). More on this later.

Tenth job, age 28, the Chinese medicine doc. I work part-time at my day job, part time for him at his local acupuncture practice. I realize that this is my calling, fly around California and Oregon seeing the best schools, get into my dream school, and then quit all the other jobs to go full-time in my business.

Age 29, pieces come together. I finally feel like I'm on my dream path, which isn't about being a millionaire, but is simply about feeling like I'm on the path I'm supposed to be on. Internally, I feel calm and the feeling of restlessness is gone for the first time in almost a decade.

***

First things first, tell me what you see here? It's messy as all hell. Don't you think I wished I could've started the right business the first time? Don't you think I wished I would've known my "calling" when I was twelve? The reality is that a lot comes up, it's infinitely harder to piece this together than I thought, and certain things have to happen in order for you to have those key aha moments.

For example, I went through five, part-time jobs just in the span of the 3 years it took me to build my business. Five goddamn jobs! I kept the data entry one the entire time, always shifting to others. I tried taking advice like "burn the ships and commit!" multiple times, and it always panned out poorly for me. Note to self: advice is almost always a bad idea unless you know yourself well and you know your situation well. Crazy important.

The big idea here is simple: each thing gave me an important piece of information, that led me to make the next decision. I wanted to really highlight a bit about my own trajectory to show you that it's way more winding than you think. Logically, it makes sense that you just find work you enjoy and it's full steam ahead, but life is anything but linear. Roadblocks come up. Mistakes happen. Opportunities materialize and vanish. Learning experiences are a daily reality. The important thing is that, if you felt as lost as I felt, just keep plugging along and putting the pieces together. Rather than a journey, think of it more like a jigsaw puzzle.

Chapter Recap: The Quest for Work I Loved—Startups, Suicide and the Winding Path of Finding Your Calling

☐ **Finding your dream job is anything** *but* **a linear search.** At the get-go, I assumed that my hustle would help me figure out the work I loved quickly. I read all the books, learned from coaches, took personality inventories and more, but none of them were very big levers. The only real information that made a big difference was Martha Beck's *Finding Your Own North Star*. The process took me up, down, left and right, for me to finally hone in on which direction to move. But if you aren't moving, doors won't open up.

☐ **It's messy.** Actually, it's messy as hell. One thing I found solace in was the stories of classical masters, from historical doctors, authors, and extraordinarily successful people—and thankfully found that the majority of them had very winding paths as well. A great example is Buckminster Fuller, who went out back in a lake to drown himself, had a spontaneous intuitive kind of awakening, and then charted an incredible turnaround. The messy part is a matter of finding out what you like, and what you don't like, and then course-correcting.

☐ **Everything gives you a piece of the puzzle.** This is really important: reflect. Reflect on what you didn't like, or what you did like. Was it the location, being around people, freedom, working on certain projects, or the subject matter? Each job or experience gives you one more piece of the puzzle.

☐ **Just keep going.** One thing (in case I didn't convey this enough here) was that I was extremely frustrated and often unhappy during this process. A lot of the jobs I had I didn't like (or they were just boring), and couldn't justify to myself wasting nine hours a day when I wasn't learning anything anymore. But I kept plugging along, shifting gears, and so on. One of the reasons why I persisted was that I told myself a little affirmation, "Okay, even if life *doesn't* get better and I hate my work until I die, I'm going to work my ass off for the next few years to see if it's possible."

CHAPTER 13

The VIP Back Door: There's Always a Secret Back Entrance

I once was talking with a friend about how she got so many job opportunities, even though she never seemed like she worked that hard or was super driven.

"I don't get it, you always have these opportunities coming your way. How do you even get them? I get stuck in the goddamn resume machine and never even get past the first round, even though I'm overqualified, and you always get through even if you don't have any related experience." I said."

"You just don't get the game—there's always a VIP back door." She replied.

I hated her.

There's always a VIP back door? When I asked her to explain, she told me about the music and fashion industry that she had been involved in. It doesn't matter if you've accomplished everything or you haven't done crap with your life—if you know people, or you know the game, you can get a backstage pass to any event with the "VIPs." Is it "unfair?" Sure. Is it all a game? For sure. But is that how the world works? Hell yes. And like it or not, it's not going away anytime soon.

So is this going to be yet another chapter on networking your way to your dream job? Nope. Not at all, at least not really. It's really a high level philosophy that helps you go from "way too many ideas" about what paths to follow, to actually honing in on a few, and then from there, rapidly testing them—so that in one hour you make more progress than you did all last year.

Cool? Let's get started.

"There Are a Million Paths I Could Go Down"

One of the feelings that I felt years ago, and that I hear a lot about when I talk to lost twenty-somethings, is this feeling that there are *way* too many options for things that could potentially be considered jobs. Not only are there too many options, there's a lot of fear behind potentially choosing the wrong path, losing a lot of time and money, and then regretting ever having decided in the first place. What if I go down the wrong path and lose a year? Sound familiar?

There's a process I go through internally with clients that often, in just a few conversations, already helps people feel better and realize that, no, there really aren't a million options. It just sounds like that in your head.

The Napkin Exercise

That infamous list sometimes sounds like this:

- Go skydiving in the Maldives
- Work for a winery and become a vagabond for a year in New Zealand
- Become an au-pair somewhere abroad
- Try being a barista at a cool coffee shop
- Move across the country and live in LA
- Move across the country and live in New York
- Write a book
- Record music
- Learn to play the guitar
- Go take a sabbatical and travel the world
- Move to Spain for a year and learn Spanish
- Hike a pilgrimage trail
- Try out Vlogging
- Go back to school for teaching
- Start some kind of business…

… And on and on. In fact, the list often goes on much longer than that. Even though when you read that to yourself you might laugh because you sound like a crazy person, that's actually often the first step to figuring out the next step. It all starts with that high level brainstorming.

When I work with people, this is often what I call the Napkin Exercise—you just go to your favorite local coffee shop on a sunny Saturday morning, grab a coffee, and then write. The point isn't to edit it because things sound silly (be a coffee tour guide in Costa Rica? *The hell was I thinking?*). The point is just to put together the master list before we go through a process here for filtering them into legitimate options. The next step is editing them down. Obviously, not all of these are really considered jobs, some of them are just trips, and others are kind of bucket list experiences. But what you want is work you actually enjoy that you do on a daily basis. So let's narrow it down. Often, we can cut the list in half with one simple exercise.

Filter #1: Careers vs. Events and the Five-Year Filter

Now, let's look at that exact same list again and break them down into two things: one-time events, and careers. One-time events are essentially trips you take, or summer adventures, and careers are things you would consider doing every day for five years. That's a big filter, obviously you probably don't want to go skydiving every day for five years, so clearly that one isn't a career for most people.

I find that lots of twenty- (and thirty-, and forty-) somethings often have all these ideas, but don't separate them into "cool experiences" and "careers." Cool experiences you can do any time, and you do them once or twice, while careers are things you want to do daily, often for years. So let's take a look at that list one more time and label each item as "event" or "possible career."

- Go skydiving in New Zealand (event)
- Work for a winery and become a vagabond for a year in New Zealand (event)
- Become an au-pair somewhere abroad (event)
- Try being a barista at a cool coffee shop (event or possible career)

- Move across the country and live in LA (possible career – doing what?)
- Move across the country and live in New York (possible career – doing what?)
- Write a book (event, but if you like doing it every day, possible career)
- Record music (potential career)
- Learn to play the guitar (event, but maybe you realize it's more for fun and not a career)
- Go take a sabbatical and travel the world (event - "this might be fun to do once")
- Move to Spain for a year and learn Spanish (event)
- Hike a pilgrimage trail (event)
- Try out Vlogging (possible career)
- Go back to school for teaching (possible career)

Almost immediately, we've cut that list in half. Maybe you realized that half of these are just one time trips or events that you can still do anytime in your life, but they aren't careers you want to investigate more, daily, to see if you really like them, you know? If you've cut down the list, that's awesome, because it means there are a lot less options, and we're getting close to the field work phase.

Look at all that's left now (four real options):

- Try out Vlogging
- Go back to school for teaching
- Write a book
- Record music

And then some potential for the moves:

- Move across the country and live in LA
- Move across the country and live in New York

We just went from almost twenty options to four we can start testing out. Feels good already, right? Another important thing is that as you gradually go through this process, you should be adding more and more things to the list continually. So maybe you realize as you try out vlogging that you love podcasting, or you love entrepreneurship— add that as a blanket category, and then later we can investigate it more.

The first step is very simple and very important: some things are awesome trips or one-time "bucket list" type of things. Some things are truly things you want to do on a daily basis for a long time, that have the potential for growth, learning, and becoming a career.

Next, another filter you can apply to narrow it down even more is "gut yes or gut no."

Filter #2: Gut Yes, Gut No

I already introduced you to that flow and gut-based philosophy, and now, I want you to run through another layer—break down the list into two things, either a very clear gut yes, or gut no. If it's unclear what you intuitively feel about it, "I'm not sure if I really want to become a food blogger... it just seems kind of cool and everyone in New York is doing it..." don't put anything next to it. If it's intuitively yes, "Hell yes, teaching would be awesome" then obviously put a yes. And if it's a no, "Ehh, I think playing guitar and being a musician isn't my thing, I just thought it was cool after I went to that hipster party in Brooklyn," then put a no.

Filter #3: The Five-Year Filter

The final filter I want you to go through is the five-year filter. This often works well when you aren't quite sure if something intuitively is worth investigating or not. Take the same list you have, after you've chopped it down using the careers vs. events filter, and then think about each one with the following criteria.

Could I do this every day for five years?

Well, think about it. Maybe being an au pair sounds great as a potential career, but now when you think about five years, it's a major "ughhhhh." Lots of things will sound cool to do for a bit, but when you think about showing up for them daily for a prolonged period of time, it very clearly narrows down the list even more.

So you've taken that master list through a few levels at this point: the career vs. event filter, the five-year filter, and the gut yes, gut no filter. What do you do with the list though?

Trenches, Wenches, and Coffee Meetings*

There's a little secret that I wish I knew going right into college, when I was forced to pick a major. That secret is simple: almost no job (from the outside) actually gives you an accurate look at what that day-to-day life really is.

For example, you see kids wanting to become doctors so that they can help people, not realizing that if they had even one conversation with a doctor they would realize a few things:

- It entails lots of paperwork
- You have less than five minutes with each patient
- You don't get to save the world in five minutes with each patient
- There's a thing called "compassion fatigue"
- There's another thing called "malpractice"
- The majority of doctors don't even recommend you become a doctor, because of the political B.S. and insurance

That's just a wee bit different from saving lives on a daily basis, helping orphans, and working with rural people in poverty.

Obviously, this is an exaggeration—there are happy doctors, you can go into private practice to control your hours, and you can do doctors without borders. But it's just to illustrate something clear: most jobs you won't have a clue about unless you talk to someone who is actually working that job.

You might think being a musician is glorious because you've seen those rock stars on the stage partying, generating crazy fame, and being the life of the party. Here's what you don't see:

- The excessive amount of traveling
- The fact that 99% of your time isn't spent on stage
- The excessive amount of partying, when you just want to relax
- The five hours a day of playing guitar, trying out songs, writing, and so on
- The inability to have a stable relationship because you're always on the road

Slightly different from the rock star you always envisioned, right? The day-to-day is very different.

What about being a writer? You might see one of your heroes giving a talk, as a well-known public figure. You can't wait for the day when you can hand out your bestselling book—signed—to all the fans raving in front of your doorstep. But then you talk to a writer, and realize the obvious:

- Most traditionally published writers don't make a lot of money from their books—so where are you going to earn money?
- Most writers have to eventually become entrepreneurs—are you willing to spend every day thinking about sales and marketing?
- Most of the selling of your book comes from the promotion (80+% of the work); are you ready to invest the effort to write your book, and then spend two years getting on hundreds of interview shows and writing guest articles to sell your book?
- Most writers (the ones who emulate what the average person is doing) stay poor and unsuccessful forever—are you willing to figure out how to become the 1%?
- It's trendy these days to call yourself a "writer"—and as a result, when you introduce yourself that way, 99.99% of the world will instantly know you're an unemployed hipster who doesn't actually have a book for purchase anywhere*

*Sorry, that one was irresistible.

Here's one final example: running a charity. You see yourself building schools in central and south America, or rural Philippines, helping kids, shooting these crazy inspirational videos, and changing lives. Here's the reality of running a charity:

- 99% of the time, you're trying to figure out how to get donors, to pay your bills, your staff, and keep the lights on.
- You spend more of your time in the office than in the field, because as the founder, it's your job to write those proposals. Every. Damn. Day.
- A few times during the year, you get to enjoy the field stuff you love.

A charity, just like anything, has a very different daily reality than most people expect. You're probably going to be in an office every day, especially for the first few years as you get funding, because you're going to have to be *selling* (yeah, what do you think about learning sales, anyway? Thought you were going to avoid dealing with money, eh…). A "day in the life" is way different in reality than you think it is.

Making Five Minutes Worth One Year

The entire purpose of me showing you this is simple: almost no clarity comes from trying to think things out and figure them out in your head. One coffee meeting or call with someone can provide more clarity on what the daily life looks like than a year thinking about it. So the next step here is obvious: let's take those things you think you'll like, and find out whether or not you're as fiery about them as you think.

As many of my friends and I were trying to get jobs, or find work we loved in New York City, or in my own area, we were trying to find ways to quickly iterate and test out interests before we committed, and soon realized that many people recommended coffee meetings as a core strategy. One conversation is all it takes, remember?

One of my friends (who is a close friend to this day) actually emailed me through my personal website with the following email:

Sub: Want to meet up?

Hey dude, I've been reading MTP for a couple months now and love what you say.

I have my own site right here which is pretty similar too: mysite.com.

I just moved into NYC and I know you said you're in there a lot, want to meet up for a quick coffee?

There are also a few online courses that I bought that I'd be happy to give you my login details for.

Alex.

This is almost word for word what my friend Alex sent to me when he moved to NYC and didn't know anyone. A cold email doesn't always work, but in this case, it worked, and we're still friends. He had a lot of the same questions that I had, namely, how to be ultra-successful at your own chosen work.

When I moved back from China, I had heard the name of a pretty well-respected and knowledgeable Chinese medicine teacher and had reached out to him several times to try and get some of his advice.

When I considered enrolling at the school where he taught, I knew I was going to be in town to shadow some of the students in the clinic and wanted some of his advice. Here's the exact email I sent to that medicine mentor of mine.

Hey <name>,

No worries on the delay—I totally understand.

I'm actually going to be in <town> on the 25th and 26th—any chance I can buy you some coffee or tea and pick your brain for five minutes about what it takes to become a master of Chinese medicine?

Best,
Alex

And here was his reply:

Am teaching a retreat at my house that weekend (do have some time in the afternoon of the 25th before the retreat starts, but won't be in town that day—my home is about 40 minutes' drive east of downtown… So, the only way that we could meet briefly in that timeframe is on Friday at my house in <town> but that may be too far to drive just for a short "hello"?

First, remember that I had emailed him about 6-7 times over the course of a year, asking simple, one-line questions. I don't know whether or not he knew me or remembered me, but I always sent the email in the same thread to build a relationship. By the time he replied with this, I was like holy shit, this is awesome! A forty minute Uber ride for $100? Not a problem at all, I would've walked five hours to make this appointment.

The "five minute" conversation turned into an hour conversation, and completely solidified that this was what I truly wanted to learn with my life. Also, I had established a relationship now with someone I really respected and wanted to learn from. Hell, I was moving across the country specifically for almost one person.

Now imagine the opposite, which is what so many of us typically do. Imagine if I was just sitting at home, drawing sketches on my notepad about all the possible career paths and choices I wanted to go down. Chinese medicine could be cool, or maybe not, I'm not sure what that really looks like. Is there any money in it? Where do I treat patients? What kind of conditions do I treat? On and on the questions would go, but one conversation answered all of them, and more, and finally planted me on the path I wanted to be on. See the difference?

The Coffee Meeting Challenge

So you have all these ideas about careers, paths, bucket list ideas, and more. And the entire point of me illustrating this was that if you can get yourself in the mindset of meeting people in that career—as quickly as possible—you will go from confusion to clarity in 1/100th the time. This is really a key success habit I wish I knew a decade ago. Don't make the same mistakes I did. So your challenge from this chapter is to find one person, in each of the jobs that has passed the three filters, and apply the following coffee meeting process.

If the person is local (e.g., you're interested in architecture and there's a local architect), try to meet them in person. If they aren't, you have Skype and your phone, so there's no excuse. How do you reach out? There are really only three things you need to know, and the first one is the most important.

How to reach out:

1. Add value
2. Find a shared bond
3. Ask for the meeting or five-minute phone call

Let's start with the most important thing: add value. Adding value is by far the most important because everyone is busy. Successful people are even busier. Famous, successful people are ten times busier. And if I, as a little blogger, get emails that are pages long, that are all solicitations on my time ("Here's my life story, can you help?"), and I get five a day like that, think about what that means for someone who is world famous. It's a nightmare.

Even though you are asking for five minutes of their time, try to add value in one of a few ways. They already get tons of emails saying, "hey, can I get your advice on this?" Well, if you have a hundred emails to answer, there is literally nothing worse than an open-ended email like that. I'm going to assume the person you are reaching out to isn't famous, but is just busy. Often, asking people flat out about a career (and a 5-minute coffee meeting—you pay) is enough. People that love their work love talking about it. Here's another sample email sequence

I've used dozens of times when I really want to ask someone about a potential career path, industry, or opportunity.

Email #1—Subject: Alex, an article you might like.

Hey Alex,

I've been reading your stuff. I'm also interested in marine biology. I also lived in <this country>, and figured you might find this really interesting, since I loved it.

Here's the link: <Cool YouTube video about cats or something>.

Your name.

Email #2—Subject: Alex, quick question

Hey Alex,

Thanks for taking the time to write me back. I'm really interested in pursuing marine biology as a career, but I'm curious what it's really like.

Do you have a few minutes where I could ask 2-3 quick questions?

Do any of the following days work for you?

Monday at 3-4 pm.
Tuesday at 6-7 pm.
Wednesday at 11 am to 12 pm.

Your name.

This is really bare bones and very simplistic. Yet it will work, because you are hopefully genuinely interested in the subject, aren't asking for a lot, and just want a five-minute conversation.

Not only have people used this on me, I've used this to make incredible connections and friendships, meet many of my mentors in person, and most of all, gain massive clarity on the path I want to go down in life. I've gotten hour-long phone conversations with

CEOs, presidents of companies (and universities), influential online personalities, and just normal people I respect and admire. And every time, one simple conversation has provided more clarity than a year of thinking and speculating.

Think about how much easier this makes your life. You just went from almost 20 ideas, and no clue which path to go down, to a very clear intuition if you want to proceed or stop, regarding certain paths. Awesome, huh? One hour used right is more valuable than one year. What this taught me is that people are often way more generous with their time than you think, especially outside the realm of business (where everyone wants money, ego, fame). If you're genuinely interested in mastery, people are way more likely to respond too.

Take your ideas on one piece of paper (you should put them on paper for a reason—clarity), go through the three filters, then validate each one of them with a coffee meeting. The next thirty days should be the most illuminating thirty days of your career life.

*What do wenches have to do with this? No clue, it just rhymed and rhyming is fun after you drink too much Rioja.

Chapter Recap: The VIP Back Door

☐ **Use the three filters strategy to narrow down ideas.** I often have clients that are confused by the seemingly dozens of ideas that are in their head, but once we go through a really basic process, they quickly realize that's not the case. Filter down the ideas using the careers vs. events filter, the gut vs. head filter, and the five-year filter. Then, move on to step two.

☐ **Make one hour worth one year of searching.** Rather than sitting down and going through career books trying to figure things out, what I found worked (by far) the best was getting in the arena. For example, if you think architecture is one of the many possible ideas you like, rather than trying to just "figure it out," ask one local architect if they have a few minutes to chat. More of them than you think will say yes. The amount of clarity that comes from having just one conversation with a real person, versus thinking for ten hours a day, is incredible.

CHAPTER 14

Time and Learning vs. Money—Forget About the Bling Bling (for Now)

*"Taking a job you hate makes no sense to me. Isn't
that a bit like saving up sex for old age?"*

— WARREN BUFFET

Not a day went by in my twenties where somebody wouldn't try convincing me to just get a high paying job - 50k, 70k, 100k, 120k - even if I hated the shit out of it. It was truly puzzling—the same people often didn't even like their own work, so what the hell were they doing giving me that advice? It was completely ass backwards.

Thankfully, I realized something important: I was confident enough that I always challenged the advice I got and filtered it in my own mind. Who was it coming from? Were they living the life I wanted? Were they happy? Were they projecting what they wanted? I decided to make a bet with myself: what would happen if I just valued learning now, instead of money? How would things turn out for me a lot later, like three, five, or ten years down the line? What about twenty years?

I had seen the trajectory of some successful people, especially entrepreneurs. I saw how they ate ramen noodles and sucked it up, ate bitter, swallowed glass, and showed up every day to build something that they wanted to build (rather than something they were stuck building). They took a financial risk in the short run, declining six figure jobs, being stuck at the poverty level, to build something more important. They took a risk. But to me, it was a bet—a bet on creating a fucking awesome life.

Think about it. Even on a boring financial level, who will make more money later? The person who takes the six figure day trading job, or the person who takes the 30k (or free) job, but gets to sit alongside one of the top traders in her industry (or the world), who spends all day learning the ins and outs of the craft? I'll put my money all day on the latter. I view skill acquisition as the multiplier—every one hour I spend now, is 10x the income in three, five or ten years. I didn't see it yet in action at the time, but I intuitively thought that it must've made sense. Many of the greats throughout history had very winding, confusing paths to finding their own calling or dream job, and I hoped (and was betting) it'd be the same for me.

For example, I spent most of my twenties earning less than $30,000. I made twelve to sixteen dollars an hour at jobs, moved back home until twenty-six, and by all external accounts I was losing the game. But I built my audience online, not even knowing you could create a business from it, but just because I wanted to share a message without knowing where it'd travel to. I wrote my books, I worked my ass off to learn how to create courses, launch products, create content that moved people, and failed a million times, iterated, improved and finally got 1% better.

While my friends were getting raises and then earning 50k, 60k, 70k or 100k—I had a hunch that they would probably cap out around age thirty-five—they'd never earn much more, later in their life. At least that's what I was banking on. But I figured if I kept doing this (even if I was God-awful now), let's just say I do the same damn thing every day for a decade, couldn't I at least make 50k a year, even if I did it all wrong? I was betting on myself that it was possible. So while all my friends had their cushy corporate salaries, I was perpetually broke, scraping by (and living at home).

I went negative half a dozen times, and earned pennies practically for the majority of my twenties. When I moved back from China at twenty-four, I moved back in with my parents until twenty-six. The only year I earned over $40,000 was my first job at twenty-two as a teaching assistant, but after China, I never made more than $30,000 in a year. I was essentially living off of $1,500 a month from multiple job sources. Then I launched my business. I suffered some more years being poor (three and a half), and then gradually earned more. I "got a raise every year"—a few thousand extra this year, then five thousand the next year, and then it *doubled* the next year.

The best part? I work on what I want to work on. I have freedom – I'm in graduate school and yet my audience is still growing. I went to Spain for a month to write this book, and my influence is still growing. I visited my girlfriend in the Philippines, and my passion projects get bigger and bigger. I have books—books! It's cool to have books when you're in your twenties. And most of all, I have a community—people I've helped, which is the best part of all. I like to think of every hour now acquiring skills as being worth ten times the fulfillment and income in the next ten years. Optimize for wisely using your time, and acquiring skills, not money, in the short run. It'll come back tenfold.

Time vs. Money

Money is like a VIP escort. Once you get a taste of what it's like (not literally, unless you're into that), you can never downgrade to anything less. Then you need more, a lot more, and you have a hard time going back to "the regular stuff." Ah, the golden handcuffs. For most people, at least what I've witnessed first-hand, a decent job that pays a lot of money is more seductive than crack. Even a dream job sitting there waiting for you (if you know what it is) often can't peel you away from security and comfort. It's really scary sometimes. And if you never learn to value the cruelest opportunist of all time—*Father Time*—you get really screwed in the end.

The last job that I officially had was—you guessed it—another opportunity to learn, and learn from a mentor, without getting paid oodles of money (although I was paid well). It was actually for a Chinese medicine practitioner that had treated me for some ongoing health problems that I wasn't getting fixed at the "normal" doctor's office. After being treated by him, and having my mind blown about this medicine I had never seen in action (but made incredible sense), I decided to be really annoying. We talked for a while, and using that coffee meeting idea, I asked him if he would be up for a five-minute coffee chat, because I wanted to know what it took to be great at Chinese medicine. I even offered to pay him for an hour of his time, straight talking. He turned the tables a bit, and instead offered, "Why not just work here part-time in the mornings? You'll learn not only

Chinese medicine with me as we talk, but you'll also learn how to run a practice (the not so fun, essential stuff)."

So once again, I voted in terms of skills, valuing my time and mentorship *more* than I valued income—and I got a huge mentor out of it, one that I'll probably have for life—that's irreplaceable. You can always earn more money, and you should earn more money, but getting more time is impossible. And in the short run, every dollar you give up to acquire hard skills and mastery is worth 10x that within three, five or ten years. It sounds far-fetched, but wouldn't you rather take the job working for a multi-millionaire, side-by-side, rather than the offer to just take a six figure salary from her without her sharing any of the core strategies she used to build her empire?

If you're smart, you'll choose the mentorship route.

Lesson: Value Learning Over Money

Here's the lesson. Take jobs or projects that guarantee learning, and ideally, something you want to actually learn about. I find a lot of twenty-somethings are fed the same B.S. spiel, "you should be so grateful you have a job!" Come on, jobs are never scarce. If you are damn good at what you do—you as a person become recession proof. Stuck between that job that pays you seventy grand but it sucks and doesn't interest you, versus a job that pays 35k and you obviously will learn a new skill that interests you and you can use later? It's a no brainer—take the job that allows you to learn skills. You'll be back at 70k in no time—with a lot more ultimate job security because you have more skills (and hopefully like it).

Use an hour a night to learn hard skills that are marketable and you can prove that you actually know them. For example, hard, marketable skills (aka skills you can prove you have acquired) that you can show to an employer might be things like the following:

- Being able to script, shoot, and edit videos (better yet—share a link to your YouTube channel)
- Being able to write blog posts that get traffic to a website (content marketing is huge with startups)
- Writing a book… and sending them the Amazon link to it
- Having a portfolio of beautiful websites you've designed
- Having a portfolio of beautiful art you've created

- Being able to set up a website (even if it's a super basic template)
- Being able to play an instrument
- Being able to speak another language

The list can go on and on here, and you get the point. The idea is that, at the end of the day, if a person asks you what skills you have, you should be able to show them very clearly. Having a bunch of good ideas means jack shit. Having hard skills you can prove you have (like speaking a language, a technical skill like programming, or editing videos) is what makes you irreplaceable.

Unless you really have to, don't take a job for the money. It'll kill your soul and ambition at the exact same time. Value time—because it's going to keep ticking whether or not you want it to—and make it count. Think about the long-term game, and suck it up for the time being by getting a crappy apartment or not going to the bar every single night.

Chapter Recap: Time vs. Money

◻ **Time is your most important gift.** We all know that time is precious, but common knowledge isn't common practice. We're also inundated with this (false) belief that since we're young, we have all the time in the world. It's a bold-faced lie. Why would you waste a year of your life when you could use it to get that much closer to your dream job or a better situation? Make it count, *especially* while you're young and failure is nothing more than a tiny setback.

◻ **Skills pay the bills.** Time is precious, but what do you really do with it to guarantee you'll make money now and later? Acquire concrete skills. A concrete skillset is what makes you marketable, whether you're looking to get hired by a company or branch out on your own. Personally, I've found that dedicating an hour a day to acquiring a skillset is more than enough to get a job or get clients within a few months.

◻ **Bet on yourself – and plan for the long run.** Naturally, people get the idea of valuing time over money, and yet still take the high paying job they hate (which sucks up all their free time). What's the middle ground? Personally, I worked for over three years before I could quit my job and go full-in on my side projects. I would work ten hours a day (either one job, or multiple), go to the gym, then spend the last three hours of the night at a café working on my freedom projects. That's how I suggest most people go about it too.

CHAPTER 15

The 1% Creative: How to Land Any Job (And Make Your Life Awesome)

It's surprisingly easy to be great and create an incredible life. And it's surprisingly easy to be better than the competition when it comes to landing jobs, finding mates, or just making your life awesome. Unfortunately, almost nobody is willing to even put in five minutes of work to accomplish this. And that's awesome for you, because that's where you can come in and excel.

Last year some time, I did a 21-day habit challenge on my wellness YouTube channel. Every single day, for an entire 21-day period, I released a brand new tiny habit video giving the audience one tiny habit per day. At the end, I was giving away three signed copies of my book, anywhere in the world, *on me*. There was one catch though: you had to follow me on social media, and then leave a comment below the video sharing your story, why you deserve it, and how it's going to help you reach your goals. Guess what? Thousands of people watched that video, and less than ten even responded with the story part (because it took a few minutes).

What's more, one person had the balls to comment, "can I have one just for asking?" Are you kidding me? I asked for a one minute (a maximum of five minutes—absolute maximum) assignment, which apparently was too much for most people, and then to add to it, you have the guts to ask me for a free book because you're too lazy to even spend half a minute acting?

Here's the simple reality: most people are just not driven enough, motivated enough, happy enough, or truly willing to even invest 5 minutes to get closer to their dream life, their dream job, that beautiful guy or girl in the bar, or any other opportunity that could change their life. It's easy for us to just, well, choose easy. The difference between greatness and mediocrity is often just 1%, just an extra minute of work to take the time and share with me your story, to actually go up and talk to that guy or girl even though you are dying inside with butterflies, or to ask a seemingly outrageous, ballsy, request. It's just 1%, we're not talking about hours a day here. So many of us think that massive change takes hours a day, but the reality is that what we can accomplish in an hour or less is incredible.

It took me over three years of working on my side project every single day—for three hours or more a day—before I could quit my job and go full-time into it. Yes, that means no drinks with friends during the week, ever. Yes, that means I often worked multiple part-time jobs during this time period, because I would quit prematurely and have to get another job (I went through about five in that period of three years). That meant no TV—in fact, I still don't even own a TV. That meant no Netflix, no partying, no girlfriend. Yes, I only saw my girlfriend on the weekend for three years. Think about that one. And yes, it really sucked, but it paid off in the end.

The funny thing is that now that I can do what I want, and I have the life experience of suffering my way to that freedom, whenever somebody wants to do the same, I offer the same advice. "Just do one hour a day." You can keep your Netflix, your daily hangout with your partner, your drinks with your friends, and so on. Just dedicate one hour a day. And guess how many people still end up complaining about that, and most importantly, don't even end up doing that? Almost everyone. Literally, almost every single one. When I used to take private coaching clients, guess how many came to me and could honestly say they dedicated one hour a day for at least a month to making progress in a project? Zero.

Yes, you read that right. Not one. The reality is that succeeding at any project is about the consistency, and it doesn't take that much extra work or effort to create a great life, find that dream job, or have an amazing relationship. One hour a day is all I took to write my first book. One hour a day is all I'm taking to write this book. In one hour a day you can search for dream jobs, or begin learning how to build your own dream job. Most people won't do anything, and I'm not asking you to do 3-5 hours a day like I did. Can you find an hour a day, to be 1% better than your former self and build a better future?

Another time, when I found "my dream," Chinese medicine, I looked at the prices of the Doctoral programs I was getting into: 130k was a pretty standard price for the school I wanted to go to. Seeing as I didn't have six figures just chilling in the bank from my magic-mike male stripping business, I had to get creative. Take debt? Work and go to school? Get a scholarship? I decided to try out two pieces of my own advice: just ask, and be 1% more creative. What if I got a full scholarship on some kind of creative grounds? Hey, it was worth a shot.

Around that time, one of my closest friends passed away, and he had the habit of writing these beautiful, wax-sealed letters with the initial of his first name. Getting one of those letters instantly made you feel special, and I figured it might be a cool wind-down ritual at night to ingrain more gratitude. So I got parchment, a wax sealing kit, and started writing the letters. In a pile full of white letters, getting one of those makes you feel like royalty, and I would never write them for the sake of "standing out," but instead, being more personal *and* standing out more than just sending another email.

Who did I send it to? Why, the president of my school of course. And the entire letter was very simple: I know you have a very hard job, and you don't get to do all the fun stuff. I can't wait to start this Chinese medicine program in the fall, but before then, here are a dozen ways to boost student enrollment. If you want to talk more about these, here's my phone number and email.

I sent the letter. Guess who emailed me a week later with a link to his assistant and a time to book the call? The president himself. I promise you that 99.999% of students in the history of that school never had the balls to do that, and I'm not special—I just thought about being 1% more creative. Even though I can't comment on whether the outcome was what I wanted, I got an opportunity that very few people got. That's what you want—one chance at bat that you might not have had before.

Adam Pacitti was a college grad in the UK who was down to his last $500 pounds and couldn't get a job for anything. In a last ditch effort, he decided to buy a billboard and put a picture of himself on it, trying to sell himself to virtually any employer. Almost overnight, he was inundated with requests, not because he was more qualified, but because he was more creative and thus stood out. Within an hour he had a job offer, and not too long after, he got over 100 offers, flat out, because he was creative, not necessarily more qualified. Let me repeat that a third time; he got tons of offers despite the fact that he was vanilla in his qualifications—he was just more creative and it cut through the clutter.[6]

The Lesson

The reality is that most people are not willing to invest even five minutes into being creative. It doesn't take massive work—just different work. Try going five minutes longer or just being a tiny bit more creative than the average person. This is something I really regret not doing better, because "I'm just not a creative person. Notice how I caught myself there? I'm in one sense just your typical, average "good student." I have a moderate amount of discipline, I do the work, and I follow the rules. But I was never a creative, out of the box thinker. And one thing that life has taught is that hardship (like a bad economy) rewards creativity. The most creative are the ones that thrive. Remember the saying attributed to Darwin? Heavily paraphrased here, the species that survives is not necessarily the strongest or smartest, but the one most adaptable to change. A recession counts as a situation that requires us to personally evolve and start doing something different.

If it comes to finding a job for example, that might mean adding a YouTube video you shot for the job as part of your cover letter. It might mean writing a short, thirty-page personal manifesto, putting it on amazon, and sending them the link. You can do this for less than $50 these days, using Upwork.com or Fiverr.com.

If it's your relationship, don't be an average Joe. I love talking about dudes at the bar, because I'm a man, and men become chimpanzees when there's a pretty girl around and alcohol is involved. If you walk up to a woman and introduce yourself and offer her a drink, I will find you, and I will stab you. Ask her opinion on something cool, interesting or unique. Just do anything other than what you see everyone else doing. If you're already in a relationship, buy your partner some goddamn flowers or write them an actual letter—and mail it to them (even if you live in the same place). For God sakes, it takes three minutes. Highly creative stuff helps you win. It doesn't matter if it's your relationship or finding a job. The more you exercise the idea muscle, the better off you'll find your life becoming.

If it's your business, try spending one hour on how to be different, which can be as simple as a logo change, a thank you for each customer that buys, or a little note.

Have more guts. Call up the CEO of a company you want to apply to, a dozen times, spaced out over every two weeks. Write a handmade letter (or twenty, or a hundred, until that mentor responds). Use your YouTube channel to get a $300/night hotel for free on your next trip, and in return, shoot a sweet promotional video for them and put it on your channel. You have no idea how many options are available now.

In other words, get creative, people. I'm one hundred percent a complete dunce when it comes to creativity, and if there was ever a person born without the creative instinct, that's me. And if I could figure some of these ideas out, you can too. I know that 99% of you are way smarter and more creative than me, so you can truly do some crazy stuff. It pays off huge. In a world of vanilla, be rocky road.

Chapter Recap: The 1% Creative

☐ **Be rocky road in a world of vanilla.** Once you start using the creative muscle, it's scary how much you can get rewarded. You land impossible jobs, you reach hard-to-reach CEOs and authors, your relationships get better, all these opportunities start manifesting that you didn't have before. Creativity is the instant multiplier that turns you into something special.

☐ **"Most people would rather resort to crime than think."** Earl Nightingale, in one of his audio programs, talks about how most people would rather resort to crime before they even think for a few minutes on how to solve a personal problem. That was me, for a very long time. All I could do was model other successful people, because the creative muscle was weak (I'm not a "creative" person by nature, at all). This is a habit, like anything else. The more you practice setting aside time to just generate cool, creative ideas from your own mind, the more you end up using this muscle.

☐ **Creativity is a multiplier and breaks all the rules.** Whether it's something as mundane as trying to get a sweet job that you aren't having any luck getting, or it's being better in a relationship, creativity is a shortcut. You can be a vanilla candidate like anyone else, think up some creative stuff, and suddenly you jump to the top of the line of candidates. It's like a cheat code for life.

CHAPTER 16

One Hour a Day to a Better Life: The Life Success Philosophy

Let's be honest here for a second: no matter how much your current life might be about as awesome as a pile of dung in the Sahara Desert, you can change it. In fact, I would argue that you can change it in an hour a day. Yeah, I get that that sounds like a cheesy Tony Robbins infomercial right before he sells you a ten-thousand-dollar life-coaching product, but bear with me for a second here.

There's a story by Earl Nightingale in one of my favorite audiobooks of his: The Essence of Success. Around the time of the great depression, he talks about passing a group of steel workers complaining about the absolute lack of work. Earl thought, "What have you been doing for twenty years, then? In your free time in two decades you could've learned to perform open heart surgery." In reality, eight hours a day not at work is an absolute ton of time, and many of us waste it. But for me, the story had another sort of importance: it illustrated just how much you can change your life in a short period of time.

One of Earl's quotes that I live by now is the following:

"One hour per day of study in your chosen field is all it takes. One hour per day of study will put you at the top of your field within three years. Within five years you'll be a national authority. In seven years, you can become one of the best people in the world at what you do."[7]

When you think about it like that, change doesn't seem so scary now, does it? Whenever I talk with people about landing their dream job, building a business, traveling the world, writing a book, getting their dream body, meditating regularly, or having an awesome relationship, two things always come up: the lack of time, and the lack of energy.

What I want to share with you now is how I challenged literally all aspects of my life with an hour a day. That means my financial life, my health, writing a book, my spirituality, my relationship with my girlfriend, traveling the world, and a lot more. One hour a day is now one of my ten commandments for change.

***

It took me one hour a day to write a three-time, #1 Amazon bestselling health and weight loss book that has gotten feedback like the following:

> *"I've read the classics, The Magic of Thinking Big, Think and Grow Rich, How to Win Friends and Influence people. I've read books from current, popular authors like Seth Godin and Gary Vaynerchuck. Your book WORKS. It's not just a health book. It's a HOW TO LIVE A LIFE YOU LOVE book!*
>
> This book has changed all the rules. If you're currently reading a book about weight loss or a book *about goal setting...PUT IT DOWN and read this. I recently paid $250 for a goal setting workshop that included one phone call a week with the presenter. I would gladly pay $250 for this book over the course."*

I've had people write me to say it was the best book on weight loss *they've ever read.* I've had recovering alcoholics and food addicts tell me that they've tried everything, and after reading my book, it was the first time they conquered food and alcohol combined for a month.

That's freaking insane! Of course, I've received mixed (and negative) feedback on the book too, but go look at the Amazon reviews. The point here isn't to brag; it's to break the myth that you need a sabbatical in Paris for a year to write any book worth reading. You don't, you just need an hour a day to write it. Who cares if it takes you three years? It's just an hour of your spare time each day. Each day I had one and only one metric for writing my book: write 1,000 words. It didn't matter if the words sucked, if the words made no sense, or if the words were stupid—I had to just write and produce. I could always go back and fix things later.

Once I had written the book, I hired a few editors, and went through the book about an hour a day to fix their edits. Then I learned how to hire designers to do the cover, and the interior and exterior. Finally, I learned the ugly self-publishing stuff, like where to publish it, how to deliver it, and so on.

Does writing a book seem scary to you now? I hope not, because I know you probably want to write one too.

Okay, so how about getting fit? I'm currently extremely fit, with a six pack year round, and I don't spend more than four hours in the gym per week. If you add up the total amount of time I spend cooking (approximately 3 hours a week, including breakfast every day by hand), that's around seven hours a week. What's that mean? About an hour a day, including my gym schedule. And that's for my own dream body. No two hour workouts here, sorry. No endless obsession with fitness.

How about building my own personal brand, Milk the Pigeon? I was actually writing a lot less than one hour a day, but if you include the time I spent writing for other sites too, then it added up to about an hour a day. I literally wrote only an hour a day—for years, mind you—to build a popular online community. So if you think that a relationship, business, brand, book, body, or any other kind of aspiration takes way more than that, you might want to reconsider. The only exception I would add to this list is building a business—however, you can do incredible things in just an hour a day.

The most important application of this hour a day philosophy though is when we come back to what Earl was talking about: acquiring new skills. And for those of you looking to change careers or really improve your financial situation, this is the *one* philosophy I'd focus on.

***

One of my friends had recently wanted to reinvent himself after getting involved in some nasty stuff in his "previous" life. Because of his "previous life" (read: prison and drugs), he was virtually guaranteed that he wouldn't be able to find a job, so he took a skill he could learn, and learned to freelance: web design. He would set aside time each day to sharpen the saw and learn the skillset—how to set up a website, how to code at a rough level, how to get clients, and so on.

Within a few months, there was his first $500 client, and then within another few months, a $1,000 client. From there, the targets just kept jumping: $3,000 client, $5,000 client, and more. He set aside one hour a day for a new skillset: hiring a team. Eventually, he branded himself as an agency, and started taking on much bigger projects, many multiples of the ones he started with. And not too long ago, four or five years after he began, he took on his first *$50,000 project*. Yes, a project that took him virtually as long as the $1,000 project, except he was making fifty *times* the amount.

That's what you call reinventing yourself, in an hour a day. He went from no skillset, to getting mid five-figure clients within five years. So you better believe he was in a completely new state financially. I know that *you* probably want a new career, a side business, or want to start freelancing because it might lead to something new. Maybe eventually you want to be your own boss. My own journey with one hour a day was originally just to acquire a new skillset to be able to find a job, but eventually it led to me being my own boss. Here's what that journey looked like to me.

From twenty-three to almost twenty-eight, I worked a string of part-time jobs (always two, sometimes up to four, including my own side projects). I deliberately had those part-time jobs because I wanted to spend my side hours cultivating specific skillsets, try starting a business, and so on. For example, here were the side skills I spent my time learning.

- First, writing—how, how much, how long, how compelling, etc.
- Second, sales—how to sell, who to sell to, what is too much selling, etc.
- Third, videos—the tech, cameras, how long, how to make it engaging, etc.
- Fourth, book writing—how to, how to write well (techniques), design, formatting, and so on.

Gradually, each one of these skills came back and served me in some way or another in my life, some of them directly, and some of them indirectly. But the most important thing is to actually set aside that time to learn hard skills. With skills, it doesn't matter where you go, and it doesn't matter what credentials you do (or don't) have. You can reinvent yourself to become whoever the hell you want to be. Skills pay the bills.

Learning a "Reinvent Yourself" Skillset in 100 Days

Any client that I work with now will start with this philosophy—want to change careers? Awesome, but most of them will require you to have a skillset (not a piece of paper). Nobody gives two shits whether you actually have a degree—they just use that to filter out the poor candidates. If you can show you have a skillset, "Hey, I'm good at web design, here's an awesome set of websites I did" then you're an easy and safe hire.

So let's get tactical and talk from my own direct experience with a skillset. I learned this skillset for my business, but it's easily something you could learn to freelance and earn $500 a month per client. Or, you could work in a corporate setting and earn a good living, if you know how to play the game right (at least a $50k/annual salary). That skillset is shooting and editing videos.

First, I'll show you how I deconstructed learning the new skill for professional-enough video, and then how I'd set a timeline for getting clients or getting good enough to find a job in it. Also, if you find yourself thinking, "A pro in 100 days? But I have friends who did four years in school to learn that..." realize that the time frame doesn't matter. A lot of people I know studied languages for four years in college, and still speak and write the language worse than a person who lived in the country for one year. Your client just sees the outside—I'm sure a professional would critique my videos a ton, but to me and to my readers, they look pro-enough. There's a certain level of quality you need to hit with your skillset, at which point it's good enough.

As a quick recap, this is how to acquire any concrete tangible skill and turn it into something you're good enough at to freelance or find a job.

Week 1: Model the Masters

I'm the most creatively stupid person you've ever met. Having said that, I also know another way to be successful (that fellow non-creatives will resonate with): model people who are really doing well. If you look at any master of the ages whether it's Einstein, Da Vinci, or some kind of athlete, they always start by modeling the masters. What they do from there is their own business, but almost everyone starts out modeling what's working.

For me wanting to learn the skill of video, (e.g., to potentially change careers and do more of it in the future), I picked ten videos that I liked, and then tried to describe on paper why I liked them. Here's what my initial analysis looked like:

- I like the blurry background in this video
- I like the way they transition between scenes in this video
- I like the way the person is in focus in this video
- I like the way they used multiple cuts of footage in this video

On and on I went—trying to describe and articulate what specifically I liked. Just saying, "I want to have cool videos" means very little if you're trying to acquire the skill of it. If you wanted to learn another skill like web design, programming, a musical instrument, or even just a fun random skillset like bartending, I would still do the same.

What do the best bar tenders do? They know how to make drinks; they know how to make drinks fast; and they know how to entertain a crowd (and potentially do cool tricks with the mixers). For web design you might want to point out the simplicity, colors, or layout of a website, by comparing it to a much uglier one.

Week 2: Learn the FAQ Skillset

Okay, so we've chosen a few examples of work we like, but how do we get there? And how on earth do we get good enough, so that we can jump ship into a new job, or even just start doing freelance work? We learn the FAQ skillset.

When I say the FAQ skillset, I just mean you ask yourself the "Frequently Asked Questions" of your skillset. For example, I saw a video I liked, and had a million beginner questions:

- "What kind of camera did they use?"
- "How do I use the right mode on the camera to get that effect?"
- "Do I need a special lens to get that effect on a camera?"
- "What do I have to do about lighting?"
- "Does my camera just pick up the audio or do I need a bonus microphone? What kinds of bonus microphones are there?"
- "How do I actually edit the videos, and what programs do I use?"

- "How should I do transition between cuts, or fix my mistakes?"

See where I'm going here? You just answer all the beginner questions about your craft. These are going to be the initial roadblocks that stop the average person on their quest to learn a skillset, just like how a beginning guitarist or pianist has to learn the scales so they can understand how to make certain sounds.

Spend one week going through the FAQ of your skillset. Compile all the top questions you have that are beginner questions and start researching. Bonus points if you just reach out to someone, because one conversation can save you a month of conflicting research.

Week 3: In The Trenches, Round One

Okay, now it's your first week in the trenches, which is code for the following: create. If it's music, time to start trying to make it. If it's a website, time to start coding one. If it's a video, it's time to make one. If it's sales you want to learn, it's time to start slingin' some dope. Here's the thing: you obviously want to try and create what you saw as an example of mastery—and yes, obviously it's not going to be good. In fact, it's probably going to suck at a level that is unacceptable for most living creatures. That's cool, and it's okay. If you want proof of it, go find anyone you admire (like a famous person) and go find some of their initial works—they're awful.

Go create something. That could be a two-minute video, it could be trying to play a song, or it could be a website. Or, try selling your mom some girl scout cookies. For me, that involved creating a video where I attempted to imitate some white screen videos that I saw on the Internet. The problem was that when I bought the screen, I had no idea that you needed so many external lights to actually get that cinematic effect. I had to buy three lights, and then I learned (even more painfully) that they had to be arranged in a certain, geometric way to get the proper light. Get it wrong, as I did, and it just makes you look like you have massive bags under your eyes. The video sucked, the content was okay, but I quickly learned more about that skillset than I did all last year. Time in the trenches of any goal = 10x as valuable as time thinking.

Week 4: Troubleshooting and Rapid Feedback

You've now created something. And it probably sucked really bad. This is where we keep plugging along—you're working on this for an hour a day I hope, right? That gives you plenty of time for mastery. With that one hour a day, for this week, you're reflecting. Okay, so I shot this video, and there's no blurred background. Why does that video I really like show people with blurred backgrounds? So I go on to do some more research. What do I learn? I need to buy a special lens, called a 50mm 1.8. The lens is around $100, so I buy it. Then I screw it onto my camera and try again. A bit blurred now, but not nearly the effect I wanted. Then I do more research and iterate yet again, and realize that I have to manually change the aperture on my camera (and I have to learn what aperture means).

The next time I go to shoot the video, I can quickly switch to manual mode, change the aperture down to 1.8, shoot, and now I have a passable blurred effect that looks pretty pro. I just have to make sure my content is solid, so that's what requires the most practice.

With your web design skillset, you might have created a website, but it's ugly as hell. It's square, things don't line up, and maybe one effect you wanted was to have a button "glow" and change color when you hover on it. You have no idea how to do that, so you start your research phase. You discover in a coding forum, that you have to use a special code, and you play around and implement that. That becomes your mastery iteration for the week.

For selling, maybe you called a client, and they shut you down before you could even say your name. Crap. What the hell am I supposed to do? You start researching, and come up with your iteration for the week: how do I overcome getting shut down right away? You read some books on sales, and realize that you have to open a conversation with warmer clients, or maybe you have to have a different script where you ask for someone's opinion instead of introducing yourself, or maybe you test a new strategy.

Your action step this week is to write down your one mastery iteration: what new skillset (as part of your overall skillset) did you learn to get better?

Week 5: Round Two of Iteration and Add a New Tactic to Your Mastery Document.

In week five, you're choosing one new tactic or iteration that you're going to be improving on. Let's take a look at what that might look like in the three example skillsets I gave:

- **Video**—get an external microphone, because the internal one sucks.
- **Web design**—how to code newsletter sign-up forms.
- **Selling**—how to overcome the "I can't afford it" sales objection.

Week 6: Round Three of Iteration and Add a New Tactic to Your Mastery Document.

In week six, we do more of what we did in week five. We add a new iteration to our skillset (aka something we've been trying to figure out how to learn to do). Here's what that might look like:

- **Video**—How to transition or fix mess ups.
- **Web design**—How to make a website more responsive.
- **Selling**—Sales cycles, and how long it takes to close certain clients within certain price points and industries.

The point is that you have new questions in your process of acquiring this new skillset, and each time you seek to answer the questions, your skillset grows. Repeat this each week up to week ten.

Week 10: Client Related, Get That $$$.

Okay, at this point, whether or not you like it, it's time to get into the true trenches—the arena—and actually get a client. It doesn't matter whether or not you want to freelance or get a new job using the skillset you've been acquiring, if you can get a client, you're once again upping the ante and improving your skills. There are some things you learn only once you're in the arena (in fact, I'd argue that you only learn 99% of the stuff you need to learn when you *are* in the trenches).

For example, one thing you might think about in private is how a video sounds, and you might think that the sound quality is paramount (which is something most pro-video people will tell you). However, when you do video work for a client, maybe you realize that the client doesn't ask a single question about sound. Maybe one thing you noticed in doing your own video work is that you prefer the blown-out background, known as *bokeh*. To you, this seems to be of paramount importance. But the first time you get a client, all they want are cool video effects, flashy transitions, sound effects, and more. To you, it's confusing and makes no sense, but to them, that's what they're paying for.

If you're doing web design stuff, what you think is the most important (like having clicky, responsive buttons on your website), may be the exact opposite of what a client asks for. The client might just want pretty colors on their website and a professional headshot, leaving you laughing to yourself. How do you get your first client? I'll share with you how I found several of mine, and give you the extreme cliff notes version.

I went to a conference (step 1) that was marginally related to shooting videos (a social media conference locally). Step 2. I talked to everyone in the room, and asked what they were working on and got their cards if I felt like I had a few ideas for their business. Step 3. A few days later, I followed up and set up coffee meetings with each of them, and offered whatever free advice I could, on building an online community or shooting video (I didn't sell anything). If I felt they could use video work, I brought it up. Of the three or so people I met there, one signed up on the spot.

Here's a "cliff notes" way to get your first client:

- **Step #1**: Go to a local event that is somewhat related to what you do. If it's video editing, you could do a local business or social media event. For web design you could do the same. For creatives, like if you're an artist, you could go to book meet ups and book signings (illustration?), art showings, and other related events. The more you think about the specific kind of people you could do work for, the easier this will be.
- **Step #2**: Talk to everyone, about what they're working on, and get their information. If you're genuinely interested in them, or think you can help them and provide advice, move on to step three.
- **Step #3**: Follow up with the people via email or a phone call, and set up a coffee meeting. If it seems like they could really use what you do, mention that it's what you do, and that you can help them. Pricing and packaging is definitely beyond

the scope of this exercise, but if you're truly just starting out, you should easily be able to get a client for $20/hour or $100/month. I always use monthly packages.

What if You Want to Change Careers?

Okay, that's great for freelancers, you might be thinking, but what if I just want to change jobs and I don't have the skills (and thus am unqualified)? The process is similar, yet different, if you want to change careers and go back into a corporate or mainstream work environment, which isn't self-employment or freelancing. Let's say right now you're in a boring marketing job, but you've started to like web design. You've gone through all the steps above to acquire the skillset and get clients, but now you really want to do it for a larger company. The most important thing for you is going to be getting clients (free or paid), to put together a portfolio. You wouldn't commission an artist without seeing their previous work, right?

Well, it's the same with most creative skillsets. Startups and most companies couldn't care less about your credentials in web design—they just want to see your work. If you can put together a portfolio on a personal website, that becomes your business card when you make introductions.

From Zero to Hero

So let's be very clear what you've accomplished here. You can literally start from zero and go through this process to become highly paid, whether you're self-employed or gainfully employed in a brand new company. Here are a few people and the transitions they made:

– **Mick,** who went from working retail (read: a B.S. under-employed job), to learning web design, getting his first $1,000 client (which was typically two weeks of work for him), getting a $5,000 client, and then building his own web design firm charging $10,000-$30,000 per client. He literally went from no skills, to creating a new skillset, out of thin air and transitioning to a very lucrative career.

- **Jill,** who went from doing an entry-level sales job, that was grinding her soul into vegemite paste, to doing marketing for a socially-responsible company. On the side, she started learning marketing by reading books, and then doing free marketing work for small businesses and turning them into case studies. She leveraged those case studies into a $20k pay raise, and a much more enjoyable job too.

- **Alex (me!),** who went from earning $12 an hour at a few part-time jobs to fully self-employed because of the skillset he acquired with writing, content creation and video editing.

The point here is pretty simple: you can re-invent your career anytime you want, without that pretty, shiny piece of paper you think you need. It's shocking how often this comes up as an objection: but I don't have a degree in that. It matters less than you think in most professions that don't require some kind of legal certification. For almost anything—with the exception of medicine, law, and a few other things—you can do this. For the average person, starting to acquire a new skillset almost always guarantees a few things: A new career that pays more and is way more enjoyable, or a side business (which then sometimes blossoms into a full-time business and self-employment).

Start setting aside that one hour a day to sharpen the saw—it's one hour a day to a better life. Does it get any better than that?

Chapter Recap: One Hour a Day to a Better Life

☐ **One hour a day to a better life.** You can literally change careers—quickly—and get a substantial pay raise, by spending an hour each day learning a hard skillset and being able to prove it. Yeah, yeah, yeah, you don't have a degree in it. In most cases, employers care less than you think, especially newer companies. They just care that you can deliver. So if you were a personal trainer, and now you want to code websites—if you can code a website since you started your "one hour a day," prove it. See the next point.

☐ **Create your brag book.** Obviously, you're acquiring a skillset from scratch, so you need to prove to employers/potential clients that you can actually deliver on this. How? Make a brag book, a portfolio, a website, or even just take pictures. You now know how to make fashionable clothing—have pictures of all your pieces on people. You now know how to shoot and edit cool videos—have a YouTube link to prove it. You now know how to do some crazy yogic stuff—have a few videos of your skills, and of the work you've helped clients do, too.

☐ **Focus on learning hard, marketable skills.** "Knowing stuff about websites" is a lot different than being able to code a website. Knowing about a guitar is different than being able to play it. Knowing a bit about fitness is different from being fit, and being able to help other people get fit. If you focus on hard skills, not only can those lead to freelance income, those are the same skills that employers hire you for—not your education (or lack thereof) or resume.

☐ **Never underestimate your ability to change.** In my case, it was 50% true that my college major had nothing to do with my life—until 29, I was employed by many different companies, mostly in marketing roles. I studied Biology and Environmental science in school. Now, I'm studying Chinese medicine (related), and even though I have a wellness business, I had to learn all those skills from zero. You're not an ant—you can change careers anytime you want.

CHAPTER 17

The Bruce Lee Rock Star Theory of Goal Achievement and Motivation

Who doesn't want to kick ass and be hardcore like Bruce Lee? Uhh, every little boy. Being born in '87, most of my childhood was in the 90s, where I obsessed with Ninja Turtles and Kung Fu movies, and like any kid thought it was the coolest thing in history. The one-inch punch? Kung Fu masters with long Taoist beards? Expeditions in the mountains to find mystics and sages? Man, I was so obsessed with this stuff, even in my twenties, that I quit my first full-time job to move to China (with a one-way ticket), to go find some masters, sages, and Kung Fu teachers.

Since childhood I had an early interest in Kung Fu and martial arts. I started taking Kung Fu lessons when I was about fifteen, went to seminars at places with names like *The Fight House* in New York City, learned how to disarm guns and knives, and overall was just trying to overcompensate for being the smallest, skinniest dude in my entire high school.

There was another thing though: I wasn't *that* good. It kind of bothered me, because I felt like I should practice more, and I felt like I could be really good, but the drive and motivation just wasn't there to do it. I was really sporadic with my efforts, too. One summer, I bought an entire kit for training iron palm and iron body, and I smacked a bean, then rock bag for a half hour to an hour every day. After bruising my skin and bones, I would use the hand liniment to prevent blood stasis and ease the bruising, and after a few months my hand looked and felt like a leather glove—it felt like I would break somebody's hand if we high-fived. But then I got demotivated and stopped training.

Another year, when I was studying a martial art called Bagua, I would walk circles for hours a day in the summer heat, or—my favorite—walk perfect circles in the snow practicing my "mud step" technique. Eventually, my interest waned with that too. Even when I moved to China, I was fiery and motivated about finding a "real" teacher in the park, and when my close friend Jeff and I found one, we trained hard. We would train in three hour sessions, year round, outside in the park at night. I was the only white foreigner at the start, so he took pleasure in kicking my ass, knocking me unconscious, or tweaking my wrists so bad that I came close to getting X-rays. He pushed it *way farther* than even the guys demonstrating techniques who were delegates and private bodyguards (at *The Fight House*).

Eventually, he raised the prices a lot, and I figured, "Eh, I'm kinda tired anyway." Yet again, I was a quitter. All the while, I couldn't figure out why I had this on-off cycle with martial arts. It really bothered me quite a lot because it was something I thought would be cool to be awesome at.

Unfortunately, it took me several more years before I finally figured out the puzzle to my lack of motivation and discipline, something that forever changed the way I pursue goals. It made me realize why so many of us fail to stay motivated on the path to reaching, well, anything, and what to do about it.

***

We have motivation and goal achievement completely backwards. Not a day goes by where I see an entrepreneur, or Forbes magazine article on motivation, suggesting that people just need to possess more grit, or know their why, or have a bigger payoff at the end of setting their goals. But what bothered me was that so many successful people I had studied and read about didn't often set goals—I mean, Einstein joked about winning the Nobel Prize (in a cocky, confident way), Steve Jobs mentioned selling a certain number of units (and failed for years before getting there), and Rockefeller sometimes planned world domination, but the majority of these people had some kind of interest or obsession that they were dead set on mastering.

I was once on a coaching call with a client who wasn't feeling super motivated to really get anything done. She mentioned that she was considering a career in music, because living in L.A. had really exposed her to that side of the music and entertainment industry.

"I'm just thinking that maybe I really want to be a songwriter and singer, you know? There are so many people here in L.A. going after that, and it sounds kinda cool." She said.

"It sounds cool, no doubt, but do you even like playing guitar three hours a day? Like on your days off, do you sit down and practice because you enjoy it so much by itself, or just because you want to be a famous musician and rock star?"

"Whoa. Good point, I guess I just find it cool..." she said as she trailed off and laughed nervously.

The Rock Star theory of goal achievement and motivation is simple: most of us want to be rock stars, without even realizing that we hate playing guitar five hours a day. If you don't love the actual process—the very skill itself, what you do every single day—the chances of becoming a rock star are slim to nil. If you don't love doing those three hours a day of writing, recording, playing guitar, it's very hard to become good enough to succeed. It's really easy to set that goal and say we want to become a famous XYZ, without asking ourselves whether or not we actually like the day-to-day.

This is what happened to me with martial arts. I realized that I loved the image of being Bruce Lee, of being a badass, of being secretly lethal, more than I loved martial arts training. I loved the endpoint, not the training, not the day-to-day, hour by hour, skill acquisition. That's why I kept quitting—I didn't truly love my three hours a day. When I realized that, I gave myself permission to quit and just be happy doing something where I loved those three hours a day. I was forcing myself because of an image I was trying to become, rather than just inherent, intrinsic motivation to explore and be curious.

What Are Your Three Hours a Day?

Let me ask you this: what image do you think is cool, or what job do you think sounds awesome? Is it being the rock star? The next Taylor Swift? Being an A-list actor? A blogger or YouTuber? What about a writer? Or maybe it's a martial artist?

Take a look at the following "three hours a day" philosophy—can you see yourself loving doing these things, or does it just look like a lot of work?

Rock Star:
- Practicing singing
- Writing songs
- Playing the guitar
- Figuring out how to pitch your stuff

Artist:
- Painting
- Training on how to improve your skills as a painter
- Meeting other artists and creatives
- Learning how to sell your art

Actor:
- Reading screenplays
- Practicing your acting (like the actual skills required)
- Going to auditions—shitloads of auditions
- Looking at yourself in the mirror to practice different roles

Blogger/YouTuber:
- Writing 1,000 words a day on something
- Shooting a video every single day, or 3-5 per week
- Learning how to sell your own projects or courses
- Reaching out to negotiate with sponsors
- Yes, learning how to sell your own merchandise

Writer:
- Writing 2,000-5,000 words a day
- Building a platform to launch your books and your writingNegotiating with book publishers, or learning how to market and sell a self-published book
- Learning how other great writers write, going to writing conferences, and improving your own writing

Martial artist:
- Practicing your core ten moves, a hundred times a day
- Weekly or daily sparring practice
- Working out
- Flexibility training
- Emulating the masters, going to fights and events, doing competitions, and so on

Doctor:
- Improving your diagnostic skills: massive memorization, practicing procedures, learning pharmaceutical contraindications, etc.
- Improving your core skillset: surgery, emergency medicine, etc.
- Reading medical journals to keep up
- Going to medical conferences
- Spending plenty of time buried in dense medical books

Now here's the big secret. When you look at that profession that you think you would like, you should read the bullet list and go hell yes, that sounds awesome. When I read the list for doctor, I get excited! It's not painful to me, because medicine is a natural interest. The same goes for writer and YouTuber—since those have become my business, it took me a few years to realize that I actually love creating videos and writing books. To other people, those are like pulling teeth.

When you read the lists, if you thought you wanted to become a musician or actor, does the bulleted list look like a lot of drudgery and hard work, or does it look like a ton of fun—or maybe what you're doing already every single day? This often explains motivation in people, because if you actually like doing something three hours a day, it's a cakewalk to become one of the greats, or at least successful. Seriously, while the entire world is filled with people forcing themselves to "grind it out" to become successful, you're pulled by a magnetic love of what you do. You're not expending all your energy on a daily basis forcing yourself out of bed to work.

The reason why I bring all of this up is simple: when you're going through that stacking the bricks process, where you throw things at the wall, and you see what sticks, often things will come up that "sound cool" or potentially are what you love. However, when you bring them through this process of filtering, you realize that maybe you didn't really love that one thing in the first place. It's also a good reason to be gentler on yourself: hey, it's okay if you didn't persist with some things. We all have these up and down phases of motivation, but sometimes it requires just a small change in philosophy to understand why that occurs.

If in your head it sounds good, but in the trenches and dirt it's awful, good luck being able to persist long enough and have the grit to succeed. It's just very unlikely.

Be gentle on yourself if you find yourself not being motivated to persist with a goal—maybe you were just trying to be a rock star, and didn't even realize you hated playing the guitar.

Chapter Recap: The Bruce Lee Rock Star Theory of Motivation and Goal Achievement

☐ **The rock star theory of achievement and motivation.** Many of us want to be famous painters, fighters, artists, musicians, authors, and so on. But I find plenty of people that "love" music, but apparently don't love it enough to practice three, four, or five hours a day to become the best. They're driven by the outcome—being famous on the stage—but not by the process. Unfortunately, the best that I've seen are drawn by a love of the process—they literally love the process more than the outcome. And that's how they get there.

☐ **We suck at figuring out what we think will make us happy.** It's funny how many twenty-somethings I talk to (or people in their thirties or older) who say, "hell yeah, fifty grand would make me a hell of a lot happier." I often used to ask people if they would be miserable as hell working twelve hours a day for $30,000 extra a year, and most said yes. But I think people philosophically like this answer, but they haven't lived it. In reality, what I find happens, is that we take a job for money, or follow an interest because "we think it's cool" but then motivation wanes. Why? We only wanted the outcome, and didn't actually enjoy the process.

☐ **The secret to motivation is loving the process more than the outcome.** This flips your life upside down when you realize it—because you stop choosing projects that you want to be awesome at, and instead, choose ones you love working on daily. The paradox is that this is how many ultra-successful people choose their goals.

☐ **Look for jobs whose process you like.** The ultimate paradox is that the work whose process you love the most is the one you're most likely to see that incredible "goal achievement" in. When you start doing things because you love doing them on a daily basis, not only are you much more likely to actually reach the "goal" you envisioned, but you start living life differently. The process becomes the reward—so every day, you've already won.

CHAPTER 18

Passion is Everything: Don't Get it Twisted

Recently I put together a doomsday document if my life ever went to hell. It's filled with the inspirational stories of other super successful people, and what their advice is on being successful. I had this crystalizing moment where I opened the document one day to find three really successful people staring at me in the face: Mark Cuban, Gary Vaynerchuk, and D'Wayne Edwards, a top shoe designer who has made shoes for Michael Jordan. Can you guess the first-damn-word out of their mouths on how to succeed? Do work that you intuitively feel so drawn to, so obsessed with, that it comes natural to you. Loving it just comes natural.

You want another little sneaky indicator of someone who is already doing work they love and find important? One thing I noticed (not in every person, but in some ultra-successful folks), is that they keep virtually the same lifestyle. They might get a slightly nicer car, or a bigger house, but you won't see the typical flashy bullshit that you find on Instagram or YouTube. And that's because they were already happy before they were ever successful. The process of doing their work every day is what made them happy.

It's funny how often people try to bash the "follow your passion" advice. It's trendy now to say things like "the myth of passion" or that "you become passionate when you get good at things." No doubt, in some situations that's true. And no doubt, anyone who is good at what they do probably likes it more. I would actually argue that many people are moderately successful (or highly successful) without any passion whatsoever for their work. They follow the grind-it-out philosophy, and they're dominating their field. And those are not the people you want to emulate.

So if I'm still a big believer in passion, as in finding work you inherently love to do every damn day, even while half of the business world is arguing against it, why do I think it's such a big deal? First, it's the nuclear reactor inside you.

When I first applied to my Chinese medicine school, I was obsessed. I was so obsessed, that I manually looked up every single professor I wanted to learn from, and emailed them—many of them, multiple times. Some of them I emailed between 5-20 times, until I heard back from them. How many students do you think did that? I was in love with my work, and as a result, I was a sponge, so I wanted to learn from whomever I could take out to coffee. The first thing about passion is that it instantly—almost overnight—changes you from someone who is a lifeless zombie showing up to work, spending 20% of your day productively, to someone who has a nuclear reactor of energy inside your chest every day.

From the outside, you might look at a successful person and wonder how in the hell they got the crazy motivation and work ethic to do what they do. But what you don't know is what's going on inside them. So you just assume they have crazy willpower and discipline. You assume that they are born that way. What you don't know is that oftentimes, before they found "their work," they were average, unhappy, frustrated, stuck people. The major shift that happened was the invisible. Internally, when you find work you love, the motivation is there almost every day.

That doesn't mean it doesn't take effort, and it doesn't mean it doesn't take discipline and ambition to still become great at what you do, but just like writing this book, it comes easy to me. It's fun. I never sit down and force myself—no, not even once. I actually look forward to it every day, and when I end up procrastinating on the other work here, guess what I do? I end up writing this book more. It's just one of those things I'm really passionate about because I feel like the message has to get shared. The internal feeling is the most important thing. Regardless of what you see externally, how "hard" I work or how "much" I work, internally, this is effortless. And that makes all the difference.

It wasn't that I have an iron discipline or that I'm special that led me to email all those professors, it was because I love the shit out of what I do. It sounds cliché, and it sounds passé, but there's a reason why passion will always go down in history as being one of the most powerful things. It's the difference in effort you put into a relationship where you feel attracted to the other person but don't feel any sort of emotional attachment, versus being completely smitten by the other person. Putting in effort comes easy, and you'll do whatever it takes to make things more awesome.

The second reason why passion is absolutely essential is that your work itself will make you happy, far beyond the rewards that come from work. This one is huge. It's almost like you've already won, and success and failure mean absolutely nothing. This one is so high-level that I don't think most people will ever realize it in their lifetime, because it's living life backwards. You know all these people talking about motivation and knowing your "why," and putting up pictures of Ferraris and big houses on their wall to motivate them? They're living life backwards.

We're told to use extrinsic motivators to reach our goals—what's the payoff, right? Well, when you do work you love, the payoff literally doesn't matter, because every single day you've already won. It completely changes your perception of time, because everyone else is "out there" pursuing their goals, waiting for that one day when they have that feeling of happiness and contentment, but you feel that every day already, so you don't even need the goals. The other thing is that success and failure will only hurt $1/100^{th}$ what they ordinarily do, versus if you're obsessed with the outcome. There's no worse person to call a failure, than someone whose entire character depends on them being a "success."

When you really love your work though, every day is an experiment, and since you've already won, who cares if one book flopped? Or one painting sucked? Or a song was awful? You still love writing books, right? You still love painting, right? You still love writing songs, right? The nuclear reactor energy is still there inside of you, driving you way beyond—through many more failures than the average ambitious person is even willing to deal with. To you, there's no other choice. This is just "your work." It's just you.

Coming back to this book, I just love writing it. It makes me happy, it's fun to do, and I'm going to be proud of it regardless of how it performs "in the marketplace." I know that this is a book that needs to be out there. More importantly, there's no amount of money, fame or impact, that will make me want to stop writing it. Compare that to someone who's dead-set on writing a "successful book." They're doing it because they want the image of being an author, and they hate the entire writing process. They spend 99% of their days hating this writing stuff, and then 1% of those days (the day it goes live), they're going to be happy. But what happens if they're 75% of the way there, hating every day, and something changes and they can't get the book out anymore?

They lose. They hated the process, *and* they didn't get the outcome. Lose, lose. That's shit city. There's a guaranteed payoff—every single day—when you love your work.

Finally, the reason why you should follow work you are called to, is that your intuition goes absolutely crazy, and leads you to awesome opportunities. When I was living in China, my buddy Jeff had enrolled at the Chinese medicine school there, and told me about this guy who seemed to really know his stuff—a guy named Dr. Heiner Fruehauf. He mentioned the guy a few times, so I bookmarked his stuff, and then forgot about it. A few years later, when I was back in the United States, I sent him an email asking about something. A year after that, I sent him a follow up question I had about Chinese medicine. And another two years after that, I told him I was checking out Chinese medicine schools, and wondered about the school where he was the dean. I had a little hunch that maybe I should just ask instead of thinking he'd shoot me down.

The rest of the story I mentioned earlier, where he invited me to his home and answered some of my biggest, burning questions I had had for years. It all came from just a little intuition that I had about who to talk to, what direction to go in, and what I might truly be interested in.

It's actually a pretty common story to hear about someone (including me) who had a life filled with resistance, roadblocks, non-stop discouragement and nothing connecting—and then when they listened to their gut, everything changed. Doors opened. Opportunities presented themselves ridiculously fast. Their path to success was literally cut down to 1/10th of what it was, with 1/100th the effort. I don't really have an explanation for this, other than the fact that when you follow your gut, and you go with what you love, life is easier, and things happen that just don't when you are iron-willing your way through your work and life.

Do You Only Have One Passion?

This brings up a really important question. Do you only have one passion? In other words, are you screwed if you don't know your "one thing" since childhood? We hear stories of Einstein, Darwin, Da Vinci and all these classical masters, and know that they're typically associated with just one thing. But is it true for the average person?

First—and this is me being 100% honest—I don't know. For me, thinking back, it was very clear that this is the path I was going to be going down, from about thirteen on. I just got talked out of my dream in my early twenties, which is why I felt lost until my late twenties. For me, yes, there's just one thing, but I have no idea what direction my life will take in the next five to ten years. Maybe I'll get bored, who knows. I don't think it's likely, but I also know that many of us are interested in and passionate about multiple things. I'm also now interested in writing more books, shooting videos, and creating an online community—and those things only started showing up once I got good at them too.

Lots of people get bored after doing one thing for a while, or we're gung-ho and on fire for about six months, and then it's on to the next thing (hobby, person, job, etc.). Are these kinds of people screwed in their work life and personal life? I don't think so. The most important thing is that you can have tons of different interests that you're passionate about, and the big idea is to follow your gut and double down on those. If you follow your gut, work hard, and go with the work that gives you that "nuclear reactor" energy, things will happen that didn't happen in your life previously—that, I can guarantee. Another thing that often shows up is that "usefulness" sneaks in the back door.

Scott Adams, in his book *How to Fail At Almost Everything and Still Win Big,* talks about one of his core success philosophies: each skill you acquire doubles your odds of success. In the book he tells a long string of his past failures, but how each failure gave him a new skill that he later fused with *yet another* new skill to create success. For me, that's how the pieces came together—but the most important thing is to always be acquiring concrete skills, even if you aren't doing work you are a hundred percent sure is your passion.

What if You Don't Have a Clue
What Your Passion Is?

Okay, I get it, you might be thinking, passion is important. Congratulations! That's not news to me at all. But how do I find mine? Do I even have a passion? Do I have multiple passions? How on earth do I get there? I've been trying to find my passion for the longest time. That's one of the key things we're going to explore here—not in a formal "how do you find your passion" way (since it didn't work for me), but more along the lines of a field guide.

Chapter Recap: Passion Is Everything

☐ **Passion is everything.** Despite the articles on *INC and in Forbes* magazine that try to argue otherwise, the vast majority of A-list successful people, mention loving their work. That kind of settles the debate for me. Work you love is way easier to show up for twelve hours a day than work you don't love. It's not rocket science.

☐ **Passion is rocket fuel.** Once I found and cultivated work I was crazy passionate about, the first thing I noticed was a dramatic increase in personal energy. And that I find is the big thing—the passion is the nuclear reactor in your chest that powers you every day.

☐ **Finding your "passion" is a winding road, too.** Like I said, for me it took five years of asking questions every day. For you, it might be longer or shorter, but I do think it's incredibly important to *never* give up on finding work you love. Even if you have to search part-time for ten years—do it.

☐ **You may not have one passion.** For me, I kind of displayed the typical passion story, where I showed an early interest in a subject (natural medicine), and then later in life "re-realized" it, and went full-steam ahead. For many people, there may not be one singular subject matter that turns you on, or there may be multiple different subjects. Go with your gut, and if you can, fuse them all into one profession or business. I have lots of other topics I'm interested in now that I'm passionate about because I'm good at them. Just work hard and keep searching, even if it's part-time.

CHAPTER 19

The Brand of You: Unicorns, Double Rainbows and Success 2.0

"I'm a business, man."

– Jay-Z

Two applicants apply for the same entry-level marketing job for a fashion company. They're both equally qualified, equally educated, and in other words, equally vanilla. They both shotgun out their resumes to hundreds of companies and hear back from less than .5%. They both are nameless applicants, in a literal sea of millions of unemployed twenty- and thirty-somethings, who have the highest rates of unemployment since the great depression.

Imagine this, though. What if one of the applicants had a personal brand? I'm not talking about having books and stuff—I'm talking about just having a few articles written on the Internet under "myname. com." What if the interviewer saw an interesting video she filmed, and a few blog posts she wrote about the future of the fashion industry, the current "state" of the industry, and her own best fashion advice? And what if, rather than just delivering her static resume, she could send them a video profiling her skillset (or demonstrating it right on video), and sent the YouTube URL to the hiring manager?

You be the judge, which one will work better? Person A: "Hey, hire me! Here's my vanilla resume." Person B: "Hey, hire me! Here's my vanilla resume, and all these cool articles and videos I wrote about the exact state of your industry, including a video I shot just for you." No brainer, right? And yet it's surprisingly difficult to find any applications ever in the history of applying for a job that dedicate 1% of their brainpower to doing something creative. I sure as hell didn't, not until I realized this.

The reality is that almost everything awesome that has happened to me, from a career and work point of view, happened because I had a personal brand: Milk the Pigeon. That's right, Milk the Pigeon got me half of the opportunities work-wise that I had in my twenties, including completely unrelated ones. And you know why? Almost every interviewer said the same thing: you're a leader. We want leaders. And it just took a few blog posts on a website to show that. I'm being very literal when I say that multiple hiring managers mentioned my blog.

This is the era of Michelle Phan shooting a Lady GaGa video, getting thirty million views, and now (years later) running a multi-million dollar company (I think it's close to 100 million now, actually), with billions of views, and fame that rivals any A-list Hollywood celebrity. This is the era of Justin Bieber playing his guitar, singing on YouTube and getting scouted by an agent and becoming an overnight sensation. It's the era of Vine stars shooting hilarious videos of themselves doing crazy shit, and becoming mainstream L.A. actors.

Newsflash: this has never existed in human history. The ability to create content that can build a community and go viral (or just get shared) has never existed before, and you have all this leverage... for free. It requires a hell of a lot of hustle and strategy, but the opportunity is free.

A couple years back, a guy reached out to me with my same name, and said, "hey dude, love your site and your bucket list—want to meet up in NYC?" I almost always say no to random requests since I'm scared of being molested by weirdos, but I said yes anyway. Who I ended up meeting was someone like me: an ambitious twenty-something, trying to figure out how to be one of the "big names" in his industry, hungry to make shit happen. And guess what? Five years later, we're still in a business and life mastermind together. He found me from my blog, and just reached out.

Another time, a big-time exec from a major media company reached out because he was feeling the pull to change gears and do some stuff differently in his life. He was being devoured by his day job, even though he was making bank. He was in NYC, from LA he said, and since I live forty minutes outside NYC I went out to meet him. We ended up hitting it off and staying friends—and yes, you guessed it—the friendship came from my personal brand.

One final story here. When I started my personal brand, I never thought of it as a business, although I wanted it to be one. As a result, at the start I would read lots of things about having an online business, like how to get more traffic to your website, how to get coaching clients, how to write and sell books, and more. And it was this binge into how to actually make a successful business work that I ended up using when I launched my online health website and business. It was this skillset that eventually let me launch an Amazon bestselling health and wellness book, and turn my business into one that let me quit my job and have the freedom to work on what I wanted.

The reality is that when you build a personal brand, which is free, you become a unicorn in a room full of horses. Damn straight, you can poo rainbows on your fellow applicants. Okay, all this personal brand talk is fine and dandy, *but I'm not an expert, I can't write or do videos, and I don't even know what I'd write about.*

That's understandable and okay. Those things don't matter for right now. What I'm trying to sell you on is this: if you put time into regularly creating content surrounding a topic you're passionate about, or even want to learn more about, it can lead to some pretty incredible things. This is an opportunity that is *free* (paid with time), and open to anyone with an Internet connection. And it opens doors that most people never seen opened. Here's how you can get started.

First, pick the medium you most connect with, and second, produce for one hour a day. That's it. That's the engine behind million dollar businesses and huge social media celebrities, and it's also the engine behind just getting an awesome job, quitting your job, or having a cool side project. Let's talk about those right now.

The Medium That Connects with Your DNA

Here's a lesson that took me three years to learn: the medium that is best is the medium that comes naturally to you. Here's how you know what comes naturally to you: you can feel it (often in your stomach) when it comes time to write, shoot videos, or record that podcast. You either feel excited and ready to roll, or you don't. A little bit of starting resistance is natural, and many of us have all kinds of insecurities coming up on video (my nose? my hair? I have to do makeup? I can't be naked? What if I'm not attractive enough?), but most of it is just those inner gremlins.

For the first three years, I wrote. I think I'm a decent writer, and I assumed that video and audio took way too much effort and technology, so I avoided them. But around the time that I was juggling working on my side project, writing my book, and more, with a ten hour a day job, I quickly learned a lesson: some things take energy, and some things give you energy. Writing took energy. Video gave me energy. Aha. That's interesting. After that time period, I went fully into video, and any articles were just transcribed, or I wrote a lot less often. Every day became a lot more effortless once I started doing that. I finally found the medium that connected with my DNA, as Gary Vaynerchuk is fond of saying.

Here's my ultimate test: if you like it enough that you can do it on a Saturday morning, then you know the medium that comes easiest and most naturally to you. Go 100% on what you already enjoy, because producing content every day for a decade isn't a walk in the park. You'll hear people say all kinds of things on the Internet: why you should be writing, blogging, or doing the next video-fad. But fads don't matter—longevity does. And the only way you're going to be able to have the discipline, grit and longevity to see the fruits of your efforts, is if you actually enjoy the day-to-day.

Next, building your brand at a high level is simple: set aside 30-60 minutes a day (or a few hours a week) to create. I'm pretty fond of the nice equal number: an hour a day.

One Hour a Day

By now, you realize that I'm obsessed with the concept of acquiring a skill in an hour a day, first introduced to me by Earl Nightingale. I've now written *two books* using this philosophy, gotten into the best shape of my life, traveled the world with a similar system, and done most of the stuff I want to do. Yes, in an hour a day.

Why an hour? First, people complain if you tell them to stop watching Netflix for three hours a day, and go work more instead. So I suggest to them one hour. Can't you watch two hours of Netflix and still do one hour a day that advances you towards the good life? It sounds more reasonable. Second, one hour a day of creating content is honestly more than enough for anyone to get their message out there and really build a personal brand, one that either is a cool side project, or one that eventually lets you quit your job, or just get your dream job. It leads to insane opportunities.

Keep Stacking the Bricks

Let's come back to that Will Smith analogy: just keep stacking the bricks. What started with me, one lost 22-year-old, just writing and complaining about how hard my twenties were, became a popular blog which helped people. That led to interviews on INC Magazine and Huffington post. That led to me creating an online health site because I realized I loved writing and video. And that has now led to multiple books, a big audience, and a platform for my thoughts—which included quitting my job and having the flexibility to choose what I work on every day.

When Seth Godin was recently interviewed, he was asked what the top three or five things were that made the biggest difference in his trajectory as a twenty-something who was seriously in the gutter. You know what he mentioned first? Daily blogging. You know how Seth had the platform to launch multiple bestselling books? His blog and audience. You know how he became a highly paid keynote speaker? His blog. You know how most of those opportunities came to him? Yup, it all started with his habit of just writing his thoughts down daily.[8]

The reality is that you genuinely have *no clue* how big or incredible your life might become if you just keep producing content every day that you enjoy making. You have no clue. If you interview and talk with most people today that are well known (have been producing content for 10+ years), many of them will tell you that they had no clue that their life could become what it is today. But they kept stacking the bricks. This is the long way of me saying, that if you keep creating, miraculous opportunities will present themselves to you in ways you can't even currently imagine.

Wake up, and start producing.

Chapter Recap: The Brand of You

☐ **Build your personal brand, starting now.** When Seth Godin says one of the top five things he did in his entire life was daily blogging—that should say something. *He's kind of a big deal.* For me, I've now seen this in my own life. It doesn't matter if you want a business or not. It doesn't matter if you're a writer or not. It doesn't matter if you really want to quit your job or just find a new one. New doors open.

☐ **Choose one medium to focus on—the one that connects most with your DNA.** I really owe three years of daily experience and Gary Vaynerchuk for helping me realize this. There's no reason to do shit you hate—and that includes the daily process of writing content. If you are writing daily and it's like pulling teeth (beyond the initial phase which is tough for everyone), maybe your medium is video or audio. If so, go full steam ahead on those. It never gets "easier" if you don't like the medium in which you are communicating.

☐ **Doors will open that you didn't even know existed.** The biggest benefit I can suggest is the intangible—opportunities materialize. You meet new people. You have this entire world that opens up that was formerly invisible to you. It's incredible. Most of the benefits I can't describe, but what I can guarantee is that incredible new things that benefit you just start happening. If you can have the grit to persist with creating for an hour a day—stuff just starts happening. Just keep going.

"HOW DO I CREATE A LIFE WORTH LIVING?"

CHAPTER 20

The Beach Bum Millionaire

Somewhere between China and the Philippines, I was sitting on a beach in Thailand, and even though I didn't have a successful business yet, I was making enough to travel and do what I wanted, when I wanted. And I was depressed as hell. How was that even possible? I had money, I had time, I had freedom, I could do what I wanted and I could work on what I wanted. In general, I thought this was what I wanted for the longest time, so it really threw me off track. As far as I was concerned, I was a millionaire. I was doing what I wanted, and I was where I wanted to be. Yet somehow, I wasn't feeling that sense of fulfillment that I thought I was supposed to feel.

Since I'm one of the least creative people I know, and a very systematic thinker, I break most things down to an equation, even if it's a flexible one. For example, until that time, my "good life" dream career equation was:

Self-employment + enough money + freedom = happiness

Then, I had all the pieces of the equation, but it didn't = happiness. So I had to rewrite it. Sitting there on the beach in Phuket with my girlfriend I took time to rewrite the equation. For me, self-employment was critical for "freedom of effort." Enough money in my twenties was literally $2,000 a month from my own business, in other words, pretty easy to attain even if I did everything wrong for a few years. So I introduced new pieces to the formula.

Self-employment + enough money + freedom + work I loved =
happiness

This time, I plugged along for another year and started adding a
bunch of side projects to my day-to-day routine, and it was fun. I was
really enjoying myself, but then even when I had fun and was creating
more wealth for myself, it was missing a certain kind of X-factor that
I couldn't explain: contribution. The feeling that what I was doing
served a purpose greater than myself. So I updated the formula this
time once more.

Self-employment + enough money + freedom + work I loved +
emphasis on contribution = happiness

Now take a look at what, for so many of us, we think the fulfillment
and happiness equation is (or at least I thought it was). Without fail,
when I talk to people who don't have as much freedom as me, they
always say the same thing. The dream is to quit the job and drink beer
on the beach.

Self-employment or self-directed work? Nope.
Time? Yep.
Freedom? Yep.
Work you love? Nope.
Any work at all? Nope.
Emphasis on contribution? Nope.

In fact, the majority of the stuff that would fill 95% of the day
wasn't even there, which was *work*. Passive income, travel, and
avoiding work just jaded me like anything else after a while. After the
very first year doing data entry and traveling to wherever I wanted
(like Taiwan for example, for a month) I thought I was in paradise. I
traveled constantly, since I didn't pay rent. I did whatever the hell I
wanted, and went where I wanted. And then I got bored. Then I got
unhappy. Then I wondered why I did this in the first place. What was
the point, anyway?

Sometimes you realize you had your ladder of success up against
the wrong wall, as the saying goes. For me anyway, it wasn't the
absence of work that produced fulfillment, it was the opposite: filling

the day with the right work, wherever I lived, no matter how much I made beyond the essentials.

It was the twelve-hour days working on stuff that I loved that left me feeling fulfilled, and made it easy to fall asleep after a long day. After that day, I was left with a lot of questions: if fulfillment wasn't the absence of work, what was it? How do I create a great life, do I just create one big bucket list and then get busy checking things off it? How do I create a life that's both awesome, meaningful, and feel like it's well lived?

One thing I learned is simple: humans don't come into this world with a roadmap to success, happiness, meaning, and fulfillment. The good part? That's where you get to create your own adventure.

Why Quitting Your Job and Traveling the World Won't Make You Happy

The good and bad stuff in life often comes in cycles, rather than life being this nice, pretty little linear path. One cycle I found myself floating in and out of was the cycle of running away. The first time I ended up quitting a job to travel the world was my China trip—I figured screw *this*, I can always come back to a life where I'm stuck in the grind working all day. So I booked a one-way ticket and took my flight towards freedom. Eventually, that got tiring, and I wasn't sure if I got what I was looking for (what *was* I looking for?), so I moved back. A year or two went by and things were back to normal, and then I felt that urge to run away again. *I'm not dealing with this society B.S. of bills, dumb bosses, and people who couldn't care less about their job.* On and on this cycle went, until—for the fourth time—I found myself quitting my job and booking a flight "anywhere but here" to magically search for something, a something that I never quite found.

It was around this time that I tried to put the feeling into words, because quitting my job and traveling the world obviously wasn't solving whatever deep emotional issue I was trying to deal with, with my quitting and moving. I just kept finding myself in the same place.

I've recently run into a lot of people who have quit their job to travel around the world, a lot like I did. And most of the time, after talking with them, I end up feeling like they've made a big mistake. More often than not, we end up quitting so that we can "get away"— and the result is that we just end up running full-speed away from something, but never towards something that intuitively draws at us.

Does quitting your job solve the problem of work? Of purpose? Of meaning? Does it help long-term? Does it make you feel like your time is worthwhile?

What happens is that we often build this life escape plan because we don't enjoy our day-to-day experience of life, and then just find ourselves right back in it once we come home. Of course, as the saying goes, you can't run away from yourself.

At the start, I envied these people. "Damn, escape your life for a bit, go off on an adventure and do something fresh and exciting. That looks awesome." Problem is, after covering about 1/4 of the world myself and meeting hundreds of people on the way, I noticed that 90% did what they did for one of two reasons: They hated their job and life, or they just ended a long-term relationship and needed a fresh start. This was surprisingly consistent.

Although there's nothing wrong with that, we naïvely assume that these things are going to make us happier long term. The truth is they won't—and just like those "mistakes" I found myself making in my early 20s, twenty-somethings are experts at avoiding the hard problems in life. Your problems or gripes with society aren't magically going to disappear because you did. Here are the biggest problems that the "quit your job and travel the world" thing doesn't solve.

Problem #1: Making Your Life Feel Worthwhile.

For a short time, you'll be thinking "Sweeeet! I'm using my time so wisely now, seeing the world, investing in experiences and not stuff." Then it'll slowly start to fade. You'll be traveling just to be traveling and you may get listless. What at first was a beautiful escape, and immensely wise use of time, has now become drudgery. You want more. Something is still missing—and you can't quite figure out what. What was "missing" from your ordinary life is also going to be missing from your travels because you've chosen to address symptoms and not the core discontent that bothers you.

When I first "quit my life" and started traveling, I didn't like a lot of things. I hated my job (like everyone else), I wanted to find more purpose and meaning in life, I needed new friends, and I just didn't want to be living a mediocre life anymore. I wanted stories to tell. I wanted adventures. I wanted to do cool things and live this "epic" *Dos Equis* guy life.

"Life is too short to be spent in a cubicle" I told myself... But guess what? When I traveled, did I get any closer to figuring out what kind of job I liked? Nope. Did I figure out how to create more meaning in my life? Nope.

That's because I didn't realize that you need to start trying things out—it doesn't matter where you are. Sitting in an ashram in India meditating is not going to materialize your dream job in front of you, it probably won't materialize that book or business you want to create, or the perfect partner you are looking for.

Finally, after the second or third time "quitting my life," the travels were no longer very happy for me. The individual days were fun and exciting, seeing new stuff, meeting new people, going on adventures, but that listlessness was finding me again.

"I still really want to live a meaningful life," I told myself. And that's when I started thinking and testing, because I realized that my escape plan wasn't helping me escape myself.

Problem #2: Creating Purpose and Meaning.

One of the problems for me was that after traveling so much just for the sake of traveling, I ended up not having a background story. Like in life, if there's no plot, adventure, or mission, events are just noise and experience strung awkwardly together. Most of us quit our jobs in the first place from a purpose based standpoint—our work sucked and felt meaningless. It felt like there were 532,234,123 other things I wanted to do than work just for the sake of existing and paying my rent.

But you don't magically find purpose and meaning by traveling. You find it by doing shit. You find it by trying new things. You find it by cultivating relationships with friends and family, or love with your spouse. You find it by creating some mission that is important to you and meaningful.

You find it by producing and not consuming. If there's one single trend I see more commonly than any other in long-term travelers, it's this: their days seem to be used wisely and they have tons of stories and life experiences, but beyond all these events there is no undercurrent of meaning. They still feel just as lost as they did in their corporate jobs, just with new, fresh surroundings.

They've got stories to tell, but they still haven't figured out shit about life. I'm not saying I have—but if you want purpose and meaning, start figuring out what gives your life meaning and purpose.... right now. If you want to do that on your travels, then do it there. You can do it sitting in your cubicle or sitting on a beach in Bali. But you need to say to yourself, "I want more meaning in my life, and I'm going to start sitting down, thinking, and testing, to see what things give my life meaning." For me, and many others, this doesn't just magically show up on the sabbatical we're on to escape "life." Today is your life. Tomorrow is your life. If vacation is not your life... then what is it?

Problem #3: Happiness.

If there's one thing I've learned from the hardest years of my life, it's this: you sure as hell can't go looking for happiness.

It's just contrary to the nature of happiness. Like success, the more you pursue happiness, the madder you become and the further you get. Rather, it's a natural side effect of doing things right. Traveling will not bring you happiness long-term, nope, no way. There are even myriad studies to show that although people's happiness peaks before/during a trip, after the return, it returns to the pre-trip levels.[2] It's fleeting. Days are more important than events.

Happiness does not come from single events.

Happiness does not come from leaving your ordinary life behind.

Happiness does not come from avoiding your problems.

You may lie to yourself and believe all of these things to be true, but I can suggest first hand: I've "ditched" reality many times, and every single time I came back to the same exact problems. Take the trip for the sake of excitement and adventure—but don't travel thinking that "quitting your job and traveling the world" magically makes you superior to cubicle dwellers or your back-home friends. You're on a temporary opiate high.

Problem #4: Balancing Adventure and Day-to-Day Ordinary Life.

One of the finest arts in life is learning how to balance adventure and reality—in other words, how to incorporate adventure into your daily life. How to *not* come off the travel high when you return to reality. The art is in learning how to have your reality constantly keep you in a state of excitement and adventure. The ultimate question, you could say, is how do you live a remarkable life in a conventional, ordinary world?

Unless you're the rare couple who plans to globe-trot nonstop for life, I assume most of us want a family and some sort of mostly-in-one-place existence. This means that there is going to have to be some balancing of income (work) and adventure (to stay sane). If your lifestyle requires you to be self-employed, are you working on that while you're traveling, or are you just saying you'll get your stuff together when the time comes?

Have you actually sat down to think about how to make your life awesome even though you're living in one place? It's easy for us twenty-somethings to say our life is awesome—many of us are untethered and can move across the world in search of freshness and excitement. And it'll work. But most of us won't end up doing that forever. So what happens when you go back? Have you thought about *that*? The art is not in creating adventure and meaning while on an adventure. That's easy, anyone can do it. That's like being happy when life is easy and going well. The art is creating an insanely meaningful and exciting life while living your day-to-day life.

Problem #5: Finding Enjoyment in Daily Life or Creating Work You Love.

Time and time again I meet people five, ten, or fifteen years older than myself that have temporarily dipped out from American society while they figure their shit out.

And it's immediately apparent after talking with them for five minutes that they haven't figured anything out. And that's pretty upsetting… I mean, great, you quit a job you hated. That's definitely good. But what now? Do you really want to teach English or teach in an international school forever? If that's what you truly love, fine. But if you're doing it because the pay is good and you can travel and have a better lifestyle for a couple of years, what's next?

Wherever you are, have you actually thought about what makes life meaningful? Have you actually thought about your "ideal" way to work and have fun? Have you actually thought about your ideal lifestyle? These things don't just come as magical realizations while you're meditating in the desert (I tried it). I hate to see so many people who start with good intentions—quit the job and find yourself—only to be lost in travel buzz drifting from place to place saying, "I'm taking it one day at a time," while failing to really meditate on life. That "one day at a time" is more often than not just a cop out, because the easy life is more attractive than the conscious life.

They fall in with the other people staying at hostels and mostly end up partying and lounging around, thinking they'll go back with some great stories and a restored sense of purpose and understanding of the world. Uhhh... *right.* Clearly that's not the case, as I meet more and more people I am repeatedly reminded that many travelers seem to have a superiority complex (can't you sniff it here?), but in reality haven't figured out much.

At first I truly envied these people. I couldn't wait to quit my job and travel. I couldn't wait to regain a life of excitement and vitality, that was full of stories and a wise use of time. And then in 2010 I started doing it, and I started getting bored. I got bored of just traveling just for traveling's sake. There was always some reality I had to come back to that needed changing and fixing, regardless of the travels. It was putting a damper on my life.

Big questions for me, like how to find meaningful work, never magically appeared upon my plate. And that's when I realized that most of us hadn't figured out anything about the real world—about how to *exist* in the world. Mostly, we just knew how to escape it, for the time being.

So here's my advice: take those trips, travel for a year, or two years, or three, or forever. Live abroad. But know that it will not solve a single problem in your life. If you can honestly tell yourself you're doing it in the spirit of adventure and excitement, you'll get the most out of it. Many of us delude ourselves into thinking quitting and traveling is a panacea, when in reality it's just another pill for the symptoms. It won't solve the problems of finding meaning, being happy, feeling your time has been worthwhile, balancing adventure and reality, or finding work you love. In this era where quitting and traveling is the cool thing to do—ask yourself, are you doing it just to escape, or will it actually bring you closer to where you want to be?

No matter how bad things might be right now, where you want to say "screw it" and just move to some beach across the world and say "sayonara" to work—do it—but realize it won't magically solve anything. Often when we're in this mental space, we need to upgrade our own definition of success.

Success for Twenty-Somethings: Then vs. Now.

In 2012, I wrote an article called *Audi R8 by 29 or Bust: Success for 20 Somethings*. The article was about how I see people pursuing arbitrary goals set by their parents or by society, and kind of unconsciously slogging through life to achieve goals that they themselves haven't set. It was almost a calling to come back to setting goals more consciously. Setting goals that you really want.

Back then, what I thought success was, was really fulfillment. Back then, waking up and doing what I wanted would be considered success. Back then, doing the work of my choice, and then financially succeeding would be considered success. Really though, I was looking for fulfillment. In many senses, fulfillment overlaps with success but is something completely different: the conditions for fulfillment are different, the path to fulfillment is sometimes different, and the feelings that are associated with fulfillment vs. success are often different.

Now, some years later, I know that what I was looking for back then wasn't just success, but fulfillment. The feeling that your life has been awesome and that it has been well lived. It's the feeling at the end of a long day, where you sit down after having done all the things you've wanted to do, where you've helped someone, or where you've done something that made such a difference in your own life or someone else's, and you drift happily off to sleep. It's the opposite of that frenetic, stressed out anxiety that comes with ambition and setting goals. Fulfillment is comfortably eating a delicious meal, rubbing your satisfied belly, and drifting off into dreamland.

Chapter Recap: The Beach Bum Millionaire

☐ **Success often doesn't satisfy people.** It's really common for me to have a conversation with someone where they say they, "just want to be ultra-successful." That's a great goal, but life often works in cycles. We work hard towards that goal for five or ten years, and then we need a new goal. Because success improved our life in some ways with money and freedom, but didn't produce fulfillment: the feeling of being *satisfied*.

☐ **The conditions for fulfillment are different than success (but sometimes overlap).** Sometimes, the two overlap. For example, writing books for me is something that combines the two. However, very often there are activities that produce fulfillment, that have no relation to success. So for example, just having dinner with some close friends, drinking a glass or two of wine, and reminiscing about life is often a really fulfilling, enjoyable experience. It didn't make you more successful though. Dating someone and going on adventures, raising kids, or pursuing work you are passionate about are all described as fulfilling, but don't always make you more successful. Many of the best, most fulfilling experiences of life are completely unrelated to the conventional definition of success.

☐ **Fulfillment requires different thinking.** Seth Godin's quote of creating a life you don't need to escape from is the first thing that comes to mind. Fulfillment is often not about goals, but about the daily process. It's also geared more towards contribution (read: other people), and thus has a lot less to do with you achieving your own personal aspirations. And, one last interesting paradox: fulfillment often comes as an unintended side effect. As Viktor Frankl said, "the unintended side effect of devoting oneself to a cause greater than oneself."

☐ **You can't escape yourself.** It sounds painfully obvious now, but I spent a lot of my twenties trying to escape myself, and unfortunately, now I see adults with families who haven't outgrown that tendency. The tendency to smoke weed, or get a little buzz on, or take little trips to escape—they're all ways we try to escape ourselves and our lives that don't fill the void.

CHAPTER 21

First Things First: What to do When Your Life Feels Meaningless

I was a really annoying kid to talk to when I was younger. I was always asking "God questions," almost always revolving around the word "why." Why am I here? What am I supposed to do with my life? Where should I go next? Why do I have to do this? To be honest, it pissed people off, I mean, for Christ's sake Jimmy, sometimes you just do stuff and don't question it, right? Just go to work, eat bitter and suck it up. Just use two cups flour and three eggs in the cake and stop thinking about "why" they are in the proportions that they are in. Just learn this material and stop asking why you'll need to know all of this to be a doctor or architect.

After I got out of the juvenile phase of life (where every "why" you ask gets a "because I said so" in return), I entered a new phase of life. More people, still asking why. Why am I here? It was weird, because I was first asking myself these questions as a kid, and now I was doing the exact same thing as an adult. Everyone is still asking why. And most people are still giving themselves, "because I said so" answers. So once again I started asking myself that age-old question: what in the hell should I do with my life? What *can* I do with my life? What am I *supposed* to do with my life? And, most importantly, what do I *want to do* during my life? What makes it feel worthwhile?

***

Survivors of all types of accidents or horrendous living conditions often share eerily similar stories. Despite the harshness of the current reality, against all odds, they maintain some special sort of reason for going on, also known as the *Stockdale Paradox*.[10] They maintain a "why" beyond just "staying alive" that keeps them going. They found some greater purpose to live for, and Viktor Frankl was one such person. He was a victim of the Nazi regime and spent several years in the Auschwitz concentration camp, while his entire family and both parents passed away (aka were murdered). As his body was slowly withering away, and as thousands of people died around him, he was deeply pondering the state of his life.

His memoir, *Man's Search for Meaning*, is interesting to me for one main reason: one can watch his mind deliberate as it searches for a meaning in all the death, suffering, and apparent meaninglessness that was going on around him. Frankl's conclusion?

> *"Life is not primarily a quest for pleasure, as Freud believed, or a quest for power, as Alfred Adler taught, but a quest for meaning. The greatest task for any person is to find meaning in his or her own life."*[11]

The words hit an eerie nerve in me, after all, I know plenty of people my age making a lot of money, who outwardly appear happy, but inwardly feel that what they are doing is pretty pointless. They feel spiritually bankrupt. So they just go ahead and do what other people are doing, to have some semblance of a sane, ordinary, normal, and supposedly happy existence. I ended up thinking about this more— the deepest human value, one that you can selectively pursue and cultivate to enrich your life, is it really happiness? Or is happiness a consequence of doing things right? Frankl chimes in here again:

> *"For success, like happiness, cannot be pursued; it must ensue, and it only does so as the unintended side-effect of one's dedication to a cause greater than oneself or as the by-product of one's surrender to a person other than oneself. Happiness must happen, and the same holds for success—success will follow you precisely because you had forgotten to think of it."*

Searching for the Wrong Thing

I think there's one particular reason why many of us feel completely lost—because we're searching for the wrong thing. Many early philosophers believed that our primary motivation in life was personal pleasure, or happiness—that's just what we strive for and that's just what our purpose is. I mean, in one way, this pleasure-seeking idea makes sense:

- What's the most important thing according to your body and your ego? You, of course. Who do you look at first in a picture? Yourself.
- We naturally shy away from, say, putting our hand on a campfire (it hurts) and enjoy doing things like eating cookies and having sex. They make us feel good.
- We help people: it either makes them feel good (which makes us feel good) or it directly makes us feel good.

There's a good argument for straight up pleasure, happiness and joy being the sole purpose of life. But what if pleasure, enjoyment and happiness were just unintended by-products? What if they were just positive consequences of doing the right thing, instead of something you could deliberately cultivate? There's a better explanation for why we're lost and why many of us constantly strive to find happiness at some point or another. Almost by default, if we do something that makes us happy, but it doesn't leave us with a lasting feeling of fulfillment, then we can't define it as meaningful.

Ready for this? The cure for being lost, and feeling like your life is meaningless, is not to re-find happiness. The way to become unlost, happy, and successful is found all in one thing: purpose. Purpose to me isn't some complex idea that requires a PhD in psychology to find—it just means living a life that *you* find worthwhile. Through purpose you create passion, you create happiness, you find drive, and you elicit meaning in an apparently meaningless existence. These all blossom, as perfect by-products. And by purpose, I don't necessarily mean "your one ultimate purpose." Purpose, like happiness, isn't static. It's not just "oh, I've always wanted to be an Astronaut, ever since I was a kid!"

For some parents, raising their kids and being a good parent is their primary purpose—but once their kids grow up and move out they suddenly find their lives feeling more meaningless. College kids that graduate university are accustomed to having a purpose: pass this class, semester after semester after semester, and finally, one last purpose—graduate. What happens once they graduate? Many lose their sense of purpose because they don't have a direction to travel towards. Normal everyday people sometimes find purpose in others—a loved one for example—and once that person leaves their life, they are crushed and fall into an existence that feels meaningless again.

Purpose, therefore, can be fleeting. But purpose—no matter how temporary—is so important because it makes you feel that what you are doing in your life actually matters. Purpose is the underlying thread that allows people to push through mountains of pain, purpose is the underlying story behind what you do, and purpose is what drives you long after the external circumstances of your life have gone to hell. And purpose is the ultimate fix for no longer feeling lost, no longer feeling like you're in a dream or an observer of your own life. It makes you feel in control.

The First Question: What Creates Meaning and Fulfillment?

"… that feeling of which so many [people] complain today, namely, the feeling of the total and ultimate meaninglessness of their lives. They lack the awareness of a meaning worth living for. They are haunted by the experience of their inner emptiness void within themselves; in addition to this, however, man has suffered another loss… No instinct tells him what he has to do, and no tradition tells him what he ought to do; sometimes he does not even know what he wishes to do. Instead, he either wishes to do what other people do (conformism) or he does what other people wish him to do (totalitarianism)."[12]

– MIHALY CSIKSZENTMIHALYI IN FLOW

The feeling of meaningless is one of those scary nagging feelings we all get at some point in our lives. We wonder if there is some grand scheme out there for our suffering, or why, after working for a couple of years in a job that's "alright," it doesn't feel like it has a point anymore. It's because both happiness and success are closely tied to purpose. It's the reason why, when you talk to so many twenty-somethings that are in their first, or second, or fifth professional job these days, they're like, "It's alright, it's just a job." *Oh, really?*

They have to convince *themselves* that what they are doing has meaning, which is a pretty sad thought if you ask me. Alright, so your life feels pointless. Either you're totally lost, or you have everything but it doesn't seem to make a difference. You're getting paid, you have a good apartment, you have a car. Now what? Here are a few things that turned it around in a big way for me. First, create a better story (or *a* story, if you don't have one). Second, give yourself a direction in which to travel (a personal treasure map). Third, determine why you are actually doing this. Fourth, go after your flow.

What's Your Story?

"You can't go on without a story any longer than you can read a book about nothing."

– DONALD MILLER

A few years ago, I had a conversation with a friend that really got me thinking: What kind of story are you living? What kind of story do you *want* to be living? The problem with not having a story is that even if you experience a lot—travel, learn, try new things—you aren't providing a *context* for all these experiences to occur in.

The experiences just become noise—they are random, chaotic, and although enjoyable, they don't come together and provide any coherent feeling of "purpose." They aren't part of a larger story line. If you don't currently have a story, there are typically four qualities inherent in any epic tale, whether it's some of the biggest movies, the oldest epics, or just a damn good life. It's the hero's journey. There's a character who wants something, who has the potential for failure, struggles (or suffers), but does *whatever it takes* to realize the story and see it through. Think about these four themes.

Without a fundamental underlying story, experiences, no matter how enjoyable or epic become noise. The story is the lifeline, the backbone, the thread that connects all experiences and makes them worthwhile.

When I moved to China around 2010, it wasn't to teach English, work, or just to randomly hang out in China. I didn't work at all except the last month there, and just lived off my saved money for a year because I went with a mission (aka a purpose). I wanted to seek out sages, mystics, monks, and Kung Fu masters. The original plan was that I would go for about five years, and come back as some kind of badass, semi-enlightened sage with mean Kung Fu skills ready to kick some ass. Think about the difference it would've been psychologically if I just, "went on a trip to China to see what was there."

It's cool to go on a trip, but there's no real purpose behind it except for fun, which is still cool. But I definitely wouldn't have stayed for a year, dealt with the ups and downs, and sure as hell wouldn't have dealt with getting punched in the face by some middle aged Chinese dude in the park, without a purpose. It was just another trip which would've gotten old after two weeks. With a purpose, I stayed over a year and it ended up playing a part in my greater life story.

Also, when you think about it, the greater purpose of me writing this book, building my own business, and doing all these things that a lot of twenty-somethings want to do is simple: I want to live my own dream life to show *you* that living your dream life is possible. That's one of the higher purposes for writing (besides loving it)—because I have to live it, to write anything about it, you know? It's so rewarding and meaningful to think that as my life gets better each year, one conversation with a person can encourage them to keep going (or maybe just start, on a dream they let go dormant).

Going after these goals would've kept me occupied for a long time, but the greater story is that of a lost twenty-something who wanted to create a meaningful life filled with the things he loved. And the reason I embarked on the adventure was that I didn't know a single person who consciously created their reality in their head, then went after it, and then lived it. I wanted to be that tiny percentage of the people on the planet who *lived it*. Otherwise, what business would I have telling people (and eventually my kids) to go after their dreams?

If you just read the features of my life, you see me writing books, shooting videos, doing coaching, and building an online community, but the greater purpose is the story behind it all: one dude against the world to *prove* that it's possible. At the end of the day, nothing scares me more than talking to people who have lost that fire to go after their biggest dreams. So I feel an obligation to society and my generation to be one who walks the talk.

The story is what keeps me going long after shit gets tough and I want to quit or just choose an easier life.

You Can't Escape Yourself

*"I find it fascinating that most people plan their vacations
with better care than they plan their lives. Perhaps
that is because escape is easier than change."*

– JIM ROHN

People seem to be goal averse. Maybe it's because setting goals sets us up for disappointment, like not losing those thirty pounds we planned to lose during the new year. Maybe it's because we are lazy. Maybe it's because we don't know what we want or haven't thought about what we want. But there is one big reason why you should set goals—even arbitrary goals like running a marathon—and that's because *they give life structure.* At the basic, most fundamental level, the easiest way to turn a meaningless life into a meaningful one is to set a random goal and go for it. Short-term fulfillment is sometimes as easy as just setting a direction to travel in.

The more facets your goal has, the better (e.g., building a business you care about is superior to learning a language, from a purpose standpoint, because it will take longer and has so many facets you can improve upon and will change your life in a bigger way). Set arbitrary fitness goals: gain 20 pounds of muscle, lose 20 pounds of fat. Make a bucket list of awesome things you want to do. Do one every week, month, six months or year. Remember these goals are random, superficial, and provide a temporary sense of purpose. They are, however, better than nothing, and are an easy step to feeling like life is worthwhile.

Why Even Bother?

"Those who have a 'why' to live for can bear almost any how."

–NIETZCHE

We already talked about the importance of having a story—a context for all the experiences that your life is made up of. But there's one other quality inherent in a meaningful life: why are you doing what you're doing? Why are you doing the work you do? For money? Or for some reason that provides real internal sustenance? Why are you going to the gym? Is it to look good for your girlfriend/boyfriend, or is it because you deep down, want to do it for yourself? It's funny, the second largest group of people I get emails from is not from people who are confused, unemployed, and unhappy—it's from people who did it all *right*, and are sitting at a job with lots of money in the bank, wondering, "is this all there is?"

Some people are more easily influenced by the "why" than others. For example, some people can really defer their happiness and job satisfaction by just working for money, because they have a family they love that needs supporting. Others get severely depressed after a short time. Similarly, some people can legitimately go to the gym and transform their bodies for another person—a guy who loses fifty pounds because his girlfriend is threatening to break up with him, for example. Other people quit soon after because they realize they are not doing it for themselves.

So when I ask "what is your why?": why learn a new skill, why start a business, why run a marathon—"just because" is a fine answer in the short-term, but to power you long-term the "why" will need to be something that deeply connects with a core value in your life. Honestly think about the following two options and tell me which one resonates with you the most:

- Starting a business so you can make much more money than you currently do in your crappy job that pays twelve dollars an hour (I spent 80% of my twenties in this scenario).
- Starting a business because you're tired of meaningless work, working for someone you dislike, working with people who dislike what they do, having your hours and schedule pre-arranged, being unable to take more than a freaking week of vacation. Also, the idea of being able to directly influence people and help them (every single day) sounds incredibly rewarding.

What is the real, emotional, deep-seated reason for doing what you're doing? The people who have surmounted the greatest obstacles in life almost always have a tremendous story or purpose behind them: the abused wife who will do anything to see her daughters not get stuck in the same situation, the guy who sacrificed his entire life and youth to accumulate money and success because he was raised in poverty, who wants to make sure his kids do work they love.

Or, you have a woman like Malala, who was deliberately targeted by the Taliban, shot in the face in an attempted assassination attempt, and now has dedicated her life to spreading peace and women's rights throughout the world. Damn. *Those* are great stories, and massive purposes for being alive.

Engage in Flow Producing Activities

Yes, by now you should know that Dr. Mihaly Csikszentmihalyi is one of the main influencers of everything I do in my life. This fourth way to avoid a meaningless life is a paradoxical one—it's less easily sought out than the other three. In a nutshell, you are looking for an *experience—flow*, to be specific. Being in *flow* is that magical moment when you do an unbelievably perfect shot during a soccer game—time freezes, the stars align, and you describe it as feeling "perfect."

Being in *flow* is the artist's muse—the concept of time evaporates, goals and structure don't exist, only enjoyment and pure engagement in the current activity exists. *Flow* is the state where most of us are happiest, where we feel in our element, where we feel challenged and as if our tasks and time are worthwhile. *Flow* is where you talk to the attractive person at the bar, and you're so engrossed in the conversation or the date that you look up, realize it's been three hours, and wonder where the time went.

We'll talk more about flow later, but there was an experience I had that quickly confirmed that this was true. I was sitting outside of a coffee shop on a warm summer day, yet again writing out a list of all the things I *could* do with my life. Move to Spain for a year. Become a scuba instructor. Go back to China? Write a book? Edit books? It was more of the same dead ends that I found myself in for the past year. An older guy I knew sat down next to me and started up a conversation, first by asking what I was working on. I jokingly told him that I was working on the formula for happiness, and laughed.

"The devil's hands are idle playthings," he said to me.

"Huh?"

"I'm sure it means a lot of things, but to me it's pretty obvious. I see a lot of people trying to figure out life, trying to figure out how to be happy, or live a meaningful life. Trying to invest effort into figuring these things out is like trying to invest *effort* into trying to sleep—it never works. The happiest people I know are the busiest people I know. The more time you have, the more you try to fidget with it and figure it out, the more those inner demons come out and the less happy you are."

It made a lot of sense to me when I thought back to the past year or so. Anytime I was in flow or engaging in some kind of peak state, whether it was snowboarding with friends, out to dinner with my girlfriend, doing judo, getting on an airplane somewhere, or just having drinks with a few people—I wasn't "specifically" doing anything most of the time to deliberately be happier. I wasn't thinking about being happy—I just was happy. Yet for some strange reason, I wrote those down as "flow producing," happy, and meaningful activities. I didn't try to make them so, they just were. And it was just because I was busy, engaged in life, and living in the moment. It was the side effect of a live well lived, like Viktor Frankl said.

Later, I'll share how I deliberately cultivated these flow activities, but for now, just remember the following. Whether or not you are "achieving" anything, flow-producing activities are inherently enjoyable, feel meaningful, and are self-described as some of the most powerful transcendent moments of life. Whether it's skiing, having sex, writing a book or just traveling—life just feels awesome.

"What matters, therefore, is not the meaning of life in general but rather the specific meaning of a person's life at a given moment. To put the question in general terms would be comparable to the question posed to a chess champion: "Tell me, Master, what is the best move in the world?" There simply is no such thing as the best or even a good move apart from a particular situation in a game and the particular personality of one's opponent. The same holds for human existence. One should not search for an abstract meaning of life. Everyone has his own specific vocation or mission in life to carry out a concrete assignment which demands fulfillment. Therein he cannot be replaced, nor can his life be repeated."

– VIKTOR FRANKL, MAN'S SEARCH FOR MEANING

The Second Question: "Is This All There Is?"

*"Often, people work long hard hours at jobs
they hate to earn money to buy things they don't
need, to impress people they don't like."*

— NIGEL MARSH

All of us, at some point in our lives, ask ourselves, "is this all there is?" My grand plan, my grand purpose, my work and my time... everything that I've worked for culminates in... this? The life I'm currently living? Shortly after, we proceed to feel like we've been really shafted by someone or something, that we're victims of fate and that we can't believe we bought into some great cosmic lie. And then we self-medicate. Most of us dull the pain of our seemingly meaningless existence by doing one of three things according to the *Flow* master, Doc. C:

#1 "As this realization slowly sets in, different people react to it differently. Some try to ignore it, and renew their efforts to acquire more of the things that were supposed to make life good—bigger cars and homes, more power on the job, a more glamorous life-style. They renew their efforts, determined still, to achieve the satisfaction that up until then has eluded them. Sometimes this solution works, simply because one is so drawn into the competitive struggle that there is no time to realize that the goal has not come any nearer. But if a person does not take the time out to reflect, the disillusionment returns: after each success it becomes clearer that money, power, status and possessions do not, by themselves, necessarily add one iota to the quality of life."

#2 "Others decide to attack directly the threatening symptoms. If it is a body going to seed that rings the first alarm, they will go on diets, join health clubs, do aerobics, buy a Nautilus, or undergo plastic surgery. If the problem seems to be that nobody pays much attention, they buy books about how to get power and how to make friends, or they enroll in assertiveness training courses and have power lunches. After a while, however, it becomes obvious that these piecemeal solutions don't work either."

#3 "Daunted by the futility of trying to keep up with all the demands they cannot possibly meet, some will just surrender and retire gracefully into relative oblivion. Following Candide's advice, they will give up on the world and cultivate their little gardens. They might dabble in genteel forms of escape such as developing a harmless hobby or accumulating a collection of abstract paintings or porcelain figurines. Or they might lose themselves in alcohol or the dreamworld of drugs. While exotic pleasures and expensive recreations temporarily take the mind off the basic question "is this all there is?" few claim to ever have found an answer that way."[13]

These are three pretty typical, superficial coping strategies. Some of us go deeper into the consume-purchase cycle. We try to chase flashier cars and pretty girls. We chase money. We buy stuff. We work our way up the ladder to earn more. We keep our mind occupied that way. You see this a lot in men who get dumped or go through some hardship and decide to channel that into "working harder than everyone else" assuming this will fix the problem. Some of us attack symptoms to keep busy. If it's our health that first gets our attention, we become fitness fanatics. If it's our work that's miserable or we don't have enough money, we become workaholics.

If it's dissatisfaction in our dating lives, we bounce around from person to person. The third typical pattern is retreat. Some of us get tired of the struggle and don't see any clear way out. We retreat. Know a friend who plays World of Warcraft® or Madden all day, or someone who smokes weed all day? Retreat. They've given up on changing their circumstances. It's an easy temporary fix, a pill for the symptoms. But like all pills they only work for so long unless the underlying conditions are addressed.

Some of us truck ahead, attack symptoms, or give up. For me it was a blend of #1 and #3—which I think are the most common. Tell me how familiar these sound—you get your first job out of college, get your new place, maybe get your new car. But then what? Assuming you don't go back to school or get married, you probably go into existential crisis mode.

What the hell do I do now? For me, I ended up just doing what everyone else did: I started partying more (since, gee, I had to use the money I earned, right!), I bought tons of stuff I didn't need and focused on increasing my earning potential. Friends reached the same point and started doing drugs again. Other friends again reached the existential crisis point and started playing video game after video game. Life for them went like this: video games before work, video games during work, video games after work. You could just as easily replace video games with drugs, alcohol, or any other means of dulling the senses. It's all the same, sometimes.

The problem is that most of us never get out of the cycle. Most of us live in this sort of "existing" phase where we are merely coping and reacting to everything happening around us. Rarely do we escape the cycle and find the opportunity to truly thrive. Again, as Doc. C says:

> *"Happiness, in fact, is a condition that must be prepared for, cultivated, and defended privately by each person. People who to learn to control inner experience will be able to determine the quality of their lives, which is as close as any of us can come to being happy."*[14]

Well, what are we supposed to do then? For starters, realize that you might be coping with existence (existing) and not actually improving it (thriving). We're being reactive to life and there's no way we can escape a crappy existence where we're getting punched in the face and doing nothing in return. We have to consciously sit down and realize, "I don't have to do mind-numbingly boring, soul-crushing work."

How do I know that no one has to get stuck? It's simple—I chose to suffer and work through it. While all my friends were smoking bowls to numb the pain and go into the dream world for just a few hours longer, I deliberately avoided it because I knew it was just prolonging my suffering in the long run. I chose the short run, multiple year depression (aka *feeling*), over turning off that reflex in my body. I knew that would be like disabling a GPS when you're lost in the woods of life.

You have to consciously sit down and realize that wasting your leisure time is shooting yourself in the foot. Your leisure time is the time when you can (and should) be digging your escape route. You have to consciously sit down and realize that after getting smashed on Friday night, you wake up exactly where you started the day before. That's fine. Unless of course you don't want to be where you were the day before. You have to consciously sit down and ask yourself what the hell you actually want from life, and if what you're doing now is getting you any closer to what you want. That goes for the job, for work, for romantic partners, for friends, and anything else.

Complacency will screw you. Comfort will screw you. Your friends will screw you. Sit down and figure out what, about your current lifestyle, makes you feel so discontent. Is it monotony and routine? Maybe you just got back from traveling and are having an impossible time settling back down into "ordinary" life. Maybe you're like a lot of twenty-somethings bouncing around in jobs because you're chronically stuck in shitty ones.

Maybe your friend group sucks (or doesn't exist, because you moved after college). Whatever it is, whatever is making you drink yourself retarded on Friday, or retreat into video games and drugs, or continue to chase the flashy cars and pretty girls but stay depressed the next day, figure out what the hell it is that is getting to you. Anything is better than not knowing "you're stuck."

It may seem overly simplistic and too vague, this advice to "think about what you actually want" for people who are stuck in the rat race (or life) in some way or another. But the truth is that the vast majority of us live in a dreamworld carefully sculpted by others, with no intention of ever realizing we're dreaming. The truth is that most of us will pass year after year just as deep into the cycle in which we were born, and never realize it. And the truth is that only by becoming aware that you are stuck can you become unstuck.

Most of us have given up and don't even realize it. Right? Look around you. How many of your friends are just sitting and occupying their piece of land. Paying three hundred, five hundred, a thousand, two thousand a month to rent a place, just so they can exist. And they work jobs they suffer through just to pay for that rent, which is just to exist on a piece of land. Years pass and nothing changes. They haven't learned anything new, they haven't traveled much or added any value to their life, they haven't changed anything about their circumstances or life experiences.

Maybe they got a promotion or two. And maybe they got their first vacation and finally saw Europe. Well, time to wait another couple years to do that again. The hell? Does nobody see how utterly insane and mindless this lifestyle is? Does nobody realize the insanity of paying just to exist on a plot of earth, or working a job, just to pay to exist on a plot on the earth, just for the sake of existing? It's like the person I mentioned earlier who died of cancer young; he realized he spent his life accumulating and existing, and none of it would be left after he was gone.

If what you're currently living is "not what you signed up for," grow a pair and start doing what you've wanted to do the whole time. Most of us cope and try and drink away the symptoms of the "is this all there is?" feeling. But when you think about it, do you really have a choice? It's either now, or forever asking yourself "is this all there is? Is this really the culmination of my whole life. *This?*"

The Third Question: What If I Feel Stuck in Life with No Way Out?

It's easy to get stuck in life. In fact, for most of us, it just happens. One day we just realize it. We get that nagging feeling that, "doing this, here, was not what I wanted to be doing." We get that nagging feeling that there's somewhere else we should be. We dream of escaping, constantly. Life has a little bit less zing to it. Happy things don't get us quite as happy, and sad things—wait, life is sad, we tell ourselves—so we suck it up.

We start telling our friends who are having hard times the age-old advice, "welcome to life. Anything you want has to be attained through struggle and warfare with life."

"Dreams? Who can afford them?"

"At least I'm paying my bills and I have a place to live."

"Ehh, that's only possible for a select few people."

For most of us, we hit that "stuck and screwed" spot right when we get the first secure job. It pays us enough so that we don't worry, we get a good enough apartment, then a good enough spouse, then a good enough marriage. And then life is, "eh, good enough" for the rest of our lives. Hearing about this "good enough" resignation from people makes me want to kick puppies.

CHAPTER 22

How to Tell if You're Stuck (and What to Do About It)

I spent a very long time in my twenties with one feeling that I hated, but couldn't quite fully describe: being stuck. Some people describe this as an existential crisis, while others describe it as depression, but for me it was one thing: stuck. No motion. No progress. No activity. I was treading water, barely keeping my head above the surface, but never making progress. Two steps forward, and two steps back. Do any of these sound familiar to you too?

#1: You Have Less Energy and Couldn't Care Less About Anything.

The most overwhelming and obvious sign of the "stuckness" is low energy and a general inability to get motivated. Everything seems like a struggle. You know you need to make friends but you don't want to put in the effort. You know you need to lose weight but you don't want to go to the gym. You want to learn how to cook but just can't be bothered to. And that basically is the essence—you just don't care anymore. You can't be bothered to really do, well, anything.

Everything is too much effort, and nothing seems to get you super aroused and happy. Usually the *only* thing that does, is when the person gets a spouse or falls in love—which is sometimes their only anchor into sanity. Underlying the signs and symptoms of depression, dullness, hollowness, don't-give-a-shit-ness, is a serious lack of motivation to do anything.

#2: Everything Seems Impossible (Even the Small Stuff).

When you get stuck, everything is a struggle. Even if you're off at five, and you usually play video games till midnight, you still complain about going to the gym and the lack of time even though you're getting fatter and fatter. When you don't have enough money for something (a vacation, an engagement ring, a new toy, a new car, etc.), you don't have the mental energy to figure out how to earn it and pay for it. You just complain, you whine about how difficult life is and how you just wish you were earning more money. This lack of energy and zest is closely tied in with symptom number three.

#3: You Rationalize Mediocre Circumstances as Being "Just the Way It Is."

What does lack of energy, and everything seeming impossible, result in? A chronic cynic. "This is just the way life is." We become a person who has no concept outside of the brutal "realities" of life. Outside of the normal paradigm for most: suffering in a job, deadly commutes, boring leisure time, jack-shit on the weekend, and an average spouse. The saddest part about this is that we're so unhappy with it, but at some point, we lie to ourselves long enough, until we've reached the full-on cynic's level: this is life.

When your car breaks down, you lose your job, and your wife divorces you—all on the same day—these kind of people say stuff like "that's life." It's like their emotional intelligence has vaporized into thin air. They are far beyond entertaining silly stuff like their dreams, passions and other stuff. Sometimes they entertain the idea of making a big life change, like moving abroad, traveling long-term, or quitting their job—but they almost never follow through. They've given up. The batteries are permanently on empty.

#4: Your Intuition Isn't Working (and You Don't Feel Anything).

Another symptom of being stuck is that you're emotionally semi-dead. When you ask people like this what they would rather be doing, or where they'd rather be, they just say, "Anywhere but here." It's like you've numbed yourself to reality to try and cope with it better— higher lows, and lower highs, but more consistency you tell yourself.

You tell yourself that smoking another bowl, drinking another glass of wine, or watching one more TV show is okay, and just what you need. But you know deep down that you're using them to self-medicate and distract yourself for one hour longer. You know that you're the most miserable you've ever been.

But here's the problem; when you're no longer connecting with your intuition—you end up doing stupid stuff because you think you should, and not because of how it makes you feel. Like trying to increase your earning potential in a job you already hate. It all sounds great to the mind, from the outside, but internally you're dying and just ignoring the dying feeling. When you turn off how you feel internally, it's like throwing your compass into the ocean while lost a thousand miles out at sea.

#5: You Get Pissed Off Over the Smallest, Most Inconsequential Things.

To me, this has always been a symptom of being stuck, or feeling trapped in the rat race. You just have to vent. You have to get that angry, bitter shit out of you, so you start cursing at drivers in traffic, calling the lady in line at Walgreens a bitch, and throwing mini tantrums whenever possible. Ever met someone who complains about traffic, kicking over the dog bowl, the new coworker, spilling their coffee, being out of shape, the dog crapping on the carpet, some rude person in the coffee line, the weather, and so on, every damn day?

Complaining is the most exciting part of their day—and it's just about the only attention they get. There's one thing about getting stuck though—it's easy, it happens naturally, and it will happen naturally, unless you invest time into not getting stuck.

How to Get Un-Stuck

If any of this sounds familiar, that's okay. You're normal. Whether you want to describe this as a depression, being stuck, or being in a rut, the twenties are a huge risk period for depression and getting stuck like this (and I spent literally years in this horrible phase).

There's one important characteristic of getting stuck, though. Ever heard stories of kids who are way bigger than their dads but are still getting beaten and abused by them years later? Have you heard stories of genius kids in the ghetto that stay stuck achieving nothing because their mom called them, "lousy pieces of garbage that will go nowhere?" Know someone who has been bullied their entire life, and still, as a grown man, won't stand up for anything, and has no self-confidence? It's because our minds have been trained to behave certain ways and believe certain things. In psychology, this is often called learned helplessness, and in rats that are repeatedly shocked no matter what direction they try to go in, or no matter what they do, they just stop trying anything.[15] Similar circumstances happen in humans too.[16]

It's like your mom always said, "Stop calling your brother an idiot! Or else one day he'll think he is one!" It's almost like that saying "If you think you can, and if you think you can't—you're right." Getting unstuck, first and foremost, is all about getting your head right.

The other day, someone I know was talking about her son. She told me she was starting to see him get stuck, she was starting to see less brightness in his eyes, he was looking sleepy—not physically—but sort of that soul weariness that comes from psychologically bearing some emotional burden for a prolonged period of time.

She looked really concerned and told me, "I just want to shake him and say *wake up*! Life has so much out there for you," she told me. "*Life has so much out there for you.*"

Chapter Recap: What to do When Your Life Feels Meaningless

☐ **Meaning is often a side-effect of living a certain way.** It took me many years and plenty of conversations with people to realize that meaning is often an "unintended side effect of dedicating oneself to a cause greater than oneself" to use Viktor Frankl's words. Pursuing meaning was like pursuing happiness for me—I never seemed to get it quite right, but when I changed the way I lived, meaning showed up. For me, the biggest source of meaning was interacting with other people, and helping *other* people to reach their goals. I suspect for most people this is true.

☐ **What many of us want isn't just happiness, but meaning.** One of the weirdest feelings was being in my early twenties, having a great job that gave me more than enough money, traveling once a year to a new country, and doing most of the things I always wanted to do, yet still feeling like, "is this all there is?" Because I no longer had a direction in which to travel, or some mission, it felt like I was just existing. I was happy, I enjoyed my days—but it felt like there was something more that I was missing—meaning.

☐ **Meaning can be cultivated.** The most important thing here is that meaning can be deliberately cultivated through projects, directions to travel in, helping other people reach their own goals, and above all, pursuing something epic (much larger than yourself).

☐ **Getting stuck happens, but often doesn't magically resolve itself.** I spent about three solid years with that stuck feeling of depression, stagnation, lack of progress, and I hated it. It wasn't until I forced myself to take action—any action—that I started making progress. I have friends who were similarly stuck, but never pushed themselves to try new things, or branch out and be uncomfortable, and years later, many are still there. I know people who are still "stuck" after ten or twenty years—the same job, the same life, the same city block—who want so much more for themselves but just won't take a risk. Until something about our daily habits change, there's no guarantee life will.

CHAPTER 23

Re-Writing Your Story: My Quest to Become The "Ultimate Dude"

Which one of these two movies are you more interested in watching? The first one is the story of a guy that travels to all fifty states in the United States. The second movie is the story of a guy who travels to all fifty states to go on one date in each state, to try and find his dream girl. Okay, most of you are probably choosing number two, unless you hate *rom coms* as much as I do, since they all end the same.

It just shows something really illuminating about human nature—an underlying story or theme is what ties together a series of meaningless events. And yes, life inherently has no meaning. The story is the golden thread that ties a great life together, but it's also what gets a person up in the morning.

For example, when I moved to China, it wasn't just to move to China—it was part of a much bigger story. My story was the quest to learn martial arts, meditation, and more, to essentially become a *gringo monk* and then come back to the USA. Because there was a story driving me, despite literally getting punched in the face, I kept going. I had a purpose for being there, and the story was my purpose.

For Victor Frankl (and I would argue, many others) the story wasn't consciously created but instead was something forcefully imposed upon him: a Nazi concentration camp. Frankl found purpose and meaning because he had a mission daily: to survive and to choose how to react, beyond being imprisoned in his cell. His story (decided after the fact) was how he ended up surviving the concentration camp, and how he found meaning during and after his ordeal.

When I started writing on Milk the Pigeon, my personal blog about figuring out your life as a millennial, it wasn't just because I felt like writing or thought I was a good writer. It was because I felt a burning emotional pain and desire to see everyone go after their wildest dreams, because I didn't see anyone doing that. I felt a lot of responsibility as a role model to go after that, realize the dream, and make it happen in my life so that others knew it was possible. Are you seeing what I'm saying? The story was about helping every twenty-something on the planet, rather than just a boy writing on his "blog." It made me physically ill to see all those people sitting at work wanting to slit their damn wrists because they gave up.

It made me physically ill seeing people behind the counter at the coffee shop who were just buying themselves time because they didn't want to ask themselves the hard questions in life, and just taking an easy way out for a few years. And it made me physically ill seeing parents forcing their kids into career paths they were obviously not suited for, forcing them to give up on their dreams—it felt like child abuse to me. My obligation was towards the whole damn *planet* to write on this blog. Yeah, you better believe that kept me motivated to keep writing. I had to do it for the whole *human race*.

***

Okay, even if you don't feel like your work is there to help the entire human race, you can always re-write your story, or choose to live a better one. One story that kept me pre-occupied for almost a decade was the story of me becoming the James Bond Alex. Almost nobody that knows me now (aka, Alex past the age of twenty-five) really knows *who I was* before now. That sounds really weird, but the Alex "before the common era" was completely different. I was about forty pounds skinnier. I was six inches shorter. I had the physical style of a kid who plays World of Warcraft all day, well, *because I did play World of Warcraft* (although not all day). I admired monks and Kung Fu masters, yet never meditated, nor did I ever train. I never had a girlfriend, didn't really do much with my life, and had left the United States only a few times.

Today, my life is very different, and it's almost the exact opposite in every single one of those categories, and it wasn't an accident. Sometime around age eighteen, when I went to college, I realized that my life sucked the way it was, and it wasn't going to get better unless I started setting some kind of goals. At the time, not much interested me besides video games and reading books on meditation and mysticism, so I didn't really have any goals I wanted to aim for. As a result, I had to come up with something unique: the kind of person I wanted to become.

That sounds pretty freaking heavy for someone who played video games for half the day, but I couldn't really figure out what I wanted to do, I just knew the kind of person that I respected. On a piece of paper, during one gin and tonic fueled-night, alongside my World of Warcraft account (level 53 hunter, *FTW*), I wrote down something important, which was just three words.

"The Ultimate Dude."

That's all the piece of paper said: the ultimate dude. In my mind around that time, I guess what I was thinking of was the Dos Equis guy, who wasn't really popular around 2005, but I had dreamed up this vision of a James Bond-type jack of all trades. I was trying to imagine who would be the guy I most respect in every category of his life. And then I started writing.

Physically, he'd be very fit. Around 185 pounds. He'd also be well groomed, muscular, but also lean. He would have a gentleman's haircut and know how to wear clothes that looked masculine and confident.

Intellectually, he would be well-read: a complete paradox. At first glance, you think he's a dumb jock, then you realize he's extremely intelligent and is incredibly intellectually savvy. He would read a book a week on anything that interested him, but especially something worth learning.

Emotionally, he wouldn't be like those old-school dudes who are all machismo—he would be extremely sensitive, internally calm and emotionally intelligent. When his kids messed up, he wouldn't immediately resort to giving them a tongue-lashing, but instead would respond (at least initially) like a sage.

He would have a girlfriend or wife who was awesome—who was always up for a new adventure each year, who wanted to do fun things, and didn't want to just stay home on the weekend. His spouse wouldn't be the classic James Bond damsel in distress, but rather a kickass life partner who valued being in an awesome relationship as much as he did. No trophy wives.

In his career, he would first and foremost do work he loved—and he would pay whatever the price to get there. He would search as many years as it took, work as many shit jobs as it took, and keep going no matter what. He would then do whatever it took to become a master, one of the greats of his generation. In other words, he would be successful—at the career and the work he viewed as his calling. He would consciously and deliberately choose the work he wanted to be successful at, something I knew very, very few people in the world ended up doing.

With his money, he would be extraordinarily generous and live with admiration for the tithing principle mentioned in the bible—giving away 10% of his income to a specific charity of his choice. He would break the myth that the "rich" aren't generous or don't care about the rest of the world.

Finally, spiritually, he would meditate every single day, model himself after the sages of the past, and do whatever it took to have that calm, friendly, sage presence that people *feel* when they walk into the same room. He would have cultivated himself to the point where he was in fact, very different internally, and it showed.

***

This might sound weird; but who the hell is this imaginary Mr. Perfect that Alex is conjuring up from his imagination? Some weird fetish or made up dude from a movie? That's what it sounds like from the outside, but to me, it sounds awesome. It sounds like the perfect vision of what to work towards, and every single one of those things sounds completely attainable to me—and I know with time I'll reach them. Some I already have. Because I was trying to change the complete trajectory of my life (in every aspect, not just fitness or career), it was really important that I had something to model myself after. Random goals didn't motivate me, and so this vision of the "The Ultimate Dude" was so motivational because it was the exact opposite of how I saw most dudes living their lives. To me, it was the most worthwhile thing of all.

One thing to think about here is the following: just how long it really took for some aspects of my life to pan out well. For example, you can become emotionally intelligent and intellectual in a short period of time—a year or two. Finding my dream career has been a messy process that I've thought about every day since age twenty-two, and only now at twenty-nine, am I firmly planted on the path. Do the math there. Seven years, and they were awful, painful years too. They weren't fun. And it's not like this was a part-time search – it was the primary obsession of my twenties.

I was also twenty-five before I got into my first serious relationship that I actually cared about. My generosity? That part of me still sucks, since I've just entered my first year of, "not being poor as all hell." Ultimately, things like spirituality never end, and they're always evolving and improving. That's what made this "ultimate dude" vision so rewarding—it's a lifelong pursuit for me that doesn't just go away.

Little did I know, during the year when I decided to become "The Ultimate Dude," I had actually set an affirmation and intention for who I wanted to become. Someone that now—over ten years later—I still think about almost every day. For me, the ultimate mark of success was this kind of life, and mastery in every aspect of life, not just the typical L.A. douche who does crossfit, dresses well, and drives a Lambo home from the gym. To me, it was the *process* of becoming that guy that became my new story.

Creating Your Story

What it took me several more years to realize was that I was essentially re-writing my own story, because the current life story sucked. There's a book entitled, *A Million Miles in a Thousand Years*, by Donald Miller, about an author who is being interviewed to make a movie about his life, when he realizes his life is boring—and it's not worth writing about.

So Miller decides to figure out what makes a good story. He compares writing a good story, or watching a good movie, to living a life that is worth living.

> *You can't go on without a story any longer than you can read a book about nothing... If you aren't telling a good story, nobody thinks you died too soon; they just think you died.*[17]

The problem with not having a story, is that having a lot of experiences—traveling, learning, trying new things—doesn't provide a context for all the experiences. The experiences just become noise, they are random, chaotic, and although enjoyable, they don't come together and provide any coherent feeling of "purpose."

Creating an Epic Story: A Character Who Wants Something

"A story is a character who wants something and overcomes conflict to get it. A character who wants something..."[18]

What's the first part of an epic story? A character has to want something. This "want" is the context for all further experiences—instead of traveling, it's visiting every country in the world to raise awareness for international peace-keeping efforts. Instead of going to the gym, it's losing fifty pounds and not ending up like both of your parents, that died young from heart disease.

Rather than making a million dollars a year in revenue, it's about creating your own legacy—building something that is beautiful, will exist long after you are gone, and will be remembered far longer than your name will be—and *then* making a million dollars. A story provides a context for all experiences. Almost all great characters and great stories are illuminated by one clear thing: clear ambition. The boy in *The Alchemist* is looking to fulfill and live his personal legend. Beowulf is looking to kill Grendel. All great stories have a character with a clear purpose. •

The Possibility of Failure

"I knew if we were going to tell a good story, it would have to involve risk... the same elements that make a movie meaningful are the ones that make a life meaningful. I knew a character had to face his greatest fears."[19]

The whole idea of *the story* is that it cannot be easily accomplished. If it is easily accomplished, it is by default not worth striving for, not special, not worth reading about. If it's easy, it's predictably attainable. That is not how an epic story goes. Nor is it how your story is going to go. No, it's going to be goddamn difficult. You're going to have to talk yourself off that ledge every week, sometimes every goddamn day, but you're going to keep going.

What makes the story great is the struggle—the question as to whether or not the person will succeed.

> *"It wasn't necessary to win for the story to be great;*
> *it was only necessary to sacrifice everything"*[20]

The story is about the character transformation. Your story is about how your character is forged through difficulty. Picking easy, predictable tasks you can succeed at easily, or can predict the outcome of, is not the making of a story others will want to read. Just imagine if the story went like this: "He got a job, then stayed at his job, and stayed at his job some more, got a promotion after five years, and then stayed at his job, and continued working..."

There is no risk. It is completely predictable. That's not how you write your story. In *The Alchemist*, the boy is constantly getting sidetracked—he gets stuck in north Africa, he runs out of money, and is forced to work at a Crystal merchant's store for years. He thinks he has failed, and temporarily, he has. His journey has numerous such setbacks, so why doesn't he give up? He doesn't give up because his failures are all in the context of a larger story. He still has a story to write—he's still in search of his personal legend.

> *"Whatever you are shooting for—whatever story you are writing—cannot, by default, be easy. It must require difficulty, it must require pain, and it must require struggle. Ask yourself if what you're doing now has a guaranteed outcome, or if it makes you nervous with the possibility of failure."*[21]

An Epic Story Sometimes Sucks While It Is Being Acted Out

> *"It would be easier not to try, not to get out of bed. I wish I could tell you I woke every morning and jumped into the thrill a character might feel inside a page-turner, but I don't; I wake every day and plod through the next page of my story, both in words and in actions.*
>
> *The reward you get from a story is always less than you thought it would be, and the work is harder than you imagined. The point of a story is never about the ending, remember. It's about your character getting molded in the hard work."*[22]

The truth about living an epic story is clear: it always looks more fun from the outside looking in. It's thrilling to watch snowboarders jump hundreds of feet into the air doing backflips, or watch fight scenes in the *Bourne* movies, or watch UFC and get pumped up.

But anyone who has done anything epic realizes that when you're in the moment—it's terrifying. It makes you queasy, weak at the knees, it takes focus, and there is the possibility of failure, injury, or death. And it's goddamn difficult. But great gain takes great risk.

> *"Remember the truth—living an epic story is infinitely harder than writing an epic story. It will be harder, take longer, and the fruits you reap won't be as great as you had anticipated. But it will be worth it. Make your story epic."*[23]

A story can happen randomly, or a person can choose to live life deliberately. If your family is kidnapped and you are the only survivor, and you spend your life looking to recover your family—you have a story. And you didn't choose it. If, however, your story is currently on the same page, year after year after year, it's time to start living life intentionally. That means deliberately choosing to create and live your story.

***

There's a saying about goals that I've always loved, that goes somewhat along the lines of the following: don't wonder if you are good enough to reach your goals, instead, wonder if your goals are *good enough for you*. In other words, your time is limited. Are the goals you're setting worth the three, five, ten, or twenty years they might take? Are they worth the trade-off—the amount of "lost" time traded in your life? You'll never be able to get that back once you sacrifice it.

Becoming un-lost means curing the superficial, introducing adventure into life, and curing the profound: finding (or creating) your story.

Your life is a story—is it worth reading?

Chapter Recap: Re-Writing Your Story

☐ **If you don't like your story—re-write a more meaningful one.**
Just like when I was in my late teens, I hated the way my story
was going. So I decided to change it and make it different. I was a
boring guy with nothing going on, so each year I set a goal to travel
somewhere near for an adventure, and learn a new skill. Over a
few years, I started having really interesting stuff to say.

☐ **My own story for a long time was becoming "The Ultimate
Dude."** This was the new focus and direction that gave meaning
and purpose to my life: becoming someone new. The process of
acquiring all these skills, abilities and experiences, all served the
same purpose: it gave me a direction in which to go.

☐ **Amazing lives all follow the principles behind amazing stories.** It
might sound like a complex process, but creating a better life story
(with more meaning) follows all the same elements of the hero's
journey from most great stories. There's something you really
want, there are an absolute ton of obstacles in the middle trying
to get there, and eventually you make some kind of progress. But
overall, it's the process, the adventure, the middle—aka the entire
story—that gives your life purpose.

CHAPTER 24

Flow Testing 101: The Art and Science of Your Happiest Moments

One thing I don't often talk about is just how depressed I got when I came back from China. I went from having the best year of my life by far, filled with adventure, filled with novelty, and filled with excitement, to moving right back into a crashed economy, sleeping in my parents' house and having no friends, and no job.

Literally overnight, I went from having a fun, adventurous life, to having nothing on my schedule, no job to show up to, and no real purpose for waking up in the morning. As a result, I got depressed. *Really* depressed. One night in the thick of it I was apparently in such a grumpy mood that my parents literally were worried enough that they said, "you should just go take whatever money you have in your savings, and go on a trip." I think they were legitimately worried I would do something stupid.

In any case, after a year of this with no end in sight, I figured I would have to try something.

I had a friend ask me, "well, what do you really like doing on Saturdays? Like if you won the lotto, what would you do?"

I literally couldn't even think of one thing I enjoyed or one thing I wanted to do. I had forgotten what made me happy, which scared the ever living crap out of me. So I decided that a little experiment was in order: a thirty-day flow test. For an entire month, I just tracked whatever scarce moments I was actually happy, or I was engrossed in an activity and forgot about how miserable my life was for a few minutes. I modeled this after the experiments that Mihaly Csikszentmihalyi had done and profiled in his book, *Flow*.[24] I put them in an Evernote document, and here's how the first twenty or so entries read:

- Stopping by the incense shop at the Renaissance faire—(Reminds me of my old days studying spirituality and the connection I felt.)
- Walking Sammy (my parents' dog) back from the mechanic and just enjoying walking in the New England air, enjoying the trees and flowers, just enjoying the outdoors.
- Hanging out with two of my close childhood friends I reconnected with—just being part of a close group. A feeling of belonging somewhere.
- Kayaking with Michelle (my girlfriend) and just talking about life and enjoying the outdoors.
- Any and all family gatherings—happiness level 10 out of 10—off the charts.
- Wine with Will, Vic, Madison and Britney (my brother, my sister, and my sister's two friends)—just life talks and enjoying life.
- Talking with a friend and my sister at the bar.
- Huge high—spending the weekend with Michelle's friend and her husband, just talking about life and drinking wine at our place.
- Talking with a close friend about Chinese medicine—in fact, I was so happy I got anxiety and adrenaline and my hands shook. Definitely my passion, calling, and destiny.
- Making dinner for Dad's birthday with all my siblings—in fact, any time hanging out with my siblings is awesome.
- Walking around Fred's (my uncle) property with family and picking up acorns—reminded me of something spiritual from childhood.
- Reading in a cafe on the weekend next to a big window with an espresso and a new book.
- Sitting in the cafe doing video editing. Realized I love doing video! How can I do more of this in my business? It was the end of my 13-hour workday but I drove home ecstatic.
- Conversation with Mitch—connecting with someone just like me was amazing.

- Scott's event—chilling at his house and meeting cool people while talking about life—that was epic.
- Just taking the train into NYC and reading an amazing book—great scenery on a sunny day on my way to meet people.
- Sitting around the dinner table with Tiela, Marie Helene (my aunts) and my parents, just talking about life. It makes me realize that my dream life involves having my family together, being surrounded by people, and having lots of long dinner parties.

A few weeks into this, I realized something big, and wrote down a few revelations. We'll talk about those in a second. So what did I realize were "flow producing" activities for me, where I forgot about my crappy life, time, and so on? Here's what those were:

- Any experience that involved other people
- Reading
- Shooting and editing videos
- Sports or the gym (gym by myself, playing tennis with friends)

Yes, for me finding *Flow* was literally that simple. Most of the days I was in an awful mood because most activities were boring, and thus were not flow producing. The biggest category surprised me the most—being around people was my #1 indicator of happiness. That was odd because I spent so much time alone (which I enjoy). So what'd I do? For the next 30 days, all I did was make sure that as many days as possible had every single one of those things scheduled, at least once.

That meant that on Saturdays, instead of sitting around my apartment being a depressed slug, I would schedule a brunch with my friend. That meant that right after eating with my friend, I'd go to my favorite café and read, then I would do some video work for a client, then I'd go play tennis with a friend, and hang out with family at night. It was so shocking how easily and quickly this boosted my mood and gave me that calm sense of fulfillment and peace that comes with actually enjoying your life. And it made me realize how you can actually engineer it if you understand things in terms of *Flow*. Doc C., I owe you a big one amigo.

The Ultimate Key to Happiness, Flow and the Lies of Being Busy

"Collectively we are wasting each year the equivalent of millions of years of human consciousness. The energy that could be used to focus on complex goals, to provide for enjoyable growth, is squandered on patterns of stimulation that only mimic reality. Mass leisure, mass culture, and even high culture when only attended to passively, and for extrinsic reasons... are parasites of the mind."

–DR. MIHALY CSIKSZENTMIHALYI

There's a horrible paradox about fulfillment and what most of us think makes a great life. There's nothing more enjoyable when you're sitting in your cubicle than pondering boarding a flight to some exotic location, renting a boat, and just cruising off into some awesome adventure. In fact, my favorite "I hate my life" activity when I had jobs I hated, was to go to kayak.com/explore, which would show you how far away you could fly from your current destination based on how much money you had. Can you imagine how cool that is?

At first, I created this huge bucket list, which involved things I thought would be awesome, like:

• Go on a shark dive in Fiji
• Bungee jump
• Sky dive
• Learn Kung Fu in China
• Hike the Camino de Santiago

On and on I placed cool little adventures and trips on the bucket list. Then, with the little money I had left over each year, I would start doing them. In fact, I'd often freelance on the side (or more commonly, work 2-3 jobs) so I could guarantee my adventure every single year.

I'd fly to Fiji, do research on giant clams for the summer, get scuba certified, go on a shark dive (and run out of oxygen—true story). It was cool. I came back with a cool story. Then I flew to New Zealand and knocked out two birds with one stone—I bungee jumped on the third highest jump in the world, and the next day went skydiving. Man, I was really kicking ass now. But something happened after bucket list activity four or five. It almost felt like I had fallen into yet another trap. I wasn't creating more fulfillment and purpose in my life, I was just checking things off a list. And the problem was that the things only happened once a year. I still hated the "every day" which was, unfortunately, 350+ days a year.

That's when I realized that a bucket list can't possibly produce fulfillment. A bucket list is filled with things you do once in a while, but your life is what you do every day. Unless you enjoy every day and find it fulfilling (no matter how ordinary it might be), fulfillment and happiness just don't exist.

There's another side of the coin here, too. During one of those perpetually lost periods of my life, I (yet again) sat down to make a list of all the best and happiest moments I was experiencing on a daily basis. When I compared myself to people constantly complaining about not living a fulfilling life, I saw something obvious: they wasted a lot of time. Around this time, I devised another theory—maybe fulfillment is just using every single hour of the day wisely. So maybe I should just be working all day, twenty-four hours a day, towards something.

Suddenly, I became one of those important "busy" people. I would show up to my job, hit the gym after, go to an important dinner, and find my favorite coffee shop to continue working. I'd write blog posts, strategize about my life, figure out the next steps, and do all the stuff that busy, important people do. Whenever somebody asked me what I was up to during the week, it was always, "sorry, too busy." I figured I was living life right, I mean, I was using every single minute to the max, which was the opposite of all those other people wasting their lives watching TV for hours. Isn't that how you create a great life? It sounded great until one day, after telling yet another person "I was busy," I stumbled upon a quote by Socrates.

"Beware the barrenness of a busy life."

Huh? The barrenness of a busy life? Isn't busy the opposite of all these turds I see wasting their lives, chilling in front of the TV for five hours a night and doing absolutely nothing?

I took a few steps back and slowed down in a café to write out everything that had been worthwhile in the last few months. Judgment aside, when did I just enjoy life, and go to sleep thinking, "that was a great day." Guess what I noticed? They were completely mundane activities, like sitting in a coffee shop reading, or going out to dinner with my girlfriend, or playing soccer on a summer day with my siblings. It was literally the most ordinary things. So much for my bucket list.

That was a great reminder to me of a surprisingly simple truth: the old-world mentality of living the simple life, surrounded by family, doing work you enjoy, is shockingly fulfilling. A once a year bucket list adventure can't produce fulfillment any more than smoking a crack pipe can. It all comes back to finding enjoyment and flow in daily life.

The Lesson: Flow Testing 101

It took me a long time to realize that the great life is not about bucket lists, and is not about being super busy and seizing every moment—it's just about living the way *you* want to live. And an easy way to see what gives you that enjoyable feeling is to do a flow test for thirty days. Personally, I recommend getting drunk every night. In November of 2012, I spent those thirty days learning about wine as part of my massive monthly effort to do little lifestyle experiments. This particular experiment was related to giving myself a flow test, and learning more about my natural strengths and inclinations.

For more than a year I have actively pursued many methods to help hone in on my "passions" and natural strengths, but many of these programs overwhelmingly had one main flaw: the fact that you can only "think it through" so much. Now, sometime between giving myself a strengths finder test and going through half a dozen books on learning what you're good at, I came across the recommendation to give myself a flow test.

This was said to be a regular exercise of Jim Collins, who wrote *Good to Great* and is a legendary business guru. Daniel Pink in his book *Drive* also recommended this. Now, before I talk about how awesome flow tests are (and how to carry them out), I want to show you why they're so important.

Stop Waiting for Love at First Sight— Start Testing The Waters

Many people make a massive error when trying to improve their work, life, or relationships. They do exactly what I did—try to work it all out in their head. It's like when you first take up a new hobby—

there are tons of assumptions in your head about how it'll be, but you realize only some of them are correct once you start. And there's *tons* of weird stuff you would never have guessed was effective, but the little experiments (reality) confirmed they were. Many of us try to work out our relationships in our head—as if we can control the future and exactly how it will pan out.

Many of us have a list of qualities and characteristics we want our ideal partner to have—only to find that, once we got that partner, they weren't that important, or we really didn't like them.

If you have no goddamn clue what you could possibly do for the rest of your life, spend as little time as possible testing as many various options as you can. A perfect example of rapidly testing ideas comes from a guy named Sean at Oneweekjob.com, who worked a new job every week for 52 weeks in an attempt to get closer to figuring out what he loves to do for work. Stop thinking you're going to be finding that one straight shot for your dream person, your dream job, or your dream lifestyle. Creating anything ideal is not about "finding" it, but about assembling each piece of the puzzle over time.

For many, many years, I figured I would just test the things out a bit. Date someone here, date someone there, and never commit, because when I found "the one," I'd know, right? I did the same for work—in one year I started (and quit) four jobs, trying to get closer to a more ideal job every time. And I did the same for life—I lived in rural areas and massive cities, I lived in cities that spoke English, and cities that spoke French, German and Chinese. I lived at home and I lived abroad. The actual lifestyle experiments themselves turned out to be much more valuable than my many thousands of hours thinking things through. Test.

What does drinking wine and getting drunk have to do with all of this? It took me a long time to realize it, but you're probably a lot like me. If you're reading this, you're probably very intellectual (read: in your head) about how you approach life. You think you can work most of the path out in your head, and then make more informed decisions in person. Unfortunately, in my experience, this is a totally false mindset—you can only feel out so much, based on limited experience. Drinking wine for thirty days was part of my experiment in learning as much about as many random topics as possible, to see what ended up sticking.

That's where the flow test comes in. I set an alarm for 5-7 different times throughout the day, and when it went off, I recorded how I felt, what I was doing, and whether or not I was in flow.

My daily alarm schedule looked like this:

- 9 am—How did I feel? What was I doing? Was I in flow?
- 11 am—How did I feel? What was I doing? Was I in flow?
- 1 pm—How did I feel? What was I doing? Was I in flow?
- 3 pm—How did I feel? What was I doing? Was I in flow?
- 5 pm—How did I feel? What was I doing? Was I in flow?
- 7 pm—How did I feel? What was I doing? Was I in flow?
- 9 pm—How did I feel? What was I doing? Was I in flow?

Much of the time, my answers looked like this:

9 am:
Feeling: Bored
Currently Doing: Working
In Flow?: Nope.

But sometimes, an interesting gem popped up, like this:

5 pm:
Feeling: Excited, motivated
Currently Doing: Writing a free guide
In Flow: Yep (For 3-5 hours straight)

6 pm:
Feeling: Happy, energized
Currently doing: Working out
In Flow: Yep

8:30 pm:
Feeling: Excited, almost manic excited
Currently Doing: Consulting a new biz owner on ways to bring in more customers.
In Flow: Yes, couldn't sleep.

4 pm:
Feeling: Insanely excited
Currently Doing: Preparing a talk for a big conference
In Flow: Yes, crazy motivated

7 Pm:
Feeling: Light, happy
Currently Doing: Making dinner
In Flow: Yes

11 Pm:
Feeling: Excited, relaxed
Currently Doing: Carving a pumpkin
In Flow: Yes

Jim Collins was said to regularly give himself flow tests to constantly improve his efficiency and find out what activities obviously weren't doing it for him, and which activities naturally made him feel happy and motivated. One thing this test will show you is the quality of your work: usually if you're not in flow, you're not getting much done. Work is segmented. There are constant interruptions. It's boring and un-engaging. It's pretty much your typical 9am-5pm office routine.

I learned that my day-job work was almost never flow-producing which was a dead giveaway that it was time to switch jobs. I also learned some new things that I had no idea were so fun: like designing online programs and writing books. They are naturally flow producing for me, and leave me in a happy, motivated state, even after I've worked for five hours.

This goes along well with what I frequently talk about—going with the path of least resistance instead of forcing yourself to be disciplined. It also showed me a new strength/passion of mine: speaking. The entire process of writing my first book *Master the Day* was flow producing for me and was fun. I was internally motivated the entire time, and not a single day did I feel resistant to writing. The entire thing was fun. That's insane! There's almost nothing in my life that I naturally feel that motivated to do. The test also went a long way towards showing me what makes me happy on a daily basis—such as activities that have a clear beginning and clear ending, with plenty of feedback along the way.

Other random things (like sitting and drinking an espresso in the afternoon with a book) made me happier than I thought. Another randomly enjoyable experience was just sitting down in a coffee shop with a friend to help them figure out a life trajectory to go down. I realized that teaching is one of my greatest passions and natural strengths. If you can't quite seem to find what makes you happy in your work, or life, give yourself a flow test, you may be surprised what it tells you about yourself.

Chapter Recap: Find Your Flow: The Art and Science of Your Happiest Moments

☐ **What makes you fulfilled might surprise you.** It took me a long time to realize that my "bucket list life" had nothing to do with making me happier on a daily basis. That really surprised me. It was only after going through this process of thinking about what really made me happy on a daily basis, not once in a while, that helped me put some pieces together.

☐ **A month of flow tests will show you things you never knew about yourself.** Things just aren't working? Do the flow test I mentioned above, then put them into an *Evernote* document so you can start spotting the trends and seeing what works.

☐ **Spot the trends in your "flow test" and schedule those into more days of your week.** When I was the least happy and satisfied with both my life and my career, I just tracked what things made me the most fulfilled on a daily basis, something I still do to this day, and then scheduled more of them into my week. For example, it could be as simple as spending more time with people, or it could be spending more time with a certain hobby you sporadically work on.

☐ **Flow is a surprisingly direct path to the present, and enjoying life.** Just as we talked about Viktor Frankl's conclusion, that a "life well lived" is an unintended side effect, life enjoyment is often the same. When you do something that's naturally flow-producing (like playing a video game or sport), you forget about happiness, get sucked into the present, and realized the last hour was tons of fun.

CHAPTER 25

Fulfillment is the Fastest Path to Success

"Success without fulfillment is the ultimate failure."

— TONY ROBBINS

Around the time of Robin Williams' death, there were lots of rumors and stories circulating about his life, about the irony of a comedian committing suicide. But more than anything, there was one story in particular that really stuck with me, which was when *Tony Robbins* was interviewed on a podcast about fulfillment versus success. When prompted about the "worst piece of life and career advice that's the most common," this was his response, first describing an experience at one of his seminars.

"... 'How many of you in this room loved Robin Williams?' And 99% of the room in Beijing, in Tokyo, in Sydney, all over the world, 98%, 99%, raise their hands. But the truth is that these people say they love him but they didn't know him. Now, was he a master of achievement? For sure. You know you want to go to Hollywood and everyone says you're full of shit. He did it. You want the #1 show? He did it. Then he wanted to have the most beautiful family, and he did it. Then he said he wanted to make more money than he could spend, and he did it. Then he wanted to win an academy award for not being funny,

and he did it. He said he wanted to make the whole world laugh, and he did it. And he hung himself. He hung himself in his own home. Leaving hundreds of millions of people around the world—he left his children and his wife scarred for life. And he was a good man. Now how do you explain that? I'll tell you how: by following the worst advice, something that got stuck in his psychology. That achievement was more important than fulfillment. It's the biggest fucking lie on the planet. And if you get it, if you wake up to it, you can actually have a life that is so rich and so beautiful. The reason you are suffering is because you are focusing on yourself."[25]

The story means a lot of things to a lot of people, but to me, it's about making sure your ladder is "up against the right wall" as the saying goes. Stephen Covey, author of the *7 Habits of Highly Effective People* once said, "If the ladder is not leaning against the right wall, each step we take just gets us closer to the wrong place, faster." In other words, if you're pursuing a goal that you *think* is going to give you that feeling of completion you're looking for, once you get there, you'll realize it was hollow all along.

And *that* is one hell of a weird feeling. After plugging along every day for five years, you get "there" (wherever that is, in space and time), and you realize it didn't exist. It's like you went to find some buried treasure and you travel across the globe following a map, arrive, and then realize you had the map upside down and the "X" was back at home.

How You Know if You Have the Wrong Goals

In the Bruce Lee chapter, I introduced you to that big, "motivation revelation" that I shared. It took me a lot of years of suffering my way through goals to realize that what motivated me, was loving the *process* more than I loved the outcome. Any project I started for an "outcome" goal, I never achieved. The inner fuel just ran out. So the first indicator of pursuing the wrong goals, is that you're too myopic— you're focusing on just getting *there*, and missing the *getting there* part.

Just like how I was with martial arts and Judo, I always wanted to be a badass, and this world champion, but I realized that I liked the idea in a romantic way more than I actually liked doing the day-to-day work. And it is the day-to-day work that makes you great at what you do. It's the day-to-day work that you either love or hate. And it's the day-to-day work that motivates you or drains you. This experience for some reason was incredibly memorable to me, and it made me realize that if you go after any goal for any reason other than loving the process, it'll almost always have emotional repercussions. There's a lot of this "grind it out all day, every day" advice from business people, but those are the same people who look like they're fifty-five by the time they're forty. Don't think you can push-push-push every day for a decade and not drain yourself.

In one sense, you see this kind of "pursuing the wrong goals" in immigrant or Asian parenting. Not to pick on Indians or Asians or anything, but the friends that I have that consistently have meltdowns come from high-pressure families where they are forced to succeed at something the parents chose. Immigrant parents sometimes sacrifice their entire lives for their kids, and put tremendous pressure on them to succeed, "because I sacrificed all of this for you—don't screw it all up." And what happens to the kids? The pressure is crushing. If you fail, you don't let down just yourself—that's the easy part. You also let down your parents, your family, your generation, your ancestors—and that's the hard part. And I have a sneaking suspicion this guilt and pressure parents put on their kids is because they themselves aren't fulfilled. That's a pretty big assumption, but I see it in the kids of parents of any ethnicity, just a lot less. It seems like parents that aren't fulfilled in their own work just drill into their kids to become successful. Sometimes it's the stereotypical "Asian tiger mom" parenting, but sometimes it's a lot like Andre Agassi's dad - he was an Olympic boxer, but never got to become the best in the world like he wanted. So he projected that dream onto his kid, drilled him from the time he exited the womb, and made him miserable (read: a drug addict), even though it also made him #1 in the world.

Another interesting thing is that sometimes we don't feel fulfilled because we're focusing just on ourselves and our own goals. Andre Agassi has one of the most fascinating life stories of anyone I've ever heard. His book Open should be required reading for anyone who wants to set and achieve world class goals, especially if you're wondering whether or not you're pursuing goals that are going to fulfill you. Since childhood, he was drilled by his insane, maniacal father, to hit a million tennis balls a year, figuring "there's no way a kid that hits a million balls a year can't become #1 in the world." His dad literally chose which house to buy for the family based on whether or not the backyard was big enough to build a tennis court in it.

As a baby in his crib, his father hung tennis balls over it, he signed him up for every tournament and competition, and eventually sent him away to tennis camps. But he hated tennis the entire time. He hated it when he was a beginner, and he hated it when he was #1 in the world. In fact, in his biography, he jokes constantly—about saying to people (including other celebrities) that "he hates tennis." They always say, "ha-ha, but you don't really hate it, do you?" And he says, "no, I really hate it. I hate tennis." They give him a quizzical look and just get on with things, almost like they don't fully believe it.

Since the goal was something his father forced him to do (he was terrified of resisting his dad), it wasn't what interested him. At one point, he expressed interest in soccer, then literature, and other interests that intuitively called to him. Every time his dad would shut him down, and he was a lot more violent than most parents that "project" goals on their kids. This is the same dad that pulled a gun on a person in traffic that cut him off, aiming the handgun an inch in front of little Andre's nose, and then laughing as the other person sped off in mortal fear. He was forced to like tennis. He didn't choose to like it. Eventually, Andre craved the feeling of matches being over—whether he won or lost, he didn't care. He just wanted them to be done. He rebelled his entire youth by getting spiked, pink hair, wearing earrings, and doing anything he could to cut class—he didn't have an outlet for the emotional time bomb that was building inside him.

Then his friend Slim introduced him to a new friend—crystal meth—and he unraveled. However, that's not what intrigued me the most about his story. The most incredible part was after he had won Wimbledon, and other major tennis competitions, that he and his girlfriend at the time (Brooke Shields) were regulars at this one restaurant, when one day a guy there (that they knew well) expressed concern that he wasn't sure if he'd be able to send his kids to college.

Andre put aside enough stock in Nike for him to ensure that when his kids went to school, it'd be enough to cover a large chunk of it. The guy's jaw dropped, and he didn't know how to thank Andre—and Andre said something incredible happened. It was that feeling he had been looking for the entire time—that feeling of completion, of happiness, of satisfaction—that he never got, even when he was #1 in the world. It was the feeling of doing something that didn't involve him, but was for someone else. After his recovery from meth and drugs, when he decided to play to raise money for charity, did he become the best in the world again, because he was doing it for a cause greater than himself. He found the right fuel.

Fulfillment is often a direction we travel in on a daily basis – it's about the things we do daily, not the things we do once in a while. I'll repeat what Viktor Frankl said because it's so important:

"For success, like happiness, cannot be pursued; it must ensue, and it only does so as the unintended side-effect of one's dedication to a cause greater than oneself or as the by-product of one's surrender to a person other than oneself."[26]

Agassi only realized that it was pursuing a goal that didn't involve himself that led to the most meaning and purpose. I realized that being driven by a process whose goal I loved, more than the outcome, gave me extra purpose and extra motivation. Most of all, purpose and fulfillment are about the little things we do on a daily basis—the coffee shop meetings, reading a book in a café, having dinner with someone you love. It's way bigger—and way simpler—than the bucket list life I was so obsessed with when I began this journey.

Chapter Recap: Fulfillment is the Fastest Path to Success

☐ **Make sure your ladder is "up against the right wall."** It's not always easy to figure out what motivates you, or what inspires you, or what goal will fulfill you or won't fulfill you. Sometimes you just learn that from experience. The best analogy I've come up with, so far, to explain this, is the rock star theory we talked about earlier. If you find the day-to-day experience of pursuing your goals fulfilling, they will almost always be that way. If you don't, no matter how successful you become you will never enjoy it. Think about that. I would argue that if you don't enjoy today, you aren't successful, and can never be successful no matter how much money you make.

☐ **Happier people are more likely to be successful.** It doesn't bear my repeating here, but Daniel Pink has written a fascinating book with this thesis. His book *The Happiness Advantage*, is a fascinating account of how happier people are more likely to be successful, and the key metrics that often lead people to being happier. Definitely check it out.

☐ **Going after a purpose larger than yourself is rocket fuel for most people.** It took me writing my first book, *Master the Day*, to really realize that what fulfilled me the most was writing a book to help my readers. Because I did it for them, when it got really good feedback, it was so fulfilling. It really had nothing to do with me, it was because the book helped them. That feeling was hard to replicate with any other goal I pursued. It was the same feeling that Agassi had when he realized that making other people's lives better was the most "complete" he had ever felt.

CHAPTER 26

Finding Your Gift and Giving it Away

"The meaning of life is to find your gift. The purpose of life is to give it away."

— ATTRIBUTED TO PICASSO

In 2015, my closest friend and I were both writing our first books and building our online communities. On a Saturday morning he called me asking for some help moving into his new apartment. My friend was one of those work 24/7, super ambitious, really-wanted-to-make-an-impact, Tony Robbins type of people. Everyone knew he was going to be the next big superstar, the next household name.

Every speaking gig within thirty miles he hosted, or knew the host, and his story of struggle from being bi-polar, to a drug addict, to being in prison, and now being a self-help personality, really attracted people. Within the last month he did over twenty-seven speaking gigs. Yes, you read that right. On Saturday, he called asking for help to move. On Sunday, we had a call together that he missed—which was very unlike him. We both joked that if we had a call at four, by three fifty-nine, we had our finger on the number ready to dial in.

On Monday, I still hadn't heard from him. And on Tuesday, when I was supposed to help him move, I called him an hour early because I forgot his address. It was extremely unusual for him not to respond, and I felt my stomach in knots. Something must've been wrong. I went on his Facebook page, intuitively assuming that if there was an accident or something went wrong, that's where I would find out.

When I read his Facebook wall, it was pure denial and a dagger to the chest—he had committed suicide the night after Valentine's Day.

***

I think as an ambitious person, it's sometimes easy for us to get caught up in our own ego. Sometimes we spend years or decades chasing this feeling of being "loved," that comes with being a success, and when we get there, we realize we had it wrong all along. All we wanted was to feel like we did something that mattered, something important, like our life was well lived and had meaning. It's the hardest thing in the world when you're miserable, depressed and broke, to try and think about doing things that fulfill you—really, it's the hardest thing in the world. The story that's more common, is going after success, realizing it didn't fulfill you, then switching gears. But to get it right from the get go is exceptionally rare.

Since that night, I've thought quite a lot about our friendship and what were the common bonds that brought us together, including lots of the lessons I learned from him (during and afterward). One of the reasons why I felt so lucky was that we had this almost cosmic friendship—I hadn't had a best friend since I was a child that I had really clicked with on an almost soul level, instantly. I had reached out to him during one of his many speaking gigs, said I'm sure we had shared ambitions, and then offered to meet up sometime. We instantly hit it off, and for whatever reason, we were kindred spirits.

You know when you meet someone and you just click in a friendship-way, like friend-soul mates? You have similar hobbies, similar ambitions, read similar books, and more? It just makes so much sense, and it's easy from day one, and you feel like you had known each other for a long time? That was a pretty cool experience for me, seeing as I had never felt that with too many people in my entire life, and zero of them I currently had as friends. It was a really unique experience.

So when he committed suicide, it felt almost like a glitch in the matrix to me—in a pretty selfish way, to be honest. I felt like I had finally found one of those soul friends I was supposed to meet, finally someone that got me, who I'd stay friends with until we were ninety and household names. I knew he'd become some great Tony Robbins figure, and I'd be well known in my own field of chosen mastery, and I joked about how funny it would be for our kids to carpool together in a helicopter to school. It just made sense. So when things changed, it really felt like there was a rift in the cosmic order. Like it wasn't supposed to happen. Something just went wrong in the cosmic DNA. Rather than feeling depressed, I just felt pretty confused. The feeling is hard to describe, but it was a non-stop feeling of denial. This wasn't supposed to happen.

Since reflecting on that, I thought about what brought us together in the first place, and I think it was one thing: hunger. We both wanted to be world class at what we did, and whether or not we said it explicitly, we wanted to be successful—we talked about fulfillment, and setting goals in every aspect of our lives (we rated our health, relationships, spirituality and more each day). But if I had to be totally truthful, both of us obviously were skewed mostly towards financial success, since we were both on our rise to the top (and I still had a job then, so I needed to focus on money).

Trying to reflect on what we talked about a lot and what we learned, I came up with a few of the following things.

1. Urgency.

We're all dying—some of us faster than others. Nothing is promised, and you genuinely have no idea when things can change, for you, for someone else, or in the world. Attack life in day-tight windows, and make those twenty-four hours count. I think in some sense, my first book, *Master the Day*, was my poor attempt to try to encapsulate that feeling—*make it count*. Not just your life. Today. Make it count.

2. Visualization literally creates your future.

Clint was the one who got me into visualization, since I thought of it as a "cool" exercise, but mostly bullshit. He was really fond of this kind of story where he'd say, "dude, it happened again!" and then would proceed to tell me about something he had visualized for a few months to a year, and then miraculously showed up in his life, in startlingly accurate detail. This is a practice I now do daily.

3. Spend as much time producing as humanly possible—while most of the world spends their time consuming.

We both made the observation early on that the producers are the ones who are successful, while consumers aren't. The "producers" was a metaphor for people that add value to the world—with products, content, books, services, movies, opinions, ideas, etc.,—while the consumers were the people who handed over their money for the value. We knew if we kept adding value to the world, everything we wanted would become a reality.

4. Contribute and inspire as many people as is humanly possible in one lifetime.

I'll never forget, Clint was pretty fond of giving unsolicited advice in the best way possible. One time he told me he just got back from the barber, and he could tell that the guy giving him the haircut was either the owner or a top performer. He proceeded to give him a pep talk, telling him to open up his own shop and "get away from these losers who don't give a shit about their work," and the dude felt incredibly inspired. That was Clint. It's funny, Milk the Pigeon really connected with people. I knew this because I wrote inspiration and was good at it—and inspiration was Clint's middle name. You never know how that one pep talk might change the trajectory of someone's life for the better.

5. Affirmations are real.

Following up on the visualization stuff, he was adamant about doing affirmations daily with his visualizations. According to him, they literally produced your reality.

6. Connect with people in an old-school way.

Another M.O. of Clint was writing handwritten notes to people that were wax sealed and written on parchment. It's funny, my mom always had me write thank you notes, which were always a chore as a kid, but after Clint, I invested in my own kit and started writing lots of handwritten notes. There's nothing like getting a letter that looks like a gift in the mail.

7. We are the next level of the "top" people— they are no different from us.

Tony Robbins. Michael Jordan. Mother Theresa. They were normal people with specific habits, a massive passion for their work and an unconquerable hunger for something. Whether we were both born thinking this way, or if we inoculated ourselves with this belief, I don't know. Nonetheless, we were headstrong in this belief (we *knew* it to be true), which I think fueled us on a daily basis. If these people weren't born special, that meant that we only needed to work hard, love our work, cultivate the right habits, and success was inevitable. Now, it's not surprising to see how that could lead to success. I think what also confirmed this suspicion was that we both had met ultra-successful millionaires, and sometimes weren't impressed. Maybe we had huge egos (pretty typical for twenty or thirty-year-old guys), but that's how we felt.

8. Habits are the secret sauce critical to achieving any level of success, happiness, fulfillment, or spiritual evolution.

Clint was one of the only other people that was hardcore about iterating on habits as quickly as possible. He's the first one that introduced me to Zig Ziglar's *Pick Four* goal tracking book, and we frequently talked about what new habits we needed at the end of each week. For us, this was also the ultimate key: anyone could change habits, so whether or not we were delusional, that fueled the belief that we could become the biggest names in the world at what we did.

9. Discipline is the secret skill standing between where you are and where you want to be.

Despite all this talk of habits and fulfillment, let me be very clear: a supreme strength and weakness of Clint's personality was the extreme reliance on iron discipline. He was a big fan of "grinding" things out, he worked seven days a week (never taking a day off), he got up at 4:30 am, slept six hours a night, and routinely worked from five am until eight pm. Hustler wouldn't even be accurate to describe him. I remember the first time we hung out, and I was being a little baby, crying about my lack of success at the time. "I feel like for someone that's as smart as me and hustles as much as me, I should be more successful." First, he felt the same, but his immediate response was, "Yeah man, but really successful people work like dogs." He was a big fan of the Jordan Belfort (the Wolf of Wall Street) approach to life. Direct, aggressive, *hustle*.

10. The purpose of life is to contribute as much value to humanity as is humanly possible in one lifetime.

Despite all our talk on outward achievement, we both really did want to make a huge impact on the world that didn't benefit us. I just think at our age, and since we were at the start of our careers, we craved personal success a lot more. We talked a lot about how we could help people on an almost daily basis, and how we could eventually raise evolved kids that were successful and contributed to humanity.

11. Always keep your word at a level that is incomprehensible to the average person.

Another funny cosmic interest we both had: we were religious about keeping our word with people. It wasn't always easy, but one of our prime virtues we aspired to was that 1800's level of reliance on "our word." If I said I'm going to be there, I'll be there, even if I have to show up late. We joked about having the opportunity to make calls with mentors, and if it was an 11:00 call, at 10:59 we'd have our fingers on the dial button. To me, the strengthening of our own character (an old-fashioned trait) was something we both highly valued. This also tied into his religious focus on one method he would use to sell to his clients. He was fond of saying things like, "If this isn't the best interaction you've ever had with a human being *ever*, I'll refund your money." And he stuck to his word. At the end of the day, having already almost lost his life multiple times from drugs, gunshot wounds, and then prison, these all embodied his extreme hunger to make sure his life counted this time around. He wanted to really make sure he mattered.

***

One lesson here is pretty clear: there's really only so much we can do for ourselves that produces lasting satisfaction. I'll repeat that, since I think it bears repeating: there's only so much you can do for yourself that'll make you happy. I was very clear ever since I was a kid on the fact that material things don't make people happy—so I never pursued a job for the money, I never accumulated lots of possessions, and focused on more meaningful things. So I was sure that I had "figured it out" when I focused on intangible things like goals. I knew that would lead to fulfillment. But I still got it wrong, after all that thinking. I *still* got it wrong. Because all my goals still had to do with just myself. I would've ended up in that mansion on the hill alone, because I didn't build any relationships or focus on almost anything else.

Over the past few years, I was trying to think back to the most fulfilling things that I did both in my life, and in my business. I defined fulfillment really simply: years later, did I feel like it was truly one of the most important experiences in my life? To me it didn't matter if money was involved, whether it was free or required money didn't matter, it was just a matter of what left a lasting impression upon me. For example, some of the most fulfilling, regular experiences in my life were the family gatherings at my parents' house every holiday. They were free (for me, not my parents) and they left me feeling 10/10 happy. But there were also paid ones too that I couldn't have done without money, like taking a trip with my girlfriend to Thailand for three weeks, or Belize for ten days.

I took a solid afternoon to begin writing out all the most fulfilling experiences, and one in recent memory came away as being a really lasting one: writing my first book, *Master the Day*. I heard from people about how the book helped them lose weight when *nothing* else worked. I heard from people who had been trying for decades to change their habits, and finally they did. I've heard from couples who were reading my book, alongside *Tony Robbins and Napoleon Hill*, in their quest for a better life.

I've heard lifelong alcoholics tell me they've "finally been sober for a week" thanks to the habit training in my book. They *knew* what to do to change, but the strategies they were implementing weren't working. And I've heard people tell me that this book made the list of the top ten they've ever read in their lifetime. Now, I don't know if I deserve that last one, but I thought long and hard about why this was so fulfilling for me too. What did I do differently this time in my goal setting process that produced so much satisfaction, the kind that didn't magically go away once I set a new goal?

The first thing, I realized, was that I wrote it for other people. The reason why I wrote the book wasn't to be considered an "expert," or as a revenue stream, or anything like that, even though those became realities too. The reason I wrote it was because there wasn't just one spot I could direct my readers, friends, and family to, in order to understand my whole "weight loss life philosophy." I wanted one work of art that I could give to people to say, "hey, if you want to see if my stuff works for you, read this first and see if you agree with me." There was almost zero interest in writing it for myself, and for the first time in my life, I did a goal solely to benefit someone else. That was pretty intriguing.

The second thing was that it directly had an impact on others. For example, getting fit is a great goal for me, and if I'm forty pounds overweight, maybe for my girlfriend too, but overall it's a selfish goal. There's nothing wrong with that, but it's a goal that directly benefits only me. As a result, there's no way to see the impact that goal has on others. There's something strange about how humans are almost wired to benefit others—almost nothing else gives us that sense of satisfaction and completion.

There was another experience that confirmed that I really needed to change how I approached setting goals. About a year ago, I opened an opportunity for ten twenty-somethings to work with me in a group coaching program to help them figure out the "next" steps in their career and life. It was really interesting to see how similar, and how different, everyone's challenges were. One thing I immediately noticed after a day: three of them were way more focused on making an impact on the world (from day one) than I was. It almost made me feel guilty. On the intake form, I had them answer questions about their top three goals for the year, so we could establish some action steps.

The three in particular I was talking about had mentioned one thing as part of their top three goals: helping other people. Something about that struck me as being so on-track that I had to re-evaluate my own goals. I'm a good person and I like helping people, but I'm not nearly as successful as I'd like to be. As a result, I was focusing all my willpower on improving my own life, but when I heard from these twenty-two and twenty-three year olds that they already knew their #1 or #2 or even #3 goal in *life* was to help people, I was impressed. I was impressed, then I felt guilty, and then I had to re-think things a bit.

They had their ladder up against the right wall to begin with.

Giving Your Gift Away

The funny paradox of creating a fulfilling life is that most of us start by living an unfulfilling one before we're forced to reconsider. It's almost like that "third world paradox" where you see old world families who are extremely family- and community-centered, with almost no material possessions, who are incredibly happy, smiling and fulfilled. You wouldn't even think they experience any unhappiness, despite how difficult their lives are. And then you see people walking down New York city streets with the latest fashions, technology, the great jobs, the high rise apartments, the BMWs, who are so busy, stressed, and miserable that they don't spot the irony. Since the time of Socrates, it looks like we don't have any more clarity about how to be happy and fulfilled.

For most of us though, who get to juggle the blessing of family life and living in this world, it can somewhat easily be remedied by one thing: setting goals that benefit other people. It might even mean doing the same goal you are right now, but changing the purpose. For example, rather than getting a job that pays you more just for the sake of more money, what if you aimed for a $20,000 raise so that you could give half to building a school in Africa? I can already *feel* more inspired setting a goal like that.

The irony of success, fulfillment, and happiness, is that they all come together, and when you focus on the single-minded pursuit of helping others, you almost always get what you want too. Most of all, you get the feeling that is so hard to replicate artificially—the feeling of your life having been well lived.

Chapter Recap: Finding Your
Gift and Giving it Away

☐ **"Giving your gift away" is a direct path to fulfillment for most people.** Many ambitious people complain about reaching their goals and achieving all the things they've always wanted to achieve, but then what? There's only so much you can do for yourself. It's like the saying that you'll "end up all alone in the biggest mansion on top of the hill." At a certain point, there's no point in doing more for yourself. It just doesn't benefit you, and definitely not from a meaning perspective.

☐ **Think about Agassi's story.** Truly, it's one of the most interesting stories I've read so far, if anything because of his own revelations on what really made his life worthwhile. He was forced into a profession (up a ladder) he didn't want. He was never understood. He destroyed himself mentally and emotionally. Eventually, he used crystal meth. All of this unraveling was that inner emotional turmoil caused by the fact that he hated his life, he was completely disconnected from how he felt (because how he felt didn't matter to him) and felt off track. Once he realized that he loved helping other people, and he put tons of his own money into charities, did he finally make his massive comeback.

☐ **Make sure your ladder is (still) up against the right wall.** I've mentioned this a few times because I still think it's one of the biggest, most important concepts to understand—I've had conversations with myself, and now with clients, that are often suspiciously similar. When they say they have a goal, I keep asking why. And then I keep asking why some more. And I keep asking it until either they are very clear that they really want it, or they're suddenly unclear why they ever wanted it. Be clear that you not only love the process more than arriving "there," but also that this goal is what *you* want, and not what your parents or society want, or what you *think* you *should* want.

CHAPTER 27

Intuition, Destiny, and the Life You Were Meant to Live

Consider yourself warned: this chapter is going into some new territory. What I'm trying to say is the following—this is some high level shit. I don't even really have proof of this, just a working theory. And that's why I'm excited to put it out into the public, because I want your thoughts on it.

During the worst years of my life, there was this undercurrent—no matter how much fun I was having, how many beers I had drank, and how many waves I had surfed—of meaninglessness. In other words, there was a feeling that regardless of whether or not I was having fun or totally depressed, there really wasn't any point to my existence. So I found it a lot easier to just kill time by playing video games, going out, drinking, and just wasting time. I didn't care, because all of it was pointless. It was that undercurrent of there being no real point to life that bothered me the most.

I would try to change all the different aspects of my internal and my external life—jobs, people, where I lived—but it never went away. It was this low level existential anxiety I couldn't quite turn off. It took me a long time before I finally found the million-dollar question: What if finding (or living) your destiny is the single most important thing you can do, to feel as if your life has been well lived?

***

Jeff and I originally met in 2009 in a Kung Fu class and then both ended up moving to China. He was laid off from an engineering job (that he hated) in 2008 after working for three years, and spent time doing some soul searching. Through an interesting set of coincidences, he ended up enrolling at the top Chinese medicine university in China, and here's how he described being on the path he feels he was "meant" to live:

> *"I've always been a happy person, even while working at my horribly boring engineering job. However, except for Kung Fu, I never knew what it felt like to have a purpose. At this stage of my life, I believe that fulfillment has two aspects.*
>
> *The first, which makes us all the same, is that we need friends and family. The second, which makes us all unique, is our purpose. Having the friends and family part is enough for most people, but to reach another level of fulfillment, I believe we need to find that "thing" that makes us want to get up and cultivate ourselves daily. If by chance you do find whatever lights a fire inside of you, that's when life becomes interesting.*
>
> *Now here's the part where I get to tell you about how my life has changed in just a year. The biggest difference I feel on a daily basis, is that I know what I'm doing on this planet. I'm not searching anymore, I'm pursuing. I feel like every step I take is a step forward. Other than that, my life is now a process of continuous cultivation. I don't feel like I'm waiting for anything; I feel like things are under my control.*
>
> *I used to worry about old age, but now I'm excited to see what kind of person I'll evolve into in five, ten or twenty years. When I was an engineer, I used to dream about retirement. Now that I've found my passion, retirement hasn't even crossed my mind. I'll be training and practicing medicine until the day I die. I can honestly say that if someone were to offer me a million dollars and let me do whatever I wanted, I would choose to stay in Beijing and continue my studies and training. To sum things up, I feel fulfilled. I feel happy. I feel like I have direction. Most importantly, I feel at peace."*

Jeff didn't magically start partying more, create some epic quest, or decide to visit every country in the world. He was just on a quest for work he loved, and that gave him direction, and *pulled him* forward every day—almost like it gave him energy, rather than draining it.

Again, this might sound really far-fetched, but what if the biggest aspect of fulfillment was just an intangible, invisible quality to your life, where you felt as if you were on the path you felt you wanted, and were supposed to be on?

Medical Anomalies, Destiny, and the Cure for Cancer

Dr. Kelly Turner (then a graduate student) was pouring through the medical research one day and noticed something interesting. One report had mentioned the remission of a cancer patient that—statistically speaking—should not have survived. They should not be alive—but they were. It was medically classified as a spontaneous remission, and then relegated to the back shelves somewhere, before being forgotten. When Dr. Turner followed up with the physicians that published these reports, she found something even more interesting: virtually none followed up with the patients to find out what they had done to aid their cancer going into remission. She found it intriguing (to say the least) that most physicians never even asked what the patients did to get better. As a result, that became the foundation and focus of her doctoral thesis: what were these "spontaneous remission" cases doing that allowed them to statistically do the impossible?

Two of the chapters in her book, *Radical Remission*, intrigued me in particular, regarding all this destiny talk. The first was the chapter on intuition, as in, the patients intuitively listening to what they (not their physician) thought needed changing, and then they changed it. The second was the chapter on having greater reasons for living—a deeper purpose. Here's a passage about one survivor who followed a deeper calling:

> *"A cancer diagnosis, however, is a wake-up call, and that means some people waking up to the fact that they may not be very excited about one or more aspects of their lives, whether it be their careers, romantic relationships, family lives, spiritual lives, communities, or hobbies. Being diagnosed with cancer tends to force people to reflect on what they would ideally like to change in order to make their remaining time on this planet — however long that may be — as enjoyable and meaningful as possible. One of the longtime survivors I met, whose cancer diagnosis allowed her to find her deeper calling, is Tami Boehmer. Tami was diagnosed at age thirty-eight with early-stage breast cancer, and when it returned six years later as stage-four breast cancer, she decided to tackle it with an integrative approach,*

combining conventional medicine with supplements, exercise, visualization, faith, and a whole-foods diet. However, despite all this, she realized that something was still missing from her life.

Despite all I was doing, I began to feel depressed and fearful about dying. Every morning I woke up with the thought, I have cancer. I certainly had strong reasons to live: my husband and especially my daughter, who was only nine at the time. I knew I had to be around to raise her. But I needed hope that this was possible, and I was getting just the opposite from doctors. Then I had a kind of epiphany. I decided to write a book about advanced-stage cancer patients and how they beat the odds. I thought it would not only be therapeutic for me but it could help others. The empty hole I was feeling started to dissipate. This was the sense of purpose I was seeking, and it gave me hope that I, too, could beat the odds and be able to nurture my daughter through adulthood. Tami's book, From Incurable to Incredible: Cancer Survivors Who Beat the Odds, *is currently fulfilling her deeper calling to spread hope to others (and herself)...*"[27]

Another person, Josie, who self-identifies as an energy healer, explained this in terms of energy:

"You've heard of the Retirement Syndrome or the Empty Nest Syndrome, where people have planned things out in their life only up to a certain point — like retirement, or when their children are grown — and they have no more goals after that. What happens a lot of times if they don't develop [their goals] is that their energy just collapses in on [itself], and often they get ill or they die really soon afterward, at a time when they're supposed to be light and free and enjoying themselves. But they haven't set any goals, and so the life force doesn't have a direction to keep being pulled forward toward something. So, that's why I say the people who still have strong dreams, strong goals of things that they want to do, and who have a strong desire to be well — those can be powerful factors in a faster healing process. For Josie and many of the other alternative healers I study, having enough goals or projects in your life that excite you is absolutely essential for bringing in enough chi to keep your body healthy and alive."[28]

Whether or not you believe any of this logically isn't what's important. What's important, is that these people found that following their intuition, and finally doing the things they always wanted to do, were key, pivotal steps in healing from cancer. I've seen women get out of abusive marriages, and the thirty or forty pounds they could never lose magically melt off—happiness matters, in a big way.

No doubt Dr. Turner's research on the nine factors play a massive role, but what I find so fascinating is that some of these people were finally given permission (via a death sentence) to go do what they had always wanted to do. And it gave them an underlying sense of peace that didn't go away. How big of a role does that really play in disease and remission? No one really knows. But one thing I can suggest from much personal experience is that *the day* I found "my thing," I finally felt like I was on the path that I was supposed to be on the entire time.

It was almost like there was a glitch in the matrix, and it had been fixed. For some reason, there was the underlying feeling of calm, that everything would be alright, and I had a reason for getting up in the morning. So many of us look for this experience of meaning, happiness, or being alive, but sometimes when you just feel like you're on the path you feel like you're *supposed* to be on—you're pursuing your destiny—all of those concerns just melt away. Any existential grief about life falls by the wayside, because you're so enthralled by being in the great river you want to play in for the rest of your life.

So let me ask you again: what if the most fulfilling, rewarding thing you can personally do *for yourself* is to follow the path you view as your destiny or calling?

Chapter Recap: Intuition, Destiny and the Life You Were Meant to Live

☐ **There's an intangible aspect to meaning—that I call "destiny."** I don't mean destiny in a mystical sense, but rather destiny in the sense that there are careers, trips, and experiences that just naturally call to you. It's like dating—sometimes you just feel that magnetic pull. Sometimes you ignore it, sometimes you go after it, but the biggest determinant of your decision is how much you listen to your own gut. Most of us ignore the "little stirrings" because the mind screams so loudly, "holy crap, how am I going to pay my rent?"

☐ **The feeling is that of "pursuit" rather than "searching" for that thing.** Jeff perfectly captured what the feeling feels like: when you're on the path you want to be on, the one you feel like you're *supposed* to be on, you feel like you're pursuing something. You already found it—there's no search—so you can't wait to see where you'll be in a few years. You have the treasure map - now it's the fun journey to the treasure. It's way different from just trying to "find it"— the anxious feeling of the clock ticking, like you're aging and not getting any closer to the path. One produces peace; the other produces anxiety.

☐ **Your intuition is the only real roadmap here.** The chapter on living in flow is one of the most important in the book for a reason—I tried so many tactics to figure out my life, my job, my own happiness, and so on. But nothing helped me more than this underlying principle that guided me. It's like being tutored by ten millionaires on how to build a business, but never wanting to get off the couch and do the work. Without the engine, nothing gets created. When you aim to live in flow and follow that thing that "speaks" to your insides, you have rocket fuel inside you.

☐ **For me, and many others, it didn't come from an "aha" moment.** Even though my story of the "aha" moment might help you think that was the case, it was hardly the case. It took seven years (yes, seven), from the day I actively set the intention to work my ass off to find or create work I loved and create this incredible life. Seven years until I fully found work I view as my calling. It's all a process of iteration.

CHAPTER 28

Hunger: The Only Real Shortcut

Within a few minutes of meeting someone, it's often easy to tell who will succeed and who won't. One of the first tiny, daily habits I started implementing in my early twenties, when I wanted to pull my life out of the gutter, was starting a mastermind. I invited a few other friends, and we started our own call group once a week, and then we'd set a goal to accomplish for the following week, before the next call.

Like I said, after a few months of doing this, it became extremely predictable who was going to make it, and who wasn't. In fact, in retrospect I realize that during the first conversation—heck, the first few minutes of our conversation—it was pretty obvious. Extremely predictable. Since then, I've started or joined 3-4 other masterminds, and the pattern is always the same. When I go to meet aspiring entrepreneurs, authors, or people just looking for jobs, it's the same. It's so simple that it's almost surprising: hunger, and how quickly people take action, is the only thing I've seen that guarantees to predict success or failure.

There's an article by Tony Robbins called, *If I Were 22: Hunger Will Destroy Your Fear of Failure,* where he talks about this a bit more:

"Achievers with youthful exuberance can do almost anything they really have *to do, but trying to* make *yourself do something is an energy that will never last. Passion wakes you up to something in life that you desire so strongly that you no longer have to push yourself to do anything. You now have a different kind of drive; a force that*

pulls *you forward. If someone asks me, 'Tony, what is the single most valuable secret to success in life? How do I live life on my terms and have choices, and become the best in my field?' I'd tell them that every great leader I've ever had the privilege to work with—whether they are a politician, an athlete, a musician, or a business savant—got there using one force above all others. And that's hunger."*[29]

I recently sat down with a business coach who charges $12,000 minimum for her coaching packages (up to $20,000). We ended up having a very similar conversation about how most people flat out don't take action. I mentioned how lucky she must be that people pay her so much, since they probably take a lot of action. Spending that kind of money must mean that her clients are incredibly invested and have taken a lot of time to think it through.

Then she dropped a bomb when she said, "Actually, that's literally the same thing I deal with: people paying me $12,000 just to ask them, 'did you do what you said you would, last week?'"

My jaw dropped. $12,000 is more than I earned some entire years in my twenties as I was freelancing, living at home, and trying to get my own businesses off the ground. At the end of the day, the path to the awesome life, job, and experiences isn't about tactics and strategies though—it's about how you show up every day. Hungry. *Starving.*

Strategies Don't Work—You Do

It's really trendy on online news sites to drop you with a list of fifteen tactics to better your life. You know what I'm talking about. Twelve ways to get more clients today. Thirty-six ways to lose weight in 2016. Fifteen ways to make more money this year. Ten ways to get your husband to listen to you. Six ways to stop clients from flaking. All of these are tactics, or success tactics. But the reason why tactics never work (guaranteed—for everyone), is because the only guaranteed way to success is to bet on the person.

It's the person who decides to keep going or to quit. It's the person who chooses whether to try a dozen tactics, and then try a dozen more if they don't work. It's the person who adapts and changes constantly to the surrounding waves and weather. The only guaranteed way to become successful is to become *the kind of person* with the drive, work ethic, creativity and hustle to see it through.

Success Has Cheat Codes

When I played Warcraft as a kid (hell yes, we're going there), you'd type a cheat code that was a shortcut: "greed is good 10,000" which would give you ten thousand gold. But this was all one big shortcut, a cheat code, because I didn't have the infrastructure in my base to keep getting gold. All the little peons I hadn't set up so that I continuously had this stream of gold coming in—I had to keep using cheat codes, expecting them to fix all my problems.

So many of us try to reach all our goals using this cheat codes approach. We want that one thing that's going to make it easy to write the book. To figure out what to do with our lives. To get the dream job. To start a successful business. But people don't realize that internally, it's so much messier than people think. When you look at the lives of the greats, they often had incredibly messy lives with twists and turns and weird unexpected paths. What makes you think your path will be any different? I know. You're in a rush. We want the tactics, but when the tactics don't work, we're out of luck. We're out of steam.

Here's the difference. A person who is craving, chasing, all these tactics and strategies and looking for the silver bullet of the week, will easily lose steam when things stop working. They quit. You know what's interesting? You take a hungry person who loves what they do, and you put every single roadblock imaginable in front of them. Literally, every damn wall you could imagine. Things don't work out. People die. They have a nervous breakdown. Truly the worst of the worst stuff—and guess what? They still succeed. Because it's hunger, and nothing else—no tactic or strategy—that gives you the borderline spiritual strength to press on. Tactics are a dime a dozen. Everyone has tactics. But not everyone makes it.

For example, I started writing my own little success booklet to myself—the secret to success—and I wrote down all the little things that have helped people succeed throughout history. This ranged from people like Einstein to normal people I knew personally who were very successful. I wrote down things like: having an irrational focus, spending one hour a day acquiring new skills, focusing on the vital few habits, showing up and doing the work, loving the process, using lateral thinking, having a niche focus, persisting and modeling what's worked. But none of those guarantee success. There are billions of people on the planet who work like absolute dogs, wearing themselves to the bone, and don't achieve any notable level of success, who barely scrape by for decades. Look at the rural Ethiopians you see on National Geographic who walk miles just to get a dirty bucket of water. They work *hard*. They *die* working hard. Yet most don't achieve even a comfortable life.

Seriously, think about that more. Work hard? There are *billions* of people who work their asses off to just feed their families. Very few of them create incredible lives. Be disciplined? Look at every person doing a menial job—they have to show up and be disciplined. Get focused? Plenty of people are just focused on their Netflix account. Do what you love? The worst person to bet your money on is someone who just wants to do what they love—they'll be focusing on creating their art and not paying their bills. You can find anyone who has "done it all right" and follows the cliché advice, the cheat codes, the success hacks. And they still haven't made it. The closest thing you can get to a guarantee is the burning fire inside you that will not quit, no matter what.

Take a messed up relationship for example, where there are a lot of things to fix. The guy is insecure, the woman is too much of a miss in-dependent overachiever at work, and in general, they are trying to work some things out together. There's no doubt that working on strategies will help: the guy works on being more secure, the woman tries to be less of a career-driven person and work fewer hours, but none of these really guarantee a great relationship. The only thing that can even come close to guaranteeing it is if they both equally believe in the importance of them staying in a relationship with each other. Hunger. The drive for it to work.

Weight loss is another great example. After having coached dozens of people, having thousands of students go through my courses, and answering tens of thousands of emails (and just as many comments on YouTube), it's clear—almost everyone wants to give up and just eat whatever the hell they want at some point. I've talked to people who have been trying for twenty years to get a body that they want and are proud of, and they've tried everything under the sun. So why do some fail and quit, and why do others keep going? Hunger. I've been in the gym four or five times a week since I was eighteen, in the pursuit of a body I'm comfortable in. That's over a decade now. Some years I saw no progress. Yes, years. That means I was putting in five hours a week for fifty-two weeks a year, for nothing.

Well, why didn't I quit long ago? Because to me, being fit is not for the sake of being fit. I'm massively hungry to achieve this goal because my old self represented mediocrity—it represented an untrained body, mind and life. It was the mediocre, easy, low level path, to just accept my body the way it was, and bitch and moan about how skinny I was for a guy. However, my life is built around the concept of hating mediocrity—I literally can't endure it for even five minutes. I physically feel weird living even one day without growing and improving. So while all my other friends and acquaintances quit years and years ago, because they too weren't see progress, I kept going.

Gradually, year after year, my body composition improved. Some years, it didn't move the needle at all. Some years, I gained ten or more pounds of muscle if I was really consistent. And now, for the first time (after ten *years*), I'm very comfortable with how I look—am I 100% at my goal? No, not yet. However, now I have that crystal clear faith that I'm the kind of person that can get there all the way.

Hunger.

It's the same kind of hunger that drives a first time author, where there's no guarantee a book is going to be a commercial success. The official statistic is that 81% of Americans want to write a book—which is 200 million people. If we applied that number worldwide, that's almost 5.8 billion people that should have books out, but last year there were roughly only a million. How many of those sell only a handful? Less than a few hundred copies? 95%? 99%? 99.9%? Many, many more people, start their books and never finish them, sometimes because they wonder who would read their book, sometimes because of imposter syndrome—wondering who am I to really be writing this?

So why do some people hit publish, or finish writing, while others don't? Some authors feel like their message isn't even about them, that it's a message that had to be shared with the world, so the purpose of having written the book is borderline spiritual. Some authors feel like the quality of books in some industry is so horrendous that they have a moral obligation to hit publish, and others just feel like they have a really important message that they think more people need to hear about.

Hunger.

At the end of the day, it's the only thing that will guarantee that you get closer to where you want to be. Nothing guarantees success, but hunger is the closest thing you have to a guarantee.

In the Pursuit of Your Dream, Time is Irrelevant and Age Doesn't Matter

Time scares the shit out of me. You see, for a long time, getting older was a reminder that I lost a year. In my head I was saying, "you've got one less year to start doing the really important stuff in life—the stuff you've always wanted to do. There's one less year to piss away."

It's not surprising then that most people also hate getting older. The clock is ticking, slowly counting down. Tick tock. Tick tock. Tick tock.

Here's another lesson that it took me a lot of years to realize: the people who are scared by time are those that aren't living the life they actually want to be living. Makes sense, right? If today, tomorrow, and the next day, you aren't enjoying life, one less day is one less day. But what about people who *do* feel they're on their chosen path?

Jeff (the friend mentioned earlier in the destiny chapter) and I recently had a conversation since he just moved back from China. We both agreed that when you find your path, when you're in a life that you feel like you're supposed to be in, time intrigues you. You think, "Wow, this stuff is awesome, I can't wait to see how much I know (or how good I'll be) in five or ten years."

It's exciting! You look forward to the coming years. You can't wait to keep following the path and see where it leads. It's the exact opposite of what most of us live. Everywhere around me I see people dreading that next birthday. It's a cultural joke now, "Ahhh Christ, alright it's my fifth twenty-fifth birthday!" When you're not "on your path," time feels like you're going away from something important.

When you've found it (or some direction), you're sprinting down a path and can't wait to see what's next. Everyone else is irrelevant; competition doesn't matter.

When you find your personal legend (as Paulo Coelho calls it), time becomes irrelevant. Many people (myself included) have this whacked out idea that, "if only I were (successful, where I want to be, married, etc.,) *now*, life would be good."

- If only I had my own business and could quit my job now, life would be good.
- If only my wife and I were living in Paris for a sabbatical, life would be good.
- If only I switched jobs and were working an awesome new job, life would be good.

We want to skip to the finale. We want to bypass all the bullshit and jump into the meat and potatoes. Obviously that can't happen though. You need a beginning and a middle for there to be an end. Time doesn't matter. It doesn't matter because you can't rush finding your "path." Scores of people I've talked to have told me about how they went after goals and things just didn't work out. I tried my best. And it didn't work. What the hell am I supposed to do now? You can't rush it—since life rarely goes according to plan.

Competition also doesn't matter. You don't compare yourself to anyone because you have found *your* path. It's no one else's but your own. You know you were born for it. Do you think young men that go into the priesthood compare themselves to their twenty-nine-year-old banking buddies making six figures in New York City? Doubt it! Different paths. Different ambitions. Different dreams. The problem is that sometimes we convince ourselves we also want what other people want (even when it's not true).

So when you're on your path, when your dad asks about your lawyer friend making 120k his first year out of grad school, you feel confident rather than insecure. "Not my path," you say to yourself. And you know it to be true.

I'm just doing my thing, and you're just doing yours.

***

Last year some time, I was in New York City meeting two friends just to catch up on life. At the time, I also had been thinking of making a move to the big city, so I figured I'd ask them each some questions on what the city life was like. I wanted an insider's perspective.

You know what's interesting? They both told me exact opposite things. One told me something that scared the crap out of me, that in the city I was going to be eaten alive and have my entire personality changed. He said I'd become a man whore, workaholic, then an alcoholic. Then leave the city once my health, prostate, and dreams were ruined.

The other said: "Look, the city is what you make it. It eats you alive only if you let it, only when you lose focus and let it eat you up, and only when you associate with people like that, too." How could that be? Two people, same place, same people, different perception. Almost 180 degrees. It made me realize something important: the people who get sidetracked and lost in life are the ones that lose their focus on the important stuff.

They're the ones who let their friends and family (or the city they live in) determine their life path. New York city is a lot like life—it'll eat you up if you let it. If you lose sight of the really important stuff, you're just going to get swept into everyone else's plan. You'll get swept into one of the million myriad other currents that are always flowing around you, with forks in the road. If you lose sight of your plan (or you don't have a plan and don't know what you want), then everything can easily sidetrack you.

Your parents' plan. Your girlfriend's plan. Your friends' plan.

You have no center to go back to and check up on. You decide to ask other people for their opinion, you crowdsource decisions, you read lots of books and essays. You try to get a massive amount of information, which gives you the illusion that you're making a smarter decision, but you're not. You're not listening to the only voice that actually matters—you're ignoring *you*.

Virtually all of us get sidetracked at one point or another. But some people never end up finding their path, and one-day wake up thinking, "how the hell did I get here?" In fact, this is one of the most shockingly common emails I get from people over forty: "I'm stuck in a life I never chose. It just happened to me. And here I am."

Sometimes, we get stuck listening to everybody else—everyone except for ourselves. If I listened to everyone else's advice, this is what I would've ended up doing.

Relationships: "If you found a great girl, stay with her and go get a good job and start a family! I'd hate to see you leave her behind." Another on the opposite side of the spectrum: "Don't ever let a woman prevent you from doing everything in life."

Work: "Go get a nice stable job and make money. Make bank now and become a workaholic so you don't have to later." Or this one: "Go off and go on adventures, work in hostels, take jobs as they come, live an adventurous life. Do everything except act in a porno. You only get one life!"

Life: "Life is tough, you gotta be realistic, hunker down, and work hard." Or how about the opposite perspective: "Dream. Do all the stuff you want. Travel, learn languages, check things off your bucket list. Do it all. Take it easy. Have fun. You only get to do it once."

***

If I listened to people, I would've been pretty screwed up in the head by now. Everyone says something different. Who in the hell am I supposed to trust? We get lost because we listen to everyone else. Stop crowdsourcing your deepest questions about life. Ignore everyone. Ignore age. Ignore time. Do what you need to do for yourself—and listen to *you*. Start doing what you know you need to do for yourself. Asking other people for advice makes us forget sometimes that they're just as lost as we are.

Stop asking outside of yourself for the answers you probably already know within you. It sounds cheesy as hell, but we western folks really suck at using our intuition. We consider logic and rational analysis to be the king of all skills. But most of the time we have an intuition about every situation and every person, yet we ignore it because we don't trust it. Oh, and don't forget to repeat this to yourself, something paraphrased from *Tuesdays with Morrie*, "people only fear age because they aren't already enjoying life and haven't found meaning, so age reminds them that they have one less year to start doing the stuff that really matters and they've always wanted to do."

In the pursuit of your dream, time is irrelevant. Age doesn't matter.

The only important thing is that you start doing for yourself what you intuitively *know* you must do to live out the dream.

CHAPTER 29

Stop Waiting to Be Chosen: Be Your Own Hero

"How… the hell do you write a book? Like, *how* does that even work?" one of my friends asked me last year.

I gave a sarcastic response, "well, technically, you just write a page a day."

"…" she stuttered for a second and then looked confused.

What she was really saying was, *who do you think you are to be writing a book?* What credentials do you have? Who gave you permission? Who chose you and declared you were the world expert on the topic? Who released the reigns, gave you a slap on the butt and said, "go for it!"?

The sad truth was that she told herself every story in the metaphorical book, besides the only one that mattered: that she actually *could* do something just like this if she wanted to. She bought the biggest lie in the world, and she believed it—hook, line and sinker.

***

So many of us could be incredibly successful, happy and fulfilled if we stopped waiting for the savior on the glowing white steed to come save us and say, "yes, you're special! Now go!" I hear it every day, and I went through it all myself.

I can't be a coach because I'm not an expert.

I won't get that job because everyone else has degrees and I don't.

I can't travel the world because it's expensive.

I can't be successful, be a great husband/wife and have a healthy family life.

All of these beliefs have the same origin: we're waiting for the white knight. We're waiting to be chosen.

Stop Waiting for Prince Charming and Your Savior (He's an Uggo, Anyways)

All of these beliefs have the same underlying mindset—we're waiting for someone to come along and give us a pep talk. *You are good enough. You can do it! Kick ass!* And those thing are great, if you have them. But if you don't, then what? *You* need to choose *yourself.* There's no more time to sit around and do affirmations hoping that you are the "chosen one," the "prodigal child," the "young grasshopper" to the sage on the mountain top. *You already are the chosen one*—you just don't know it.

I've witnessed these incredible transformations when the switch is flipped. You see a person who is on the fence, or who is highly doubting herself, and the second you share this mindset—that 100% of her excuses are legitimate bullshit—she opens up. She takes action. The fear goes away just 1%—enough to allow her to see success. She finally commits, takes off, and then things happen.

What changed? Almost nothing! I gave her permission and I said, "these are all B.S.—literally every person that has ever done anything, has gone through this—so get creating and get started." It's amazing what actually happens when you give someone permission to act— they act. It's almost like you smashed the B.S. meter in their head to pieces and they wake up from the spell and realize, "Oh, really? Whoa, cool. So *that's* how this works." So many people are sitting around telling themselves some story about why they aren't doing well.

I'm an introvert, I suck at making friends.

I'm a first time business person, I don't have any skills.

I've never done this before and I don't know any other people (in this field).

How in the hell do I even do this, anyway?

At the end of the day though, I didn't possess some magical confidence—the only thing I possessed was an utter hatred of my daily life, imagining the cubicle existence of the average person who dies before having done anything they want in life. The people who have died before ever having lived.

How I Chose Myself (And Figured It Out)

When I started my personal blog, Milk the Pigeon, I started it because I didn't see a single person that was living out their dream. In other words, living a conscious life they had created mentally, that they then created in the physical world. I didn't know a single one.

I figured, "Screw it, I'll be the first then." Even though I later realized that there are lots of people like this (thanks Internet), for whatever reason, I was frustrated and pissed off enough that I told myself I would do it and figure it out.

The very first article I ever wrote was, *"The Generation of Dreamers is Dead."* I wrote how I was beyond frustrated that I couldn't find *anyone* that was committed—as long as it took—to create that dream life they saw in their head. I didn't have a single friend who was willing to be poor for a decade, start and quit seven, eight, nine, or ten jobs (yes, did that), and suffer to the point of depression because he or she had so much commitment to the dream.

Not one. Needless to say, it's been a long (and often lonely) few years, but here's the important concept: I chose myself. I didn't wait for the magical rainbow to illuminate my path. It's almost that perfectionism, similar to the feeling that a lot of men in their twenties have, that, "I can't get married or settle down until I'm already successful."

Clearly it makes no sense. But if you wanted to theoretically acquire the skills required to be skilled enough to be paid for your skills, here's a little afterthought. Don't forget, the line between expert and non-expert is blurry. Does it require a PhD? An M.D.? 10 years' experience? Or just the ability to get people results? For example, I wrote my first book which became an Amazon bestseller, but a lot more importantly, has great reviews because it's helped people. I've never once called myself an expert, but lots of people do once they see my book and the reviews it's gotten. All I cared about was writing a book that helped people, and ultimately, that's all that people cared about.

What does an expert know that you don't? Well, most experts I've met know a lot more than the average person, but that's really not that impressive since the average person knows very little and watches endless TV rather than taking time to read, grow and improve. Here's how I view an "expert" on writing, for example:

- They've read other experts on writing
- They know the basic principles of writing
- They've written and have spent time in the arena

They know about the subject (self-education). They know the basic principles (the skillset). They've written (concrete experience). Was I an expert when I put pretentious professional pictures on my website? When I wrote my first article? When I wrote my hundredth article? When I wrote better? When I wrote my first book? When my first student lost five pounds? When one of my students lost 100+ pounds? When I've had a hundred students lose dozens of pounds? When I enrolled in a doctoral program? At what point are you the expert that is finally ready to act? The line is extremely blurry. Whether or not you act then, comes down to one thing: your beliefs.

Stop Waiting—All The Greats "Figured" It Out

"It had long since come to my attention that people of accomplishment rarely sat back and let things happen to them. They went out and happened to things."

— LEONARDO DA VINCI

When I was younger and wanted to learn all the success secrets from the greats of their industries, I asked some really stupid questions. I would ask generic things like, "how do you become successful?" and get stupid, generic answers like, "work hard and be passionate." Those helped me as generically as the questions I asked. This was my first introduction to the old concept that the quality of our questions determine the quality of our answers.

What you never hear from successful people is what really goes on behind the scenes. That no matter how good (or bad) the mentor, how good or bad their life, how good or bad the circumstances were, they all did one thing: they figured it out. They started stacking those bricks, and each brick led to one brick that was a little bit less crappy and more solid. It was a little bit more inspiring. They followed their intuition and pivoted, moved, quit, and started in alignment with it. They went with their gut regarding what projects called to them, and what businesses they should avoid.

They inched closer, today a half inch, tomorrow a foot. Tomorrow, back two feet, and the next day, forward six inches. They relentlessly plowed ahead, swallowing failure after failure. They knew that each action, whether it succeeded or failed, was one brick—which would always lead to a new brick. Each step, no matter how much in the dark it seemed, was one step closer on the drunken staircase. They knew that with enough hunger, they could finish it—and figure anything out.

And most of all, they realized the greatest success principle of all. It's the one that no one will tell you, but all who have succeeded already know deep down: *you already are the chosen one.*

"For, in the end, it is impossible to have a great life unless it is a meaningful life. And it is very difficult to have a meaningful life without meaningful work. Perhaps, then, you might gain that rare tranquility that comes from knowing that you've had a hand in creating something of intrinsic excellence that makes a contribution. Indeed, you might even gain that deepest of all satisfactions: knowing that your short time here on this earth has been well spent, and that it mattered."

– JIM COLLINS, GOOD TO GREAT

Appendix A: What the Hell Does "Milk the Pigeon" Mean, Anyway?

If you didn't know me before reading this book, you might be wondering what in the hell a pigeon with its nipples sticking out has to do with, well, *anything*. To "Milk the Pigeon" is an old English phrase that means to attempt the impossible, like trying to milk a pigeon. As far as I know, it was first written down in a dictionary called *the 1811 Dictionary of the Vulgar Tongue,* by Francis Grose (a soldier at the time) which compiled the slang of commoners that was often used in the eighteenth century.

When I started my personal blog, Milk the Pigeon, in 2011, I started it because I didn't see many dreamers that were in their 20s and hadn't settled for a life they didn't want. It became my own personal travelogue of experiences, advice, and frustrations on the path to realizing my own dream, and hopefully inspiring other people in the process. At that time, I didn't know anyone personally who had set their goals on paper about what they wanted from every aspect of their life, and then lived it, so to me this was essentially doing the impossible. As far as I was concerned, I would be the first. Obviously, this wasn't true, but based on the people I saw around me, I was apparently the first one that I knew that apparently wanted more from life.

When you combine the symbolism of "attempting to Milk a Pigeon" with the fact that I could stare at a pigeon, indecently exposing itself every day, as I logged in to write, it was a no brainer.

The Road Ahead:
Milking Pigeons and Your
Quest for an Awesome Life

Hopefully, at this point, you should feel so jacked up on inspiration, that you're like a hamster on meth. You should also have a little bit of an idea of which direction to go—maybe a little intuition here or there suggesting something.

Remember that you have your own internal GPS, the internal compass of your gut. The internal compass always knows what you want, but the thing that determines whether or not you listen to it is another thing.

The biggest obstacle standing between where you are and where you want to be is the following: the presence or lack of courage. It took me writing hundreds of pages to realize that the one thing that will get you anywhere is courage. It's the fear monster that stops you from writing that book. From booking that flight. From saying, "I do" or "I can't do this anymore." It's the fear monster that tells you that one day you'll do all the things you want to do. And it's the fear monster that ultimately will drive you to an early, empty grave. The fear monster ensures you die without ever having lived.

It took writing hundreds of pages to boil down the advice to my former self in one word: Courage. Sometimes, you're going to be scared shitless by the future, and when everything seems dark and foreboding, when everything has gone to hell, it's that spiritual strength you have to pull out of you—faith—and then take a step into the darkness. And most of all, you have to take that step when every bone in your body is screaming at you to do the opposite, and through it all, know that *you will get there.*

Endnotes

1 This Is What Millions of Young People In China And India ... (n.d.). Business Insider. Retrieved October 21, 2016, from http://www.businessinsider.com/united-nations-supports-ispeak-china-india-adrian-fisk-2011-10

2 The quarterlife crisis: Young, insecure and depressed ... (n.d.). *The Guardian.* Retrieved October 21, 2016, from https://www.theguardian.com/society/2011/may/05/quarterlife-crisis-young-insecure-depressed

3 The Real Colonel Sanders: More Than A Fast-Food Icon—*TIME*. (n.d.). Retrieved October 21, 2016, from http://content.time.com/time/nation/article/0,8599,2019218,00.html

4 Hoy, A. (2015). Stacking the Bricks. Retrieved November 26, 2016, from https://unicornfree.com/stacking-the-bricks

5 Adam Pacitti who spent last £500 on billboard begging for ... (n.d.). *The Daily Mail.* http://www.dailymail.co.uk/news/article-2279261/Adam-Pacitti-spent-500-billboard-begging-job-spends-pay-packet-say-thanks.html

6 Nightingale, E. (1969). This is Earl Nightingale. Garden City, NY: Published in co-operation with J.G. Ferguson Pub. by Doubleday.

7 How Seth Godin Manages His Life. *Four Hour Blog.* http://fourhourworkweek.com/2016/02/10/seth-godin/

9 "How Vacations Affect Your Happiness." *New York Times.* http://well.blogs.nytimes.com/2010/02/18/how-vacations-affect-your-happiness/comment-page-9/.

8 "Jim Collins. Concepts." *Jim Collins.* http://www.jimcollins.com/concepts.html.

9 Frankl, Viktor E. *Man's Search for Meaning.* Boston: Beacon Press, 2006.

[10] Csikszentmihalyi, Mihaly. *Flow: The Psychology of Optimal Experience*. New York: Harper & Row, 1990.

[11] IBID

[12] IBID

[13] Seligman and Beagley. "Learned Helplessness in the Rat." Comparative and Physiological Psychology. (1975): 534-41 Web. http://www.ncbi.nlm.nih.gov/pubmed/1150935

[14] Miller, William R., and Martin E. Seligman. "Depression and Learned Helplessness in Man." *Journal of Abnormal Psychology* 84.3 (1975): 228-38. Web.

[15] Miller, Donald. *A Million Miles in a Thousand Years: How I Learned to Live a Better Story*. Nashville, TN: Thomas Nelson, 2009. Print.

[16] IBID

[17] IBID

[18] IBID

[19] IBID

[20] IBID

[21] IBID

[22] IBID

[24] Csikszentmihalyi, Mihaly. *Flow: The Psychology of Optimal Experience*. New York: Harper & Row, 1990.

[25] Ferriss, Tim. Tony Robbins – On Achievement Versus Fulfillment. *Four Hour Blog*. Retrieved November 26, 2016, from http://fourhourworkweek.com/2016/08/10/tony-robbins-on-achievement-versus-fulfillment/

[26] Frankl, Viktor E. *Man's Search for Meaning*. Boston: Beacon Press, 2006.

[27] Turner, Kelly A. *Radical Remission: Surviving Cancer against All Odds*. HarperOne, 2015. Print.

[28] IBID

[29] Robbins, Tony. "If I Were 22: Hunger Will Destroy Your Fear of Failure." Linkedin Pulse News. https://www.linkedin.com/pulse/20140527113908-101706366-if-i-were-22-to-succeed-you-need-to-be-hungry.

Printed in Great Britain
by Amazon